QUOTATIONS FOR KIDS

QUOTATIONS FOR KIDS

COMPILED AND EDITED BY
J. A. SENN

ILLUSTRATIONS BY STEVE PICA

THE MILLBROOK PRESS   BROOKFIELD, CONNECTICUT

To quote a couple words Babe said in *Babe the Gallant Pig*

by Dick King-Smith, I dedicate this book to "my mum."

J. A. Senn

Design by Tania Garcia

Published by The Millbrook Press, Inc.
2 Old New Milford Road
Brookfield, Connecticut 06804
Visit us at our Web Site

library: 5   4   3   2
trade: 5   4   3   2   1

Quotations for kids / compiled and edited by J. A. Senn.
          p.   cm.
Includes bibliographical references and indexes.
Summary: An illustrated reference work offering more than 2000
quotations ranging from the Bible to folklore to children's literature.
ISBN 0-7613-0267-0 (lib. bdg.)
ISBN 0-7613-1296-X tr hcvr)
1. Quotations, English. [1. Quotations]
I. Senn, J.A. PN6081.Y63 1999
082—dc21   98-40310
                                   CIP
                                   AC

Contents

Introduction

For many years dictionaries and encyclopedias especially designed for children have opened worlds of knowledge in forms that young people can readily understand and use. With the somewhat recent publication of children's atlases, almanacs, thesauruses, and even a rhyming dictionary, young people now have more reference information available to them than ever before. With the publication of *Quotations for Kids*, there is now the first book of quotations that specifically addresses the needs and interests of young readers and that draws quotations from works that are familiar and important to them.

I could have never succeeded in this enormous undertaking without the help and guidance from school and public children's librarians across the country and all of the others listed in the Acknowledgments. Together, we embarked on an extensive survey of children's literature with the goal of bringing together from a wide variety of sources — including fantasy, poetry, historical documents, speeches, and song lyrics — a major body of quotations in which each quotation is either interesting, enjoyable, relevant, or helpful to young people.

The search for quotations began with children's classics such as *Alice's Adventures in Wonderland, Black Beauty*, and *Tom Sawyer*. We also included quotations from almost all of the Newbery Award winners as far back as 1960 — although not always from the books for which they were cited. For other sources of quotations, we consulted prestigious booklists such as the Women's National Book Association's list of *Eighty Books for 21st Century Girls* and the *American Library Association's Best of the Best for Children*, edited by Denise Perry Donavin.

During the extensive gathering process, it became clear that we could not include all of the authors we thought should be represented in this book of quotations for young people. We learned that it was the writing style and, perhaps, even the personality of individual authors that made their books either conducive or not conducive for deriving quotations. As a result, the number of quotations from any particular author in *Quotations for Kids* in no way signifies that author's worth or value compared with any others.

Another important issue arose as we searched for quotations from poetry, biographies, and historical works. If we were to quote from primary sources, many of those books would be inaccessible to students in their school libraries, and even if they were available in public libraries, the majority of them would be difficult for young people to read. As a result, we decided to draw poetry quotations whenever possible from collections that would most likely be in children's libraries — such as *Rainbows Are Made: Poems by Carl Sandburg*, selected by Lee Bennett Hopkins, and *The Random House Book of Poetry*, selected by Jack Prelutsky. We also looked for biographical and historical quotations from significant secondary sources such as Russell Freedman's Newbery Award-winning biography of Abraham Lincoln and other child-oriented nonfiction books such as *Herstory: Women Who Changed the World*, edited by Ruth Ashby and Deborah Gore Ohrn.

We faced a similar decision involving quotations from Shakespeare. We felt that most quotations directly from Shakespeare would be difficult to understand out of context, and most young people would have trouble reading Shakespeare's original texts on their own. We chose, therefore, to introduce young people to the stories of Shakespeare by quoting from Bernard Miles's *Favorite Tales from Shakespeare*. Similarly, we have included quotations from Geraldine McCaughrean's *The Random House Book of Stories from the Ballet*. All of these secondary sources are indicated by the words *found in* preceding the title in the source line following a quotation. (*As a guide to librarians and other interested adults, we have listed all secondary sources in a bibliography starting on page 222.*)

In actuality, these decisions were relatively easy to make since the objective of this book is to be — first and foremost — a reference book for young people. If a young person especially enjoys a particular quotation or wants to know more about what an author or character is saying in a quotation, I wanted that child to be able to find the source of that quotation easily in order to be able to read that quotation in context.

As a reference book, *Quotations for Kids* goes far beyond mere entertainment — although fun and enjoyment certainly are valid reasons for young people and adults alike to use this book. Young people, for instance, can also use this book as a source of quotations for reports, as a source of opinions about important matters, as a basis for journal writing, as a sampler of books to be read, and, in general, as a window to the world. Librarians, teachers, and parents will also find many valuable ways to use this book to enrich learning and family life: to locate quotations to serve as springboards for writing assignments or research projects, to stimulate interest in reading entire books, and to serve as starting points for discussions of historical events or present-day values. Librarians also may find this book to be a helpful source of titles to add to their collections.

Finally, I want to state clearly and unequivocally that in a book of this scope, comprehensiveness is not possible — neither is proportional representation. Although a herculean effort was made to include as many significant historical people and as many titles by as many authors as possible, I know that there are still many other quotations that should have been in this first edition. I'm hoping, however, that all of the librarians, teachers, parents, and young people who enjoy this book will send those missing quotations to me so I can put them into future revised editions.

J. A. Senn

Acknowledgments

Quotations for Kids would have never become a reality without the enormous help I received from so many! However, there was one radiant guiding light that was with me from the beginning to the end. That never-flickering support came from

Marian Amodeo,
then the Head of Children's Services
and since then the Director at the
Lucy Robbins Welles Library in Newington, CT.

I'm also enormously indebted to Marian for the incredible selection of books in her library and her extremely helpful staff—including Helen Malinka, who has since then been appointed Head of Children's Services, and Jane Machowski.

All across the country, there were other librarians who, in addition to their full-time jobs, were willing to help by recommending books and even participated in the search for quotations themselves. My two best quotation finders by far were

Sue Geiger, School Library Media Specialist
at the Clearspring Elementary School
in Damascus, MD,
and
Louise Turner, Children's Librarian at the
Fort Smith Public Library in Fort Smith, AR.

There is no way to calculate their help! Others who also willingly offered their help were Joyce Brown, Library Media Specialist at the Cottonwood Point Elementary School in Overland Park, KS; Mary Cox, Library Media Specialist at the Belle Vue Middle School in Tallahassee, FL; Mary Oates Johnson, History Specialist in Andover, MA; Rhonda Peterson, Library Media Specialist at the Armand Larive Middle School in Hermiston, OR; Dr. Shirl Schiffman, Instructional Designer at the Columbia International University in Columbia, SC; and Anette Wilson, Library Media Services with the Grand Rapids, MI, Public Schools. In addition, I count among my best quotation finders the following students in Rhonda Peterson's Armand Larive Middle School Library Club: Nicole Allstott, Tyler Bendixsen, Shannon Boettcher, B.J. Branson, Autumn Cutting, Alex Gray, Rebecca Heihn, April Heyworth, Stacy Marie Nevin, Christina Surber, Sarah Swoboda, and Andy Williams.

Less directly involved but still essential in getting this book off the ground were the following people: Dr. Patricia Breivik, Dean of the Libraries and Library Services at Wayne State in Detroit, MI; Ruth Lumpkins, Director of the Grand Rapids Public Schools Library Media Services, Grand Rapids, MI; Allan Ragsdale, Director of Educational Media in Tallahassee, FL; Jenny B. Petty, Assistant Professor and Periodicals Librarian at the Ouachita Baptist University in Arkadelphia, AR; and Diane Skorupski, School Library Media Specialist in Tucson, AZ.

Finally there are those close to home who helped in one way or another—and often in many ways—throughout the process of compiling this book. They are Joey Fusco, Timmy Fusco, Catherine Kunze, Marcy Lomen, Susan Potter, and Laura Wieleba.

How To Use This Book

Basically you can use *Quotations for Kids* in three ways: to browse for fun and information, to locate quotations about a specific subject, and to find quotations by a specific author. If you want to read simply for pleasure, start at the beginning of the book and skim through the various topics that are listed in alphabetical order until you find one that catches your attention. As you "surf" through the book, you will get ideas for other sources of quotations about a particular subject under some topic headings. For example, under the topic *Mothers*, you will see a note in parenthesis that says, (*See also* Parents.) Look throughout the book, as well, for other cross-references — such as under Athletics, (*See* Sports).

Subject Index. The best way to find quotations about a specific subject is to look at the Subject Index that begins on page 240 and continues to the end of the book. All of the subjects and fictional people covered in this book are listed there in alphabetical order. For example, you will find a listing for *Anger, Bears, Brothers and Sisters, Civil War, Colors,* and *Determination* — to name just a few of the more than three hundred entries. Under the listing *Poems*, you will even find references to all of the poems or lines from poems that appear throughout the book. Following is a typical listing in the Subject Index.

The numbers 1-15 following the subject tell you that Baseball is a main heading in the book, and there are 15 quotations in that section.

Baseball 1-15
   See also: Brothers and Sisters 3; Disabilities 1; Excellence 1; Heroes 1; Life 17; School 8; Writers and Writing 4

Following the main heading are other references to baseball throughout the book. For example, quotation number 1 under the subject Heroes *is also about baseball.*

You can find the section on *Baseball* by looking at the guide words at the bottom of each page. Just like the guide words in a dictionary, they will tell you what subjects are covered on each page. Once you locate the 15 quotations in the *Baseball* section, you will notice that they are listed alphabetically by the last names of the authors of the quotations or by the last names of the people who said them. For example, the first quotation in the *Baseball* section was said by Hank **Aaron**, and the last one was written by Ernest **Thayer**.

In the Subject Index, you will also find topics that do not have a main heading in the book — such as the following one for *Discouragement*.

Discouragement
See: Birds 3; Determination 10; Home 10; Inventions and Inventors 5

Since there are no numbers after the subject *Discouragement*, look for individual listings underneath it. For example, the third quotation under the subject *Birds* is about discouragement.

People Index. On page 226, just before the Subject Index, you will find another index, the People Index. Turn to that index if you are looking for quotations from the books of a favorite author — such as Betsy Byars or Walter Dean Myers. Also listed in the People Index are the names of all of the real people — both famous and historical — whose words are quoted in this book — people such as George Washington and Amelia Earhart. Since the People Index is set up exactly like the Subject Index, you should have no problem tracking down quotations by your favorite author or quotations by someone like John Adams for a report you might be writing.

Notice that this entry about John Adams includes not only quotations that he said but also a quotation someone else said ABOUT him.

Adams, John (2nd President) Government 1, 2; The Presidency 1, 2, 3; Revolutionary War 1, 2, 3; ABOUT Adams: Peace 1

Bibliography of Secondary Sources. Before the People and Subject Indexes is the Bibliography of Secondary Sources, beginning on page 222. This section lists all of the secondary sources of quotations used in this book. Refer to this list when you are looking for reference books or collections of songs and poetry.

Symbols Used within the Quotations. Once you begin reading some of the quotations in this book, you will repeatedly come across some symbols. For example, you will see three periods (. . .), called an ellipsis, which are used to show that some words have been dropped from a quotation. You will also find brackets ([ ]) enclosing letters, words, or phrases. Brackets enclose words from a previous sentence that have been added to make the meaning of a quotation clearer, or they show that only

Sources of the Quotations. The quotations in this book are from many different sources: current popular fiction, classic fiction, historical fiction, nonfiction, newspapers, and magazines. The source of every quotation is listed directly under the quotation so that you can find the quotation in its context and read more about it. The following example explains each part of a source line.

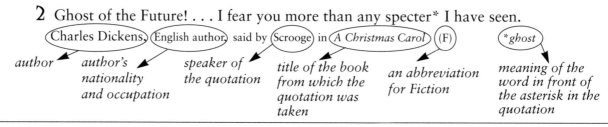

2 Ghost of the Future! . . . I fear you more than any specter* I have seen.

Charles Dickens, English author, said by Scrooge in A Christmas Carol (F)   *ghost

author   author's nationality and occupation   speaker of the quotation   title of the book from which the quotation was taken   an abbreviation for Fiction   meaning of the word in front of the asterisk in the quotation

Abbreviations Used in Source Lines. Throughout the book, abbreviations are used to keep the source lines short. If you don't know what a particular abbreviation means, just look for its meaning in the following list of general abbreviations.

General Abbreviations

arr. = arranged
c. = around the time of
Capt. = captain
CEO = chief executive officer
Col. = colonel
coll. = collected
Com. = commander
comp. = compiled
ed. = edited
F = fiction
Gen. = general
Gov. = governor
Ibid. = in the same place

Jr. = junior
KJV = King James Version of the Bible
maj. = major
NAACP = National Association for the Advancement of Colored People
NF = nonfiction
NIV = New International Version of the Bible
NW = northwest
Rev. = reverend
sel. = selected
v. = verses
vol. = volume

part of a longer quotations is included. Also, a difficult word within a quotation will be followed by an asterisk (*). Another asterisk appears at the end of the source line of that quotation. Beside the second asterisk is the meaning of the difficult word.

Uses for the Quotations. At the top of the list of reasons to use *Quotations for Kids* are fun and enjoyment. Browse through it and stop when you see a quotation or even a picture that you think is interesting because there's always a quotation to go with each picture. (The quotation with the star behind the number is the quotation that goes with the illustration on the page.)

There are, of course, many other uses for this book in addition to entertainment — such as any or all of the following:

- To find quotations by famous people such as George Washington, Abraham Lincoln, and Eleanor Roosevelt to include in a social studies report.
- To find quotations about important subjects such as animals, pollution, and technology to add to a science report.
- To find an interesting topic to write about.
- To find quotations that give you ideas for journal entries.
- To find quotations to add to book reports or biographies.
- To find books that sound interesting to read.
- To find sources for additional information for research projects.
- To find additional titles of favorite authors.
- To find quotations for a daily calendar.
- To use as a guide in creating your own book of quotations.

Accomplishment

1 Whatever accomplishment you boast of in the world, there is someone better than you.

> African proverb

2 For what shall it profit a man, if he shall gain the whole world, and lose his own soul?

> Bible, Mark 8:38 (KJV)

3 You never know what you can do until you have to do it.

> Betty Ford, founder of the Betty Ford Clinic for substance abuse and wife of the 38th US President, found in *Contemporary Heroes and Heroines*, ed. by R. B. Browne (NF)

4 A hundred [points] out of a hundred, the perfect performance, never before reached by man and dog in the whole history of the sheepdog trails, but now achieved by man and pig, and everyone went mad!

> Dick King-Smith, English author, *Babe the Gallant Pig* (F)

5 The greatest accomplishment is not in never falling, but in rising again after you fall.

> Vince Lombardi, US professional football coach, found in *Instant Replay* by J. Kramer (NF)

6 It is an achievement for a man to do his duty on earth irrespective* of the consequences

> Nelson Mandela, South African President and former political prisoner, in the Jan. 1992 *Biography Today* (NF)
>
> *regardless

7 3 Cheers for Bear!
(*For where?*)
For Bear—
3 Cheers for the Wonderful
Winnie-the-Pooh!
(*Just tell me, somebody*—WHAT DID HE DO?)

> A. A. Milne, English author, words to the "Anxious Pooh Song" in "We Say Good-bye" from *Winnie-the-Pooh* (F)

8 Accomplishments have no color.

> Leontyne Price, US opera singer, found in the *Book of Black Heroes, Vol. 2* by T. Igus (NF)

9 The feeling of accomplishment welled up inside of me . . . three Olympic gold medals. I knew that was something nobody could ever take away from me, ever.

Wilma Rudolph, US track star, found in *Wilma Rudolph: Champion Athlete* by T. Biracree (NF)

10 I liked to make money, but money wasn't the only thing. It was also the sense of accomplishment.

Dave Thomas, US founder of Wendy's, in the Apr. 1996 *Biography Today* (NF)

Action

1 One thing you should know about tears: They're utterly useless. No point in weeping. . . . We need to get busy and do something.

Lloyd Alexander, US author, said by Dr. Tudbelly, *The Cat Who Wished To Be a Man* (F)

2 When you're the shortest kid your age—even shorter than the girls—you make a point to act big.

Tom Birdseye, US author, said by Ryan, *Tarantula Shoes* (F)

3 Instead of . . . griping, get in there and make things better.

George Bush, 41st US President, in the Dec. 1, 1996 *Parade* magazine (NF)

4 I guess [people] don't get excited about a thing until somebody starts taking it away from them. Then they wake up and fight for it.

Oliver Butterworth, US author, said by Dr. Ziemer, *The Enormous Egg* (F)

5 Do something. Do anything. But don't just stand there and let people beat on you and then thank them for doing it.

Vera and Bill Cleaver, US authors, said by Mary Call, *Where the Lilies Bloom* (F)

6 A man has a right to be judged by how he acts, not by how someone may have *told* you he acts.

Allan W. Eckert, US author, said by Mr. MacDonald, *Incident at Hawk's Hill* (F)

7 Brave actions never want a trumpet.
English proverb

8 It won't do you a bit of good to know everything if you don't do anything about it.

Louise Fitzhugh, US author, said by Ole Golly, *Harriet the Spy* (F)

9 Well done is better than well said.

Benjamin Franklin, Revolutionary statesman, the 1737 *Poor Richard's Almanack* (NF)

10 I am telling young people that if you're dissatisfied with the way things are . . . get out there and occupy these positions in government and make the decisions.

Barbara Jordan, member of US Congress and educator, found in the *Book of Black Heroes, Vol. 2* by T. Igus (NF)

11 When people made up their minds that they wanted to be free and took action, then there was change.

> Rosa Parks, US civil rights activist, found in the *Book of Black Heroes, Vol. 2* by T. Igus (NF)

12 That's what being a man is all about. . . . It's just doing what's got to be done.

> Robert Newton Peck, US author, said by Rob's father, *A Day No Pigs Would Die* (F)

13 For those who are willing to make an effort, great miracles and wonderful treasures are in store.

> Isaac Bashevis Singer, Polish-American author, said by Rabbi Moshe, "A Tale of Three Wishes" from *Stories for Children* (F)

Adventure

1 Can't keep still all day. . . . I like adventures, and I'm going to find one.

> Louisa May Alcott, US author, said by Jo, *Little Women* (F)

2 Do you want an adventure now, or would you like to have your tea first?

> J. M. Barrie, Scottish author, said by Peter Pan, *Peter Pan* (F)

3 I've stayed in the front yard
   all my life.
 I want a peek at the back
 Where it's rough and untended
   and hungry weed grows.
 A girl gets sick of a rose.

> Gwendolyn Brooks, US poet, "A song in the front yard," found in *Women's Words: Columbia Book of Quotations by Women* by M. Briggs

4 Never say "no" to adventures. Always say "yes," otherwise you'll lead a very dull life.

> Ian Fleming, English author, said by Com. Pott, *Chitty Chitty Bang Bang: The Magical Car* (F)

5 To ride a horse with real Indians would be an adventure, a wonderful adventure.

> Kristiana Gregory, US author, *The Legend of Jimmy Spoon* (F)

6 Life is either a daring adventure or nothing.

> Helen Keller, US author and humanitarian, found in *Helen Keller: Humanitarian* by D. Wepman (NF)

7 [Harry Crewe] had always suffered from a vague restlessness, a longing for adventure that she told herself severely was the result of reading too many novels when she was a small child.

> Robin McKinley, US author, *The Blue Sword* (F)

8 We [hobbits] are plain quiet folk and have no use for adventures. Nasty disturbing uncomfortable things! Make you late for dinner!

> J. R. R. Tolkien, English author, said by Bilbo Baggins, *The Hobbit* (F)

YES!!

Advice

1 Mind grammar, spelling, and punctuation, use short words, and express as briefly as you can your meaning.

> Louisa May Alcott, US author, in an Oct. 24, 1878 letter to John Preston True, found in *Great Americans in Their Own Words* (NF)

2 Be glad you are a cat! Let me tell you about men: Wolves are gentler. Geese are wiser. Jackasses have better sense.

> Lloyd Alexander, US author, said by the wizard Stephanus, *The Cat Who Wished To Be a Man* (F)

3 Eat no green apples or you'll droop,
   Be careful not to get the croup,
   Avoid the chicken-pox and such,
   And don't fall out of windows much.

> Edward Anthony, US poet, "Advice to Small Children," found in *The Random House Book of Poetry for Children*, sel. by J. Prelutsky

4 Be careful . . . of the wind you choose.

> Avi, US author, said by Zachariah to Charlotte, *The True Confessions of Charlotte Doyle* (F)

5 So one thing I want to say about life is don't be scared and don't hang back, and most of all, don't waste it.

> Joan W. Blos, US author, written by Catherine Hall Onesti, *A Gathering of Days* (F)

6 Don't listen to the advice of bad companions; if you do, you will repeat it!

> Carlo Collodi, Italian author, said by Blackbird, *The Adventures of Pinocchio* (F)

7 Advice to a fool goes in one ear and out the other.

> Danish proverb

8 Whatever you do in this world, no matter how good it is, you will never be able to please everybody. All you can strive for is to do the best it is humanly possible for you to do.

> Jeri Ferris, US author, said by Marian Anderson's mother, *What I Had Was Singing* (NF)

9 If you are ever in real trouble, don't panic. Sit down and think about it. Remember two things, always. There must be some way out of it, and there must be humor in it somewhere.

> Louise Fitzhugh, US author, said by Sport's father, *Sport* (F)

10 Don't hurry, don't worry. You're only here for a short visit. So be sure to stop and smell the flowers.

> Walter Hagen, US professional golfer, in the May 22, 1977 issue of *The New York Times* (NF)

11 When kids ask me for advice on how to do well in school, I always tell them: Stop watching so much TV and start reading at night.

> Lee A. Iacocca, US business executive and author, in the Jan. 1992 *Biography Today* (NF)

12 Expect everything, I always say, and the unexpected never happens.

Norton Juster, US author, said by the Whether Man, *The Phantom Tollbooth* (F)

13 Advice from friends is like the weather. Some of it is good; some of it is bad.

Arnold Lobel, US author and illustrator, the moral in "The Baboon's Umbrella" from *Fables* (F)

14 Never let your head hang down. Never give up and sit and grieve. Find another way. And don't pray when it rains if you don't pray when the sun shines.

Attributed to Leroy "Satchel" Paige, US professional baseball player

15 [S]tay positive and stay on top of things.

Gary Paulsen, US author, *Hatchet* (F)

16 Believe there is a great power silently working all things for good, behave yourself and never mind the rest.

Beatrix Potter, English author, *Journals 1881–1897* (NF)

17 [G]row up gentle and good, and never learn bad ways; do your work with good will, lift your feet up well when you trot, and never bite or kick even in play.

Anna Sewell, English-American author, said by Black Beauty's mother, *Black Beauty* (F)

18 Good medicine tastes bad . . . just as good advice hurts your ears.

Yoshiko Uchida, Japanese-American author, said by Rinko's mother, *The Best Bad Thing* (F)

19 [G]et plenty of sleep, and stop worrying. Never hurry and never worry! Chew your food thoroughly and eat every bite of it. . . . Gain weight and stay well.

E. B. White, US author, said by Charlotte, *Charlotte's Web* (F)

20 You shouldn't give advice you don't follow.

Patricia C. Wrede, US author, said by Queen Cimorene, *Calling on Dragons* (F)

Age

(See also Children)

1 I'm not a minute older than I was yesterday. Bless that generous-hearted dwarf!

Lloyd Alexander, US author, said by Maibon, "The Stone" from *The Foundling and Other Tales of Prydain* (F)

2 With age comes wisdom.

American proverb

3 Everyone faces at all times two fateful possibilities: one is to grow older, the other not.

Anonymous saying

4 Rise in the presence of the aged, show respect for the elderly and revere your God.

Bible: Leviticus 19:32 (NIV)

5 Shall I *never* get any older than I am now? That'll be a comfort, one way— never to be an old woman—but then— always to have lessons to learn! Oh, I shouldn't like *that*!

Lewis Carroll, English author, said by Alice, *Alice's Adventures in Wonderland* (F)

 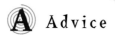

6 *One* can't [help growing older] perhaps . . . but *two* can. With proper assistance, you might have left off at seven.

Lewis Carroll, English author, said by Humpty Dumpty, *Through the Looking Glass* (F)

7 I am long on ideas, but short on time. I expect to live to be only about a hundred.

Thomas A. Edison, US inventor, in the Apr. 1931 issue of *Golden Book* magazine (NF)

8 All would live long, but none would be old.

Benjamin Franklin, Revolutionary statesman, the 1749 *Poor Richard's Almanack* (NF)

9 Will you still need me,
    will you still feed me
  When I'm sixty-four?

John Lennon, English musician and composer, words from the song "When I'm Sixty-four," written with P. McCartney

10 Pooh, *promise* you won't forget about me, ever. Not even when I'm a hundred.

A. A. Milne, English author, said by Christopher Robin, "An Enchanted Place" from *The House at Pooh Corner* (F)

11 How old would you be if you didn't know how old you was?

Leroy "Satchel" Paige, US professional baseball player, in the June 8, 1984 issue of *The New York Times* (NF)

12 Eleven is just about the best age for almost anything.

Zilpha Keatley Snyder, US author, said by Ivy, *The Changeling* (F)

13 When you get old
  And think you're sweet
  Pull off your shoes
  And smell your feet.

"When You Get Old," anonymous poem, found in *For Laughing Out Louder*, sel. by J. Prelutsky

Ambition
(See Goals)

America and Americans
(See also Native Americans)

1 America! America!
  God shed his grace on thee
  And crown thy good with brotherhood
  From sea to shining sea!

Katharine Lee Bates, US editor and author, words to the song "America the Beautiful," first published on July 4, 1895, found in *The Faber Book of America*, ed. by Ricks and Vance (NF)

2 Would America have been America without her Negro people?

W. E. B. Du Bois, US educator and author, *The Souls of Black Folk*, found at the beginning of *Our Song, Our Toil*, ed. by M. Stepto (NF)

3 To find a man who has not benefited by [Thomas] Edison . . . it would be necessary to go deep into the jungle. I hold him to be our greatest American.

Henry Ford, US car manufacturer, found in *The Thomas A. Edison Album* by L. F. Frost (NF)

4 When I was a child, my parents were always talking about "home." They meant America, of course, which sounded so wonderful I couldn't understand why they had ever left it.

Jean Fritz, US author, *China Homecoming* (NF)

5 This land is your land, this land is
      my land
   From California to the New York island;
   From the redwood forest to the Gulf
      Stream waters;
   This land was made for you and me.

Woody Guthrie, US folksinger and composer, music and words to the song "This Land Is Your Land," found in *Gonna Sing My Head Off!*, coll. and arr. by K. Krull

6 The distinctions between Virginians, Pennsylvanians, New Yorkers and New Englanders are no more. I am not a Virginian, but an American.

Patrick Henry, Revolutionary leader, in a speech to the Continental Congress on Sept. 1, 1774

7 America is not like a blanket—one piece of unbroken cloth, the same color, the same texture, the same size. America is more like a quilt—many patches, many pieces, many colors, many sizes, all woven and held together by a common thread. . . . [A]ll of us fit somewhere.

Jesse Jackson, US civil rights activist, in a July 16, 1984 speech to the Democratic National Convention

8 What the people want is very simple. They want an America as good as its promise.

Barbara Jordan, member of US Congress and educator, in a June 16, 1977 speech

9 And so, my fellow Americans: ask not what your country can do for you—ask what you can do for your country.

John F. Kennedy, 35th US President, in his Jan. 20, 1961 Inaugural Address, found in *The American Reader*, ed. by D. Ravitch (NF)

10 Oh, say, does that star-spangled banner
yet wave
O'er the land of the free, and the home
of the brave!

Francis Scott Key, US lawyer and poet, words to the song "The Star-Spangled Banner," which became the national anthem in 1931, found in *The American Reader*, ed. by D. Ravitch (NF)

11 [W]e here highly resolve . . . that this nation, under God, shall have a new birth of freedom—and that government of the people, by the people, for the people, shall not perish from this earth.

Abraham Lincoln, 16th US President, in his Nov. 19, 1863 Gettysburg Address, found in *The Faber Book of America*, ed. by Ricks and Vance (NF)

12 [Americans] made us many promises, more than I can remember, but they never kept but one; they promised to take our land, and they took it.

Manuelito, member of the Navajo tribe, in an 1865 speech before Congress

13 America was discovered accidentally by a great seaman who was looking for something else; when discovered, it was not wanted; and most of the exploration in the next fifty years was done in the hope of getting through it or around it.

Samuel Eliot Morison, US historian, *The Oxford History of the American People* (NF)

14 *E pluribus unum.* (Out of many, one.)

Motto on the Seal of the United States, adopted on June 20, 1782

15 I love to see the starry flag
That floats above my head.
I love to see its waving folds
With stripes of white and red.
"Be brave," say the red stripes,
"Be pure," say the white.
"Be true," say the bright stars,
"And stand for the right."

"Our Flag," anonymous poem, found in *Celebrating America*, comp. by L. Whipple

16 I pledge allegiance to the flag of the United States of America and to the Republic for which it stands, one nation under God, indivisible, with liberty and justice for all.

The Pledge of Allegiance, officially adopted in 1942, found in *The American Reader*, ed. by D. Ravitch. (NF)

17 History and destiny have made America the leader of the world that would be free.

Colin Powell, US Chairman of the Joint Chiefs of Staff, in a Sept. 28, 1993 speech

18 I wanted children now to understand more about the beginnings of things . . . what it is that made America as they know it.

Laura Ingalls Wilder, US author, found in *Laura Ingalls Wilder: A Biography* by W. Anderson (NF)

19 Your country needs you!

World War I recruiting slogan

Anger

1 Too bad,
So sad,
You're mad,
I'm glad.

Anonymous folk poetry, found in *And the Green Grass Grew All Around*, comp. by A. Schwartz

2 Do not let the sun go down while you are still angry.

Bible, Ephesians 4:26 (NIV)

3 There's nothing so strong as rage, except what makes you hold it in—that's stronger. It's a good thing not to answer your enemies.

Frances Hodgson Burnett, English-American author, said by Sara, *A Little Princess* (F)

4 The first fourteen years of [Sara's] life all seemed the same. . . . Now . . . she was filled with a discontent, an anger about herself, her life, her family, that made her think she would never be content again.

Betsy Byars, US author, *The Summer of the Swans* (F)

5 [I]f people could make me angry, they could control me. Why should I give someone else such power over my life?

Benjamin Carson, US surgeon and author, *Gifted Hands* (NF)

6 If you are patient in one moment of anger, you will escape a hundred days of sorrow.

Chinese proverb

7 I admire Mom, even when she's mad at me, and I know she loves me. I'm not so sure about Dad, who never gets mad at me. Maybe he doesn't care enough.

Beverly Cleary, US author, written by Leigh, *Strider* (F)

8 I am angry at the condition of society that creates problems for blacks and women. But I think there are ways anger can be turned into something positive.

Jewel Plummer Cobb, US biologist and educator, found in the *Book of Black Heroes, Vol. 2* by T. Igus (NF)

9 There is no sight so ugly as the human face in anger.

Louise Fitzhugh, US author, said by Mrs. Hansen, *The Long Secret* (F)

10 Take this remark from *Richard* poor and lame, Whate'er's begun in anger ends in shame.

Benjamin Franklin, Revolutionary statesman and inventor, the 1734 *Poor Richard's Almanack* (NF)

11 *Anger* is never without a Reason, but seldom with a good One.

Benjamin Franklin, Revolutionary statesman and inventor, the 1753 *Poor Richard's Almanack* (NF)

12 Give it time. Anger might die down by the change of a couple of seasons.

Virginia Hamilton, US author, said by Mayhew, *The House of Dies Drear* (F)

13 [D]id you ever feel so angry you could see the blood inside your eyes?

Karen Hesse, US author, said by Nyle, *Phoenix Rising* (F)

14 Anger in its time and place
May assume a kind of grace.
It must have some reason in it,
And not last beyond a minute.

Charles and Mary Lamb, English poets, "Anger," found in *The Book of Virtues for Young People*, ed. by W. J. Bennett

15 It's funny how you can be mad at someone one moment and want to hug them the next.

Anne Lindbergh, US author, *Travel Far, Pay No Fare* (F)

16 It was a pointless fight: the kind that switches from one thing to another without ever touching the important issue.

Ibid.

17 Anger has overpowered him, and driven him to revenge. . . . Anger makes us all stupid.

Johanna Spyri, Swiss author, said by Klara, *Heidi* (F)

18 A temper's like a snake. Can be coiled up, quiet as can be, and first thing you know—*wham* and you're bit.

Mary Stolz, US author, said by Mr. Wheatley, *Quentin Corn* (F)

19 One day Princess Miserella rode out of the palace in a huff. (A huff is not a kind of carriage. It is a kind of temper tantrum. Her usual kind.)

Jane Yolen, US author, *Sleeping Ugly* (F)

Animals

(See also Cats, Dogs, Horses, Mice and Rats, Pets, Rabbits, *and* Zoos)

1 Many people deny animals the *power of reasoning.* They never watched a pride of lions operating in strategic formation during a hunt, every move of each individual controlled by thought communication and working with precision until the kill is secured.

Joy Adamson, Austrian wildlife conservationist and author, "What Animals Can Tell Us about Ourselves," found in *The Golden Treasury of Animal Stories and Poems*, ed. by L. Untermeyer (NF)

2 All things bright and beautiful,
     All creatures great and small,
     All things wise and wonderful,
     The Lord God made them all.

> Cecil Frances Alexander, "All Things Bright and Beautiful," found in *The Random House Book of Poetry for Children*, sel. by J. Prelutsky

3 There was something rare and secret like the spirit of the woods about [the fox] and back of his calm, straw-gold eyes was the sense of a brain the equal to a man's.

> Paul Annixter, US author, "Last Cover" from *The Best Nature Stories of Paul Annixter* (F)

4 Consider the poor hippopotamus:
     His life is unduly monotonous.
         He lives half asleep
         At the edge of the deep,
     And his face is as big as his bottom is.

> Anonymous poem, found in *A Nonny Mouse Writes Again!*, sel. by J. Prelutsky

5 How much wood would a woodchuck chuck
     If a woodchuck could chuck wood?

> Anonymous tongue twister

6 Great green gorillas growing grapes in a gorgeous glass greenhouse.

> Graeme Base, English-Australian author and illustrator, *Animalia* (F)

7 All animals are our cousins in a way. Very distant, of course, but it's a scientific fact, all the same. . . . [I]f you think about the study of evolution, you'd find we had something in common with all living creatures.

> Nina Bawden, English author, said by Nina's mother, *Henry* (F)

8 God made the wild animals according to their kinds. . . . And God saw that it was good.

> Bible, Genesis 1:25 (NIV)

9 The turtle looked at me. There was no doubt, none whatsoever, that it had a soul.

> Bruce Brooks, US author, thought by the grandson, *Everywhere* (F)

10 If I were running this country, I would hang every-one who dumps animals [by the side of the road].

> Beverly Cleary, US author, said by Barry, *Strider* (F)

11 I know how to milk [a cow], feed it, slaughter it, skin it, drain it, quarter it, roast it, and eat it.

> Pam Conrad, US author, said by Julia Creath, *My Daniel* (F)

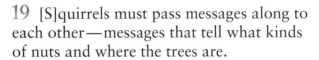

12 Take a ride on the elephant and feel, for yourself, man's domination of the greatest creature on earth.

Gillian Cross, US author, said by Michael Keenan, *The Great American Elephant Chase* (F)

13 If a man's going to keep animals to work for him and feed him, he's got an obligation to treat them right. A man who mistreats a poor, dumb beast is no better than a beast himself.

Cynthia DeFelice, US author, said by Nathan, *Weasel* (F)

14 I had seen a herd of elephants traveling through dense native forest . . . pacing along as if they had an appointment at the end of the world.

Isak Dinesen, Danish author, *Out of Africa* (NF)

15 The giraffe, in their queer, inimitable,* vegetative gracefulness, act as if it were not a herd of animals but a family of rare, long-stemmed, speckled gigantic flowers slowly advancing.

Ibid. *matchless*

16 Porcupines wear their fear on the outside. . . . They bother nothing, and nothing bothers them. They allow us the gift of their beauty.

Michael Dorris, Native American author and anthropologist, said by Moss's mother, *Guests* (F)

17 All creatures bleed the same blood, be they man or be they beast. Our fates are intermingled. Wheresoever spills the blood of any of earth's creatures, there spills the blood of man.

Susan Fletcher, US author, *Dragon's Milk* (F)

18 Extinct is forever.

Friends of Animals advertising slogan

19 [S]quirrels must pass messages along to each other—messages that tell what kinds of nuts and where the trees are.

Jean Craighead George, US author, said by Sam Gribley, *My Side of the Mountain* (F)

20 [Miyax] had been watching the wolves for two days, trying to discern which of their sounds and movements expressed goodwill and friendship.

Jean Craighead George, US author, *Julie of the Wolves* (F)

21 In the High and Far-Off Times the Elephant . . . had no trunk. He had only a blackish, bulgy nose, as big as a boot, that he could wriggle about from side to side; but he couldn't pick up things with it.

Rudyard Kipling, English-American journalist and author, "The Elephant's Child" from *Just So Stories* (F)

22 The camel's a mammal
    who grouches and grumps.
I think that he wishes
    he didn't have humps.

Maxine W. Kumin, US poet, "Camel," found in *To The Zoo: Animal Poems*, sel. by L. B. Hopkins

23 No animal should ever jump up on the dining-room furniture unless he is absolutely certain that he can hold his own in the conversation.

Fran Lebowitz, US humorist and author, *Social Studies* (NF)

24 [W]hen, on the still cold nights, [Buck] pointed his nose at a star and howled long and wolflike, it was his ancestors, dead and dust, pointing nose at star and howling down through the centuries through him.

Jack London, US author, *The Call of the Wild* (F)

25 The saddest spectacle . . . were the animals, rabbits, coyotes, mountain lions, deer, driven by the fire to the edge of the mountain, taking a look at the crowd of people and panicking, choosing rather to rush back into the fire.

Anaïs Nin, French-American author, "Forest Fire" from *The Diary of Anaïs Nin 1947–1955* (NF)

26 Care taking of a pig can keep a body as nervous as a longtail cat in a room full of rocking chairs.

Robert Newton Peck, US author, said by Rob's father, *A Day No Pigs Would Die* (F)

27 Benny, [the Little Blue Ox of Paul Bunyan], grew two feet every time Paul looked at him.

Carl Sandburg, US poet and biographer, "Paul Bunyan of the North Woods" from *The People, Yes* (F)

28 The destruction of a species is final.

George Schaller, US naturalist and field biologist, in the Feb. 2, 1997 *Parade* magazine (NF)

29 I meant what I said
And I said what I meant . . .
An elephant's faithful
One hundred per cent!

Dr. Seuss, US author, said by Horton, *Horton Hatches the Egg* (F)

30 Why did God make owls, snakes, cats, foxes, fleas, and other such loathsome, abominable creatures? [The mouse Abel] felt there had to be a reason.

William Steig, US author and illustrator, *Abel's Island* (F)

31 Wake not a sleeping lion.

Turkish proverb

32 There is no sight more beautiful in the animal kingdom than that of a full-grown bull in action. Its bravery, pride, majesty, and strength cannot be matched by any other animal.

Maia Wojciechowska, Polish-American author, said by an old man, *Shadow of a Bull* (F)

Appearances

(See also Beauty*)*

1 It really does not pay to pretend to be what you are not.

Aesop, Greek writer, the moral in the fable "A Wolf in Sheep's Clothing," found in *The Children's Treasury*, ed. by P. S. Goepfert (F)

2 Even in my day, mortals had a deplorable tendency to mix appearances with fact. I should hate to tell you how many numbskulls put crowns on their heads—as if a metal hoop had anything to do with being a king.

Lloyd Alexander, US author, said by the wizard Arbican, *The Wizard in the Tree* (F)

3 [Mrs. Bertha Flowers] had the grace of control to appear warm in the coldest weather, and on the Arkansas summer days it seemed she had a private breeze which swirled around, cooling her.

Maya Angelou, US poet and author, *I Know Why the Caged Bird Sings* (NF)

4 Every person has a kind of animal they got their soul mixed up with way back when the world was made. You can tell [what it is] by what they look like.

Bruce Brooks, US author, said by Dooley, *Everywhere* (F)

5 I think how you look is the most important thing in the world. If you *look* cute, you *are* cute. If you *look* smart, you *are* smart, and if you don't look like anything, then you aren't anything.

Betsy Byars, US author, said by Sara, *The Summer of the Swans* (F)

6 I know I place too much importance on the way I appear to the outside world, and I keep things inside too much. I [just] don't like to give pieces of myself away.

Julie Reece Deaver, US author and illustrator, thought by Morgan, *Say Goodnight, Gracie* (F)

7 How large unto the tiny fly
　　Must little things appear! —
　A rosebud like a feather bed,
　　Its prickle like a spear.

Walter de la Mare, English author and poet, "The Fly" from *The Complete Works of Walter de la Mare*

8 Appearances are deceitful.

English proverb

9 [W]hen I think of your good heart, you no longer seem to me so ugly.

Clifton Johnson, said by Beauty, a retelling of *Beauty and the Beast* (F)

10 [Mr. Smith] looked as though he'd been manufactured to fit his name. Average height, brownish hair, pale skin, medium build, middle aged. He was the sort of person you began to forget the minute you met him.

Robert Lipsyte, US author, "Future Tense" from *Sixteen* (F)

11 Thenceforth, in the nature of things, [the wolf cub] would possess an abiding distrust of appearances. He would have to learn the reality of a thing before he could put his faith in it.

Jack London, US author, *White Fang* (F)

12 I'm sure you're much nicer than you look!

Eleanor H. Porter, US author, said by Pollyanna to Mr. Pendleton, *Pollyanna* (F)

Arithmetic

1 There was an old man who said, "Gee!
I can't multiply seven by three!
   Though fourteen seems plenty,
   It might come to twenty—
I haven't the slightest idee!

Anonymous limerick, found in *Laughable Limericks*, comp. by S. and J. Brewton

2 Asa loudly lamented the great injustice that he must struggle with Arithmetic while Cassie and I, indeed, all we girls [in 1831] are excused by reason of our Sex from all but the simplest ciphering, and the first four rules.

Joan W. Blos, US author, written by Catherine Cabot Hall, *A Gathering of Days* (F)

3 [Harriet] hated math. She hated math with every bone in her body. She spent so much time hating it that she never had time to do it.

Louise Fitzhugh, US author, *Harriet the Spy* (F)

4 [In school] I acquired fair writing pretty soon . . . but I failed in the arithmetic, and made no progress in it.

Benjamin Franklin, Revolutionary statesman, found in *Benjamin Franklin* by R. R. Potter (NF)

5 Two plus two equals four. . . . When two plus two doesn't equal four, anything can happen.

Louis Sachar, US author, said by Mrs. Jewls, *Sideways Stories from Wayside School* (F)

6 Arithmetic is where numbers fly like pigeons in and out of your head.

Carl Sandburg, US poet and biographer, "Arithmetic," found in *Rainbows Are Made*, sel. by L. B. Hopkins

7 Arithmetic is numbers you squeeze from your head to your hand to your pencil to your paper till you get the answer.

Ibid.

8 Arithmetic is where you have to multiply—and you carry the multiplication table in your head and hope you won't lose it.

Ibid.

9 Math and me don't get along too well. I figure that's because my head is round and math is very square and logical. So all that square math just bounces off my round head and never gets in there.

Robert Kimmel Smith, US author, said by Bobby, *Bobby Baseball* (F)

10 I give my dad credit for singlehandedly keeping my math grades high enough so I wouldn't be held back [in school].

Steven Spielberg, US movie director and producer, in the Jan. 1994 *Biography Today* (NF)

Athletes

(See Sports)

Baseball

1 I never want them to forget Babe Ruth. I just want them to remember Aaron.

Hank Aaron, US professional baseball player, in a 1982 speech upon his induction into the Baseball Hall of Fame

2 I would forget to eat because of baseball.

Roberto Clemente, Puerto Rican professional baseball player, found in *Champions* by B. Littlefield (NF)

3 When I was young, I was so interested in baseball that my family was afraid I'd waste my life and be a pitcher. Later, they were afraid I'd waste my life and be a poet. . . . They were right.

Robert Frost, US poet, found in *A Restless Spirit: The Story of Robert Frost* by N. S. Bober (NF)

4 The mound is a mountain. You are at the bottom trying to hit uphill. The pitcher is King Kong.

Joe Garagiola, US professional baseball player, *Baseball Is a Funny Game* (NF)

5 They throw the ball, I hit it; they hit the ball, I catch it.

Willie Mays, US professional baseball player, in the July 25, 1970 *Sporting News* (NF)

6 Our lives are loops
or line drives
bunts, grounders, towering
home runs
and death a stumpy shortshop
or a tall guy out in left field
waiting to gather us up.

Lillian Morrison, US poet, "Fair or Foul" from *The Sidewalk Racer and Other Poems of Sports and Motion*

7 Take me out to the ball game,
Take me out with the crowd.
Buy me some peanuts and
    Cracker Jack,
I don't care if I never get back.

Jack Norworth, US actor, words to the song "Take Me Out to the Ball Game," published in 1908, found in *Gonna Sing My Head Off!*, coll. and arr. by K. Krull

8 It got so I could nip frosting off a cake with my fastball.

Leroy "Satchel" Paige, US professional baseball player, *Maybe I'll Pitch Forever* (NF)

9 [Jackie Robinson's] courage forced open doors of the sport to people of color from all over the Western Hemisphere. But it wasn't easy, especially that first year.

Lawrence S. Ritter, US author, *How It All Began* (NF)

10 I was even with baseball and baseball was even with me. The game had done much for me, and I had done much for it.

Jackie Robinson, US professional baseball player, found in *Jackie Robinson: Baseball Great* by R. Scott (NF)

11 I hit big or I miss big. I like to live as big as I am.

Babe Ruth, US professional baseball player, found in *Baseball, the American Epic* by Ward and Burns (NF)

12 Throwing a fastball by Henry Aaron is like trying to sneak the sun past a rooster.

Curt Simmons, US journalist, in the Nov. 19, 1973 *Sports Illustrated* (NF)

13 Personally I wish that girls never got into playing [Mustang League] baseball. Girls do nothing but mess up a team. They can't throw and they can't catch and some of them run funny.

Robert Kimmel Smith, US author, said by Bobby, *Bobby Baseball* (F)

14 The biggest thing in my life is baseball. . . . I think about base-ball a lot. Like most of the time. I also dream of baseball. Even when I'm awake.

Ibid.

15 But there was no joy in Mudville—mighty Casey has struck out!

Ernest Lawrence Thayer, US poet, "Casey at the Bat," found in *From Sea to Shining Sea*, comp. by A. L. Cohn

Basketball

1 I believe that basketball is the most phys-ically grueling* of all professional sports.

Bill Bradley, US professional basketball player and senator, *Life on the Run* (NF)   *demanding

2 A professional basketball player must be able to run six miles in a game, a hundred games a year—jumping and pivoting under constant physical contact.

Ibid.

3 When trapped into playing basketball, I made my own rule: always run away from the ball. No one ever complained, or, as far as I know, noticed.

Beverly Cleary, US author, *A Girl from Yamhill: A Memoir* (NF)

4 I keep both eyes on my man. The basket hasn't moved on me yet.

Julius Erving, professional basketball player, in the Mar. 14, 1977 *Sports Illustrated* (NF)

5 I can accept failure. Everyone fails at something. But I can't accept not trying.

Michael Jordan, US professional basketball player, *I Can't Accept Not Trying* (NF)

6 Once I get the ball, you're at my mercy. There is nothing you can say or do about it. I own the ball. . . . When I'm on my game, I don't think there's anybody that can stop me.

Michael Jordan, US professional basketball player, in a Mar. 1989 interview

7 My definition of losing is not somebody who loses a game. . . . Losing is giving up. . . . Everyone can be a winner in life.

Cheryl Miller, US basketball player and sports commentator, found in the *Book of Black Heroes, Vol. 2* by T. Igus (NF)

8 Basketball players
already tall
rise on springs
aspiring for the ball,
leap for the rebound
arms on high
in a dance
of hallelujahs.

Lillian Morrison, US poet, "Forms of Praise" from *The Sidewalk Racer and Other Poems of Sports and Motion*

Beauty

(See also Appearances)

1 Of course, a dog is a pretty poor judge of human beauty, but I'd seen enough fashion magazines to give me a rough idea.

Ann Braybrooks, US screenwriter, said by Pongo in Walt Disney's adapted film version of *101 Dalmatians* (F)

2 If it had grown up . . . it would have made a dreadfully ugly child; but it makes rather a handsome pig.

Lewis Carroll, English author, said by Alice, *Alice's Adventures in Wonderland* (F)

3 Beauty is but skin deep.
English proverb

4 Looks ain't everything in this life, unless you happen to look like a turkey buzzard, and then they're pretty crucial. It's hard to be friendly to something that ugly.

John R. Erickson, US author, said by Hank, *Hank the Cowdog* (F)

5 As a beauty I'm not a great star,
  There are others more handsome by far,
    But my face I don't mind it,
    Because I'm behind it—
  'Tis the folks in the front that I jar!

Anthony Euwer, "My Face," found in *The Classic Treasury of Silly Poetry*, ed. by J. P. Resnick

12 Remember that the most beautiful things in the world are the most useless: peacocks and lilies, for instance.

John Ruskin, English author, found in *The International Thesaurus of Quotations*, comp. by Ehrlich and De Bruhl (NF)

6 Common-looking people are the best in the world; that is the reason the Lord made so many of them.

Abraham Lincoln, 16th US President, in the Dec. 24, 1865 diary entry of Lincoln's secretary, found in *Lincoln: A Photobiography* by R. Freedman (NF)

7 There weren't two ways about it—the girl had no beauty, and in a royal Princess that is a serious flaw.

Phyllis McGinley, US author, *The Plain Princess* (F)

8 [Harry Crewe] had never much cared for beauty, although she was aware that she lacked it and that her position might have been a little easier if she had not.

Robin McKinley, US author, *The Blue Sword* (F)

9 Mrs. Thomas said I was the homeliest baby she ever saw . . . but that my mother thought I was perfectly beautiful. I should think a mother would be a better judge than a poor woman who came in to scrub.

L. M. Montgomery, Canadian author, said by Anne, *Anne of Green Gables* (F)

10 [W]hat makes you think we ever know how beautiful we are? No one knows.

Sylvia Peck, US author, said by Ruby, *Seal Child* (F)

11 I cannot tell you how many times people have come up to me to compliment me on my lavish figure.

Miss Piggy, muppet, *Miss Piggy's Guide to Life*, as told to H. Beard (F)

13 Generally, by the time you are Real, most of your hair has been loved off, and your eyes drop out and you get loose in the joints and very shabby. But these things don't matter at all, because once you are Real, you can't be ugly, except to people who don't understand.

Margery Williams, English-American author, said by the Skin Horse, *The Velveteen Rabbit* (F)

Birds

1 The sad young bluejay flew away.
He'd had a most distressing day,
For shame and scorn were all he got
For trying to be what he was not.

Aesop, Greek writer, the moral in "The Jay and the
Peacock," a retelling by Tom Paxton from *Androcles and the
Lion and Other Aesop's Fables* (F)

2 Many birds were so astonished at the
sight [of two double rainbows] that they
stopped flying and fell to the ground, or
collided with each other in midair.

Joan Aiken, English author, *The Last Slice of Rainbow* (F)

3 It didn't work.
I planted birdseed in the ground
And wild weeds sprouted all around.
I know it sounds a bit absurd
But I couldn't grow a single bird.

Brod Bagert, US poet, "Birdseed," found in *For Laughing
Out Louder,* sel. by J. Prelutsky

4 Said Orville Wright to Wilbur Wright;
"These birds are very trying.
I'm sick of hearing them cheep-cheep
About the fun of flying."

Rosemary and Stephen Vincent Benét, US poets,
"Wilbur Wright and Orville Wright" from *A Book of
Americans*

5 Nothing in the world is quite as
adorably lovely as a robin when he shows
off—and they are nearly always doing it.

Frances Hodgson Burnett, English-American author,
The Secret Garden (F)

6 Over increasingly large areas of the
United States, spring now comes unheralded
by the return of the birds, and the early
mornings are strangely silent where once
they were filled with the beauty of bird song.

Rachel Carson, US environmentalist and author, *Silent
Spring* (NF)

7 A bird in the hand is worth two in the
bush.

English proverb

8 The early bird catches the worm.

English proverb

9 I wish the bald eagle had not been
chosen as the representative of our
country: he is a bird of bad moral character
. . . generally poor, and often very lousy.

Benjamin Franklin, Revolutionary statesman, in a Jan.
26, 1764 letter to Sarah Bache

10 Out of the sky, from a pinpoint of a
thing, would dive my beautiful falcon.
And, oh, she was beautiful when she made
a strike—all power and beauty.

Jean Craighead George, US author, said by Sam about
Frightful, *My Side of the Mountain* (F)

11 Here and there great branches had been
torn away by the sheer weight of the snow,
and robins perched and hopped on them in
their perky conceited way, just as if they
had done it themselves.

Kenneth Grahame, English author, *The Wind in the
Willows* (F)

16 There were fussy and chatty grey doves like Grandmothers . . . and greeny, cackling, no-I've-no-money-today pigeons like Fathers. And the silly, anxious, soft blue doves were like Mothers.

P. L. Travers, Australian-English author, *Mary Poppins* (F)

17 It ain't any use to tell me a blue-jay hasn't got a sense of humor, because I know better.

Mark Twain, US author, "What Stumped the Blue-jays" from *The Complete Short Stories of Mark Twain* (F)

18 [Wilbur and I] could not understand that there was anything about a bird that could not be built on a larger scale and used by man.

Orville Wright, US inventor, found in *The Wright Brothers* by R. Freedman (NF)

12 A parrot . . . is a tropical zygodactyl bird (order psittaciformes) that has a stout curved hooked bill, is often crested, brightly variegated and an excellent mimic. In other words . . . a parrot is a little bird with a big mouth.

Deborah and James Howe, US authors, said by Chester the cat, *Bunnicula: A Rabbit-Tale of Mystery* (F)

13 Birds look free but they're not. . . . They're prisoners, really, of their own territory. They can't move easily from one territory to another.

M. E. Kerr, US author, said by Buddy's grandfather, *Gentlehands* (F)

14 [Mockingbirds] don't eat up people's gardens, don't nest in corncribs, they don't do one thing but sing their hearts out for us. That's why it's a sin to kill a mockingbird.

Harper Lee, US author, said by Miss Maudie, *To Kill a Mockingbird* (F)

15 The little birds sang as if it were the one day of summer in all the year.

L. M. Montgomery, Canadian author, *Anne of Green Gables* (F)

Books

(See also Reading *and* Writers and Writing*)*

1 A book is a friend.
American proverb

2 [Laura Ingalls Wilder] wanted her books to be known as true stories, accurate in every historical detail.

William Anderson, US author, *Laura Ingalls Wilder: A Biography* (NF)

3 The twentieth century was often called the Era of the Book. In those days, there were books about everything from anteaters to Zulus. . . . They illustrated, educated, punctuated, and even decorated. But the strangest thing a book ever did was to save the Earth.

Claire Boiko, US playwright, said by Historian in the play *The Book That Saved the Earth* (F)

4 When I type a title page, I hold it and I look at it and I think, I just need four thousand sentences to go with this and I'll have a book!

Betsy Byars, US author, *The Moon and I: A Memoir* (NF)

5 What is the use of a book . . . without pictures or conversation?

Lewis Carroll, English author, said by Alice, *Alice's Adventures in Wonderland* (F)

6 Through the use of books I had the whole world at my feet: could travel anywhere, meet anyone, and do anything.

Benjamin Carson, US surgeon and author, *Gifted Hands* (NF)

7 In the seventh grade . . . I found a place on the [library] shelf where my book would be if I ever wrote a book, which I doubted.

Beverly Cleary, US author, *A Girl from Yamhill: A Memoir* (NF)

8 Books have been [Oprah Winfrey's] friends for as long as she can remember, sometimes her only friends. And, she says, they made her who she is today.

Marilyn Johnson, US journalist, in the Sept. 1997 *Life* magazine (NF)

9 A book is just a way to *remember* a story, like a photograph is a way to remember a friend.

Anne Lindbergh, US author, said by Parsley, *Travel Far, Pay No Fare* (F)

10 If the First Amendment means anything, it means that a State has no business telling a man, sitting alone in his own house, what books he may read or what films he may watch.

Thurgood Marshall, US Supreme Court Justice, in an Apr. 7, 1969 legal opinion

11 The daughter learned to love books, particularly adventure novels where the hero rode a beautiful horse and ran all the villains through with his silver sword.

Robin McKinley, US author, *The Blue Sword* (F)

12 This Book is to be Read in Bed.

Dr. Seuss, US author, the Foreword to *Sleep Book* (F)

13 [Encyclopedia Brown] read more books than anyone in Idaville, and he never forgot a fact. His pals said he was like a library and a computer rolled into one, and more user-friendly.

Donald J. Sobol, US author, "The Case of the Fifth Word" from *Encyclopedia Brown and The Case of the Disgusting Sneakers* (F)

14 Mongoose just sat there [in the library], like he was hypnotized by the book in front of him. Other books were spread across the table, like he was taking a bath in books.

Jerry Spinelli, US author, "Mongoose" from *The Library Card* (F)

15 [In Amanda Beale's suitcase] there were fiction books and nonfiction books, who-did-it books and let's-be-friends books and what-is-it books and how-to books and how-not-to books and just-regular-kid books.

Jerry Spinelli, US author, *Maniac Magee* (F)

16 Many adults feel that every children's book has to teach them something. . . . My theory is a children's book . . . can be just for fun.

R. L. Stine, US author of the Goosebumps books, in the Apr. 1994 *Biography Today* (NF)

17 My books are water; those [books] of the great geniuses are wine. Everybody drinks water.

Mark Twain, US author, found in *Mark Twain: America's Humorist, Dreamer, Prophet* by C. Cox (NF)

18 I think I was born with the impression that what happened in books was much more reasonable, and interesting, and *real*, in some ways, than what happened in life.

Anne Tyler, English author, found in *The Writer on Her Work*, ed. by J. Sternburg (NF)

19 People put down [in books] what happened before you were even born, and you can understand and not make the same mistakes. Like history, books let things in.

Cynthia Voigt, US author, said by James, *Homecoming* (F)

Brothers and Sisters

1 A good sister to me all these years in spite of the utter unlikeness of our tastes, temperaments & lives. If we did not love one another so well, we never could get on at all.

Louisa May Alcott, US author, speaking of her sister Anna, found in *Louisa May* by N. Johnston (NF)

2 Many things in my story truly happened; and much of *Little Women* is a reflection of the life led by us four sisters.

Louisa May Alcott, US author, in an Aug. 7, 1875 letter to Mrs. H. Koorders-Boeke, found in *Great Americans in Their Own Words* (NF)

3 It was a great thrill to be on the [San Francisco Giants] team with my two younger brothers. Three brothers playing together is something that was never accomplished before.

Felipe Alou, Cuban-American professional baseball player and manager, referring to Matty and Jesus Alou, found in *Famous Hispanic Americans* by Morey and Dunn (NF)

4 My mother and father didn't plan for me to be an only child, but that's the way it worked out, which is fine with me because this way I don't have anybody around to fight.

Judy Blume, US author, said by Margaret, *Are You There, God? It's Me, Margaret* (F)

5 [Matthew] knows what he would like to do but he's not sure where he could find a rocket that would shoot [his sister] Vanessa to Mars.

Paula Danziger, US author, *Earth to Matthew* (F)

6 I was dumbfounded. It was the first time in my life I'd ever heard my brother, with his great brain, admit he didn't know everything.

John D. Fitzgerald, US author, said by J.D., *The Great Brain* (F)

7 I knew that I loved [my younger brother Arliss] as much as I did Mama and Papa, maybe in some ways even a little bit more.

Fred Gipson, US author, said by Travis, *Old Yeller* (F)

8 I *have* a half-sister
I *have* a whole-sister
I *have* a step-sister
That adds up to three.

I *am* a half-brother
I *am* a whole-brother
I *am* a step-brother
There's just one of me!

Mary Ann Hoberman, US poet, "Half-Whole-Step" from *Fathers, Mothers, Sisters, Brothers*

9 You might call [feeling like part of a team] caring. You could even call it love. And it is very rarely, indeed, that it happens to two people at the same time — especially a brother and a sister.

E. L. Konigsburg, US author and illustrator, *From the Mixed Up Files of Mrs. Basil E. Frankweiler* (F)

10 We get to play with each other, and you always have a friend. There's nothing bad about being a twin.

Mary-Kate and Ashley Olsen, US actresses, in the Sept. 1995 *Biography Today* (NF)

11 My brother built that robot
to help us clean our room,
instead it ate the dust pan
and attacked us with the broom.

Jack Prelutsky, US poet, "My Brother Built a Robot" from *Something Big Has Happened Here*

12 One sister for sale!
One sister for sale!
One crying and spying young sister
   for sale!
I'm really not kidding,
So who'll start the bidding?

Shel Silverstein, US poet and illustrator, "For Sale" from *Where the Sidewalk Ends*

13 I think growing up with three brothers made me really tough and competitive because I always wanted to beat them in everything.

Charlotte Smith, US professional basketball player, found in *Women in Sports* by J. Layden (NF)

14 [My sister's] such a brain and a good athlete that I know I can't compete so I rebel.

Todd Strasser, US author, said by Jake, *Help! I'm Trapped in My Teacher's Body* (F)

15 Brothers and sisters are like hands and feet.

Vietnamese proverb

16 From the time we were children, my brother Orville and myself lived together, played together, worked together and, in fact, thought together.

Wilbur Wright, US inventor, found in *The Wright Brothers* by R. Freedman (NF)

Bugs

1 Oh, say, can you see
Any bedbugs on me?
If you do, pick a few,
And we'll have bedbug stew.

Anonymous folk poetry, found in *And the Green Grass Grew All Around*, comp. by A. Schwartz

2 A centipede was happy quite,
  Until a frog in fun
Said, "Pray, which leg comes after which?"
She lay distracted in the ditch
  Considering how to run.

Anonymous poem, found in the *Oxford Book of Poetry for Children*, comp. by E. Blishen

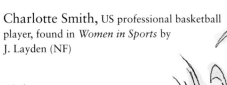

3 They came suddenly—the way [fireflies] always do. First there was a black sky, then there were hundreds of gold and yellow lights sparking up the darkness.

Patricia Beatty, US author, thought by Hannalee, *Be Ever Hopeful, Hannalee* (F)

4 So what would you call it if you saw a grasshopper as large as a dog? As large as a *large* dog? You could hardly call *that* an insect, could you?

Roald Dahl, English author, *James and the Giant Peach* (F)

5 All the insects in all the world
  About the Scroobious Pip entwirled.
    Beetles and (bookworms) with
      purple eyes,
    Gnats and buzztilential flies,
  Grasshoppers, butterflies, spiders, too,
  Wasps and bees and dragonflies blue.

Edward Lear, English artist and poet, *The Scroobious Pip*

6 Every bee that ever was
was partly sting and partly . . . buzz.

Jack Prelutsky, US poet, "Bees," found in *Animal Poems,*
comp. by P. Richardson

9 The spider does not weave his web for
one fly.

Slovenian proverb

BUZZZZ Z Z ZZZZZ¹ʳ¹ʳ...

BUZZZZ ZZ Z ZZZZZ ¹ ¹ ¹ ¹ ...

BUZZZZZZZZ¹ ¹ ¹ ¹ ¹ ...

7 Hunt no living thing;
Ladybird, nor butterfly,
Nor moth with dusty wing,
Nor cricket chirping cheerily,
Nor grasshopper so light of leap,
Nor dancing gnat, nor beetle fat,
Nor harmless worms that creep.

Christina Rossetti, English poet, "Hurt No Living
Thing," found in *The Random House Book of Poetry
for Children,* sel. by J. Prelutsky

8 You can tell the temperature with
crickets. You count the number of chirps
in a minute, divide by four and add forty.
They're very intelligent.

George Selden, US author, said by Mario, *The Cricket in
Times Square (F)*

**10 A young spider knows
how to spin a web without
any instructions from anyone. Don't you regard that
as a miracle?**

E. B. White, US author, said by Dr. Dorian,
Charlotte's Web (F)

11 [T]he line of ants closed in, chanting
and snuffling and breathing out some kind
of dark, thick smell.

Jane Yolen, US author, "Harlyn's Fairy" from *Twelve
Impossible Things Before Breakfast* (F)

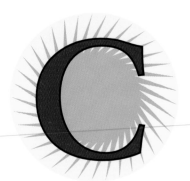

Careers

(See Occupations)

Cats

(See also Pets)

1 A cat is a lion to a mouse.
Albanian proverb

2 A catalog is where cats come from. It's a big book full of pictures of hundreds and hundreds of cats. And when you open it up, all the cats jump out and start running around.

Ann Cameron, US author, said by Julian, "Catalog Cats" from *The Stories Julian Tells* (F)

3 I didn't know that cheshire cats always grinned; in fact, I didn't know that cats *could* grin.

Lewis Carroll, English author, said by Alice, *Alice's Adventures in Wonderland* (F)

4 The Rum Tum Tugger is a terrible bore: When you let him in, then he wants to be out; He's always on the wrong side of every door, And as soon as he's at home, then he'd like to get about.

T. S. Eliot, American-English poet and playwright, "The Rum Tum Tugger" from *Old Possum's Book of Practical Cats*

5 When the cat's away, the mice will play.
English proverb

6 Farm cats have a pretty good time. They may not be petted or cosseted* but it has always seemed to me that they lead a free, natural life.

James Herriot, English veterinarian and author, *Moses the Kitten* (F)   *pampered

7 I don't know if you've ever watched a cat try to decide where to sit, but it involves a lot of circling around, sitting, getting up again, circling some more, thinking about it, lying down, standing up, bathing a paw or tail and . . . circling!

Deborah and James Howe, US authors, said by Harold the dog, *Bunnicula: A Rabbit-Tale of Mystery* (F)

8 [S]ome town cats are nothing better than prisoners, kept indoors all the time. Well treated, maybe, well fed and fussed over, but just as much prisoners as those rabbits [in the cage].

Dick King-Smith, English author, said by Martin's father, *Martin's Mice* (F)

9 Cats are patient. Even when they are anxious and frightened, they will wait quietly, watching to see what happens.

Ursula K. Le Guin, US author, *Catwings Returns* (F)

10 Cats definitely have their own opinions.

Ann M. Martin, US author, found in *Ann M. Martin: The Story of the Author of the Baby-sitters Club* by M. Becker R. (NF)

11 When he wanted to go outside, Max would look my father straight in the eye and shred a piece of furniture.

Paul Meisel, US illustrator, from *Purr . . . Children's Book Illustrators Brag about Their Cats*, ed. by M. J. Rosen (NF)

12 Cats sleep fat.
They spread out comfort
   underneath them
Like a good mat,
As if they picked the place
And then sat;
You walk around one
As if he were the City Hall
After that.

Rosalie Moore, US poet, "Catalogue," found in *Cat Poems*, sel. by M. C. Livingston

13 The trouble with a kitten is
THAT
Eventually it becomes a
CAT.

Ogden Nash, US poet, "The Kitten," found in *Custard and Company*, sel. by Q. Blake

14 Finally and most important, cats do not have nine lives. You only have one life, and if you lose it, no more cat.

Phyllis Reynolds Naylor, US author, said by Carlotta the cat, *The Great Escape* (F)

15 If man could be crossed with the cat, it would improve man, but it would deteriorate* the cat.

Mark Twain, US author, *Notebook* (NF)   *worsen

16 Ignorant people think it's the *noise* which fighting cats make that is so aggravating, but it ain't so; it's the sickening grammar they use.

Mark Twain, US author, "What Stumped the Blue-jays" from *The Complete Short Stories of Mark Twain* (F)

17 There's just something in me that doesn't trust a cat.

E. B. White, US author, said by the mouse Stuart, *Stuart Little* (F)

Change

1 All of us, at one time or another, grow a little weary of what we are. Sometimes, I tire of being a wizard. Sometimes you tire of being a cat. It's quite normal. Very well. You shall be—oh, let us say, a badger. For a few days. A refreshing change.

Lloyd Alexander, US author, said by the wizard Stephanus, *The Cat Who Wished To Be a Man* (F)

2 The odds are very good that worrying is a waste of time. And besides, worrying won't change what happens anyway, will it?

Judie Angell, US author, said by Mr. Meyer, "I Saw What I Saw" from *A Whisper in the Night* (F)

3 The need for change bulldozed a road down the center of my mind.

Maya Angelou, US poet and author, *I Know Why the Caged Bird Sings* (NF)

4 Everything don't change much. . . . There's eatin' and sleepin' and talkin' and settin' that goes on. One day might be different from another, but there ain't much difference when they're put together.

William H. Armstrong, US author, thought by the boy, *Sounder* (F)

5 Things just are, and fussing don't bring changes.

Natalie Babbitt, US author, said by Mae Tuck, *Tuck Everlasting* (F)

6 The grass withers and the flowers fall, but the word of our God stands forever.

Bible, Isaiah 40:8 (NIV)

7 [T]o stay young always is also not to change. And that is what life's all about—changes going on every minute, and you never know when something begins where it's going to take you.

Joan W. Blos, US author, written by Catherine Hall Onesti, *A Gathering of Days* (F)

8 The things I don't like, I will try to change.

Medgar Evers, US civil rights activist, found in *Contemporary Heroes and Heroines*, ed. by R. B. Browne (NF)

9 I am sure no doll ever underwent so great a change in two short weeks. No butterfly emerged more resplendent* from its cocoon than I from the hands of Miss Milly Pinch.

Rachel Field, US author, said by Hitty, *Hitty: Her First Hundred Years* (F)   *brilliant

10 And then the most extraordinary transmogrifications (which is just a long word for "changes") began to occur.

Ian Fleming, English author, *Chitty Chitty Bang Bang: The Magical Car* (F)

11 The only sure thing about luck is that it will change.

Bret Harte, US author, "The Outcasts of Poker Flat" (F)

12 I was myself last night, but I fell asleep on the mountain, and they've changed my gun, and everything's changed, and I'm changed, and I can't tell what's my name, or who I am!

Washington Irving, US author, said by Rip Van Winkle, *Rip Van Winkle* (F)

13 Where there is hope there is life, where there is life there is possibility, and where there is possibility change can occur.

Jesse Jackson, US civil rights activist, found in *My Soul Looks Back, 'Less I Forget,* ed. by D. W. Riley (NF)

14 We were content to let things remain as the Great Spirit made them. [The white men] were not, and would change the rivers and mountains if they did not suit them.

Chief Joseph, leader of the Nez Perce, found in *Bury My Heart at Wounded Knee* by D. Brown (NF)

15 I give thanks for things that time nor circumstances can never change — a mother's love, a song.

Sally M. Keehn, US author, said by Regina, *I am Regina* (F)

16 When people change, old pictures of them don't change along with them.

Anne Lindbergh, US author, said by Parsley, *Travel Far, Pay No Fare* (F)

17 Good-bye is always hello to something else. Good-bye/hello, good-bye/hello, like the sound of a rocking chair.

George Ella Lyons, US author, *Borrowed Children* (F)

18 Isn't it strange
  That however I change,
  I still keep on being me?

Eve Merriam, US poet, "Me, Myself and I" from *Rainbow Writing*

19 Everything [Mandy] knew about life was suddenly broken into pieces, like the bright shards in a kaleidoscope. Telephones, computers, homework, buses, everything was utterly changed now that the world had elves in it.

Ann Turner, US author, *Elfsong* (F)

Children

(See also Age)

1 Let the little children come to me . . . for the kingdom of heaven belongs to such as these.

Bible, Matthew 19:14 (NIV)

2 If you ask me, being a teenager is pretty rotten— between pimples and worry about how you smell!

Judy Blume, US author, said by Margaret, *Are You There, God? It's Me, Margaret* (F)

3 Of course, I'm "young," and politics are conducted by "grown-ups." But I think we "young" would do it better. We certainly wouldn't have chosen war.

Zlata Filipovic, Sarajevian diarist, *Zlata's Diary*, Nov. 19, 1992 entry (NF)

4 Parents can only give good advice or put [their children] on the right paths, but the final forming of a person's character lies in their own hands.

Otto Frank, Dutch father of Anne Frank, quoted by Anne, from *Anne Frank: The Diary of a Young Girl*, July 15, 1944 entry (NF)

5 Many of us allow our children to eat junk, play with junk, watch junk [on TV], listen to junk, and then we're surprised when they come out to be social junkies.

Jesse Jackson, US civil rights activist, found in *Jesse Jackson* by A. Kosof (NF)

6 We are the world, we are the children
We are the ones who make a brighter day
So let's start giving.

Michael Jackson and Lionel Richie, US singers and composers, words and music to the song "We Are the World"

7 [My owners] thought [my father] had spoiled his children, by teaching them to feel that they were human beings.

Harriet A. Jacobs, US diarist, *Incidents in the Life of a Slave Girl* (NF)

8 Children learn from their parents.

Japanese proverb

9 All kids need is a little help, a little hope, and somebody who believes in them.

Earvin "Magic" Johnson, US professional basketball player and businessman, *My Life* (NF)

10 Being a kid in America is hard work.

Athena V. Lord, US author, *Today's Special: Z.A.P. and Zoe* (F)

11 [Mrs. Goodgame] was one of those rare unhappy grown-ups who are profoundly irritated by the fact that children exist.

Ian McEwan, English author, *The Daydreamer* (F)

12 Childhood Is the Kingdom Where Nobody Dies.

Edna St. Vincent Millay, US poet, poem title

13 Way we're raised around here [in the hills of West Virginia], children don't talk back to grown folks. Don't hardly talk much at all, in fact. Learn to listen, keep your mouth shut, let the grown folks do the talking.

Phyllis Reynolds Naylor, US author, said by Marty, *Shiloh* (F)

14 The airways seemed filled with the children of broken homes, migrating like birds [between parents].

Richard Peck, US author, thought by Jim Atwater, *Father Figure* (F)

15 If I had it to do over, I'd get started [playing golf] at about 10, 11, or 12. You develop a more natural swing if you start as a kid.

Betsy Rawls, US professional golfer, found in *Women in Sports* by J. Layden (NF)

16 [B]eing grown up is something you decide inside yourself.

Mary Francis Shura, US author, thought by Greg, *The Josie Gambit* (F)

17 It is quite possible that an animal has spoken civilly* to me and that I didn't catch the remark because I wasn't paying attention. Children pay better attention [to animals] than grownups.

E. B. White, US author, said by Dr. Dorian, *Charlotte's Web* (F)   *politely

18 The world is a wonderful place when you're young.

E. B. White, US author, said by a goose, *Charlotte's Web* (F)

Choices

1 Is it better to be wise if it makes you solemn and practical, or is it better to be foolish so you can go on enjoying yourself?

Natalie Babbitt, US author, said by Uncle Ott, *Knee-Knock Rise* (F)

2 [O]nce I had brains, and a heart also; so, having tried them both, I should much rather have a heart.

L. Frank Baum, US author, said by Tin Woodman, *The Wonderful Wizard of Oz* (F)

3 Choose for yourselves this day whom you will serve. . . . But as for me and my household, we will serve the Lord.

Bible, Joshua 24:15 (NIV)

4 [Y]ou have to make your own choices. And then live with them.

Ilene Cooper, US author, said by Jonathan's father, *Choosing Sides* (F)

5 I spent that day mostly in the woods, having the alternative before me — to go home and be whipped to death, or stay in the woods and be starved to death.

Frederick Douglass, US abolitionist and author, *Escape from Slavery*, ed. by M. McCudy (NF)

6 When someone makes out a guest list, the people not on it become officially uninvited, and that makes them the enemies of the invited. Guest lists are just a way of choosing sides.

E. L. Konigsburg, US author and illustrator, said by Ethan Potter, *The View from Saturday* (F)

7 [W]e have no choice of what color we're born or who our parents are or whether we're rich or poor. What we do have is some choice over what we make of our lives once we're here.

Mildred D. Taylor, US author, said by Mama, *Roll of Thunder, Hear My Cry* (F)

8 Samuel Simpson was generally called Seesaw because of his difficulty in making up his mind. Whether it were a question of fact, of spelling, or of date, of going swimming or fishing, of choosing . . . a stick of candy at the village store, he had no sooner determined on one plan of action than his wish fondly reverted to the opposite one.

Kate Douglas Wiggin, US author, *Rebecca of Sunnybrook Farm* (F)

9 No choice is also a choice.

Yiddish proverb

10 Sometimes it's better to rise up out of the ashes, singing.

Jane Yolen, US author, "Phoenix Farm" from *Twelve Impossible Things Before Breakfast* (F)

Civil Rights

(See also Equality and Racism)

1 There are those who say to you — we are rushing this issue of civil rights. I say we are 172 years late.

Hubert H. Humphrey, US politician, in a July 14, 1948 speech to the Democratic National Convention

2 Until justice is blind to color, until education is unaware of race, until opportunity is unconcerned with the color of men's skins, emancipation will be a proclamation but not a fact.

Lyndon B. Johnson, 36th US President, in a May 30, 1963 speech at Gettysburg, PA

3 [T]he rights of every man are diminished* when the rights of one man are threatened.

John F. Kennedy, 35th US President, in a June 11, 1963 speech to the nation on civil rights   *reduced

Civil War
(1861–1865)
(See also War)

1 What armies and how much of war I have seen, what thousands of marching troops, what fields of slain, what prisons, what hospitals, what ruins, what cities in ashes, what hunger and nakedness, what orphanages, what widowhood, what wrongs and what vengeance.

Clara Barton, US nurse and founder of the American Red Cross, found in *Angel of the Battlefield* by I. Ross (NF)

2 My menfolk didn't go to war for the Confederacy because they favored slave holdin' but only because they was Southerners and they couldn't abide the idea of anybody sayin' they was slackers.

Patricia Beatty, US author, said by Hannalee's mother, *Be Ever Hopeful, Hannalee* (F)

3 I worked night and day for twelve years to prevent the war, but I could not. The North was mad and blind, would not let us govern ourselves, and so the war came.

Jefferson Davis, President of the Confederacy, in a July 17, 1864 letter

4 I was eleven years old and desperate to kill a Yankee before the supply ran out.

Paul Fleischman, US author, said by Toby Boyce, *Bull Run* (F)

4 Every American ought to have the right to be treated as he would wish to be treated, as one would wish his children to be treated. This is not the case [in America today].

Ibid.

5 The fight must go on. The cause of civil liberty must not be surrendered at the end of one or even a hundred defeats.

Abraham Lincoln, 16th US President, in a Nov. 19, 1858 letter to Henry Asbury

6 We are not fighting for integration, nor are we fighting for separation. We are fighting for recognition as human beings.

Malcolm X, US Black Muslim leader, in a 1964 speech in New York City

7 You can't hold a man down without staying down with him.

Attributed to Booker T. Washington, US educator and author

5 My task was to keep a regiment of 1,000 North Carolina men healthy. Many were felled* long before we saw battle. . . . Typhoid and measles raced through the ranks. Scurvy and pneumonia claimed victims as well.

Paul Fleischman, US author, said by Dr. Willam Rye, *Bull Run* (F)   *died*

6 I propose to fight it out on this line [before the Spotsylvania Court House], if it takes all summer.

Ulysses S. Grant, Union general and later the 18th US President, in a May 11, 1864 dispatch to Washington, D.C.

7 No terms except an unconditional and immediate surrender can be accepted.

Ulysses S. Grant, Union general and later the 18th US President, in a Feb. 16, 1862 message to Gen. Simon Buckner at Fort Donelson

ABRAHAM LINCOLN

8 The war is over—the rebels are our countrymen again.

Ulysses S. Grant, Union general and later the 18th US President, telling Union forces not to cheer Gen. Lee's surrender on Apr. 9, 1865

9 I think that the beginnin's of this war has been fanned by hate till it's a blaze now; and a blaze kin destroy him that makes it and him that the fire was set to hurt.

Irene Hunt, US author, said by Bill Creighton, Across Five Aprils (F)

10 After four years of arduous* service, marked by unsurpassed courage and fortitude, the Army of Northern Virginia has been compelled to yield to overwhelming numbers and resources.

Robert E. Lee, Confederate general, in his farewell to his army on Apr. 10, 1865   *very difficult

11 Go home now, and if you make as good citizens as you have soldiers, you will do well, and I shall always be proud of you. Good-bye, and God bless you all.

Robert E. Lee, Confederate general, in his farewell to his army, found in Be Ever Hopeful, Hannalee by P. Beatty (F)

12 My paramount object in this struggle is to save the Union, and is not either to save or destroy slavery.

Abraham Lincoln, 16th US President, in an Aug. 22, 1862 letter, found in Lincoln: A Photobiography by R. Freedman (NF)

13 Enough lives have been sacrificed. We must extinguish our resentments if we expect harmony and union.

Abraham Lincoln, 16th US President, said to his cabinet on Apr. 14, 1865, a few hours before he was shot at Ford's Theatre

14 After my father and brother were killed, I hated all Yankees, but now I understand that there were good men fighting on both sides.

Carolyn Reeder, US author, written by Will, Shades of Gray (F)

15 The war wasn't about slavery — it was about states' rights! People in the South were tired of being told what to do by a government hundreds of miles away in Washington. They wanted to live under laws made by their own state governments instead.

Carolyn Reeder, US author, said by Will, *Shades of Gray* (F)

Clothes

1 It is not only fine feathers that make fine birds.

Aesop, Greek writer, the moral in the fable "The Jay and the Peacock" (F)

2 And why do you worry about clothes? See how the lilies of the field grow. They do not labor or spin. Yet I tell you that not even Solomon in all his splendor was dressed like one of these.

Bible, Matthew 6:28-29 (NIV)

3 With clothes the new are best; with friends the old are best.

Chinese proverb

4 Today I discovered two kinds of people who go to high school: those who wear new clothes to show off on the first day, and those who wear their oldest clothes to show they think school is unimportant.

Beverly Cleary, US author, written by Leigh, *Strider* (F)

5 [B]ear in mind that it is not fine clothes that make the gentleman, but rather clean clothes.

Carlo Collodi, Italian author, said by Geppetto, *The Adventures of Pinocchio* (F)

6 Was it clothes that made a prince . . . just as rags made a street boy?

Sid Fleischman, US author, thought by Jemmy, *The Whipping Boy* (F)

7 [T]he Rhinoceros took off his skin and carried it over his shoulder as he came down to the beach to bathe. In those days it buttoned underneath with three buttons.

Rudyard Kipling, English-American journalist and author, "How the Rhinoceros Got His Skin" from *Just So Stories* (F)

8 [For the national Miss Teen USA pageant] I wanted to get an inexpensive dress to prove the point that it's not the dress, it's what is inside the dress.

Charlotte Lopez, Puerto Rican-American who was the 1993 Miss Teen USA, in the Apr. 1994 *Biography Today* (NF)

9 [A]fter all, what does it matter if your trousers do have different coloured legs, so long as they cover you up and keep you warm!

Bernard Miles, English actor and author, the retelling of *A Midsummer Night's Dream* from *Favorite Tales from Shakespeare* (F)

10 Clothes, to Marjorie Beasley, were a legal necessity having no useful function whatsoever except in wintertime.

Phyllis Reynolds Naylor, US author, *Witch's Sister* (F)

11 Even now she knew that this was one of those mysterious garments in which she always felt happy.

Ruth Park, New Zealand-Australian author, *Playing Beatie Bow* (F)

12 [The hermit] Dave was dressed in rabbit skins, stitched together. His feet were wrapped in tree bark and moose-moss. An owl sat on his head.

Daniel Manus Pinkwater, US author and illustrator, *Blue Moose and Return of the Moose* (F)

13 Wouldn't they make enchanting coats? . . . For spring wear, over a black suit. We've never thought of making coats out of dogs' skins.

Dodie Smith, English author, said by Cruella de Vil, *The 101 Dalmatians* (F)

14 I blame that [ugly green] jacket for those bad years. I blame my mother for her bad taste and her cheap ways.

Gary Soto, Mexican-American author, "The Jacket" from *Small Faces* (F)

15 [Indian Chief] Saknis brought [Matt] a pair of moccasins. They were handsome and new, of moosehide, dark and glistening with grease, tied down with stout thongs that were long enough to wrap about his ankles.

Elizabeth George Speare, US author, *The Sign of the Beaver* (F)

Colors

1 Violet, you're turning violet, Violet!

Roald Dahl, English author, Violet's mother, *Charlie and the Chocolate Factory* (F)

2 Any color, so long as it's black.

Attributed to Henry Ford, US car manufacturer, when he explained the choice of color for the Model-T Ford

3 By candlelight, the warmth of the colors [of the spools of thread] made me think the thread would throw off a perfume like a garden of flowers.

Paula Fox, US author, thought by Jessie Bollier, *The Slave Dancer* (F)

4 When you're feeling sorry for yourself, everything looks beige and gray. Even people.

E. L. Konigsburg, US author and illustrator, said by Phillip, "At the Home" from *Throwing Shadows* (F)

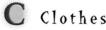

5 [King Corlath's] eyes were yellow as gold, the hot liquid gold in a smelter's furnace.

Robin McKinley, US author, *The Blue Sword* (F)

6 [I]sn't pink the most bewitching color in the world? I love it, but I can't wear it. Redheaded people can't wear pink, not even in [their] imagination.

L. M. Montgomery, Canadian author, said by Anne, *Anne of Green Gables* (F)

7 You, whose day it is,
Make it beautiful.
Get out your rainbow colors,
So it will be beautiful.

Nootka, North American Indian tribe, found in *The Trees Stand Shining*, sel. by Hettie Jones

8 At night all cats are gray.
Russian proverb

9 For the life of him, he couldn't figure why these East Enders called themselves black. . . . [T]he colors he found were gingersnap and light fudge and dark fudge and acorn and butter rum and cinnamon and burnt orange. But never licorice, which, to him, was real black.

Jerry Spinelli, US author, *Maniac Magee* (F)

10 I wish we could have real rose red T-shirts, and the writing should be black or maybe pink. . . . Every color looks beautiful with rose red.

Vera Williams, US author, said by Elana Rosen, *Scooter* (F)

11 [The cats] were tabby, gray, white, tortoiseshell, ginger, seal brown, and every other cat color in the world except a proper and witchy black.

Patricia C. Wrede, US author, *Calling on Dragons* (F)

Computers

(See Technology)

Confidence

1 The first time I shot the hook, I was in fourth grade, and I was about five feet, eight inches tall. . . . I was completely confident it would go in and I've been shooting it ever since.

Kareem Abdul-Jabbar, US professional basketball player, in the May 1986 *Star* (NF)

2 Nobody will think you're somebody, if you don't think so yourself.
African-American proverb

3 If you think you can, you can. And if you think you can't, you're right.

Mary Kay Ash, US founder of Mary Kay Cosmetics, in a 1985 issue of *The New York Times* (NF)

4 I'm tough. I'm indestructible. I'm like the coyote in "Road Runner" who is always getting flattened and dynamited and crushed and in the next scene is strolling along, completely normal again.

Betsy Byars, US author, said by Joe Melby, *The Summer of the Swans* (F)

5 I didn't care if someone [in high school] thought I was a geek because I wouldn't drink a beer or because I played bluegrass music.

Vince Gill, US country singer and songwriter, in the Apr. 7, 1996 *Parade* magazine (NF)

6 Throughout his life Hercules had this perfect confidence that no matter who was against him, he could never be defeated.

Edith Hamilton, German-American author, "Hercules," slightly adapted from *Mythology* (F)

7 I felt happier than I had felt in weeks. We had found confidence down there on the corner of Randolph and Wabash, seventy-eight cents of confidence, and the glow it gave us was a wonderful experience.

Irene Hunt, US author, thought by Josh, *No Promises in the Wind* (F)

8 I am somebody.
  I may be poor,
    but I am somebody!
  I may be uneducated,
  I may be unskilled,
    but I am somebody!
  I may be victimized by racism,
    but I am somebody!
  Respect me. Protect me. Never
    neglect me.
  I am God's child.

Jesse Jackson, US civil rights activist, found in *Jesse Jackson: A Biography* by P. McKissack (NF)

9 [T]he best thing in the world . . . was to be quite sure of yourself, but not to expect admiration from other people.

A. A. Milne, English author, said by the Princess in the one-act play *The Ugly Duckling* (F)

10 You are your most valuable asset. Don't forget that. *You* are the best thing you have.

Gary Paulsen, US author, said by Brian's teacher, *Hatchet* (F)

Constitution

1 The Constitution of the United States was made not merely for the generation that then existed, but for posterity — unlimited, undefined, endless.

Henry Clay, US politician, in a Feb. 6, 1850 speech to the US Senate

2 The Constitution of the United States . . . covers with the shield of its protection all classes of men, at all times, and under all circumstances.

David Davis, US Supreme Court Justice, in his 1866 opinion in *ex parte Milligan* (NF)

3 The Constitution of the United States knows no distinction between citizens on account of color.

Frederick Douglass, US abolitionist and author, found in *My Soul Looks Back, 'Less I Forget*, ed. by D. W. Riley (NF)

4 Our Constitution is in actual operation; everything appears to promise that it will last; but nothing in this world is certain but death and taxes.

Benjamin Franklin, Revolutionary statesman, written in 1789, found in *George Washington* by R. Bruns (NF)

5 The Constitution . . . is unquestionably the wisest ever yet presented to men.

Thomas Jefferson, 3rd US President, in a Mar. 18, 1789 letter to David Humphrey

6 Our Constitution is the envy of the world, as it should be, for it is the grand design of the finest nation on earth.

Thurgood Marshall, US Supreme Court Justice, *We the People* (NF)

7 We, the people of the United States, in order to form a more perfect union, establish justice, insure domestic tranquility, provide for the common defense, promote the general welfare, and secure the blessing of liberty to ourselves and our posterity, do ordain and establish this Constitution for the United States of America.

Preamble to the United States Constitution, June 21, 1788

8 There is no higher law than the Constitution.

William H. Seward, US statesman, in a Mar. 11, 1850 speech to the US Senate

Conversation

(See also Talking)

1 A proverb is the horse of conversation.
African proverb

2 [T]here was at least one rule: As long as there was food to eat, there was no conversation.

Natalie Babbitt, US author, *Tuck Everlasting* (F)

3 If [kittens] would only purr for "yes" and mew for "no" . . . so that one could keep up a conversation!

Lewis Carroll, English author, said by Alice, *Through the Looking Glass* (F)

4 [W]hen it slowly resumed, it was that regrettable sort of conversation that results from talking with your mouth full.

Kenneth Grahame, English author, *The Wind in the Willows* (F)

9 Animals talk to each other, of course. There can be no question about that; but I suppose there are very few people who can understand them.

Mark Twain, US author, "What Stumped the Blue-jays" from *The Complete Short Stories of Mark Twain* (F)

Courage

1 It is easy to be brave from a safe distance.

Aesop, Greek writer, the moral in the fable "The Wolf and the Kid" (F)

2 [T]he soldiers put on their bravery with their caps.

Ray Bradbury, US author, "The Drummer Boy of Shiloh" from *The Machineries of Joy* (F)

3 I'm very brave, generally . . . only today I happen to have a headache.

Lewis Carroll, English author, said by Tweedledum, *Through the Looking Glass* (F)

4 Your father had strong convictions* and he followed them. That takes courage.

Jane Leslie Conly, US author, said by the rat Nicodemus to Racso, *Racso and the Rats of NIMH* (F)   *beliefs

5 [I]f people expect you to be brave, sometimes you pretend that you are, even when you are frightened down to your very bones.

Sharon Creech, US author, said by Salamanca, *Walk Two Moons* (F)

5 Up here in the hills [of West Virginia], you hardly ever get down to business right off. First you say your howdys and then you talk about anything else but what you come for, and finally . . . you say what's on your mind. But you always edge into it, not to offend.

Phyllis Reynolds Naylor, US author, said by Marty, *Shiloh* (F)

6 [I]n all my life I had never been able to speak with the dead, though many times I had tried.

Scott O'Dell, US author, said by Won-a-pa-lei (Karana), *Island of the Blue Dolphins* (F)

7 It was wonderful, indeed, how I could have heart-to-heart talks with my dogs and they always seemed to understand. Each question I asked was answered in their own doggish way.

Wilson Rawls, US author, said by Billy, *Where the Red Fern Grows* (F)

8 [Billy Buck] told Jody how horses love conversation. He must talk to the pony all the time, and tell him the reasons for everything. . . . A horse never kicked up a fuss if someone he liked explained things to him.

John Steinbeck, US author, *The Red Pony* (F)

6 To be afraid and to be brave is the best kind of courage of all.

Alice Dalgliesh, US author, said by John Noble, *The Courage of Sarah Noble* (F)

7 Who has no courage must have legs.
Italian proverb

8 Great crises produce great men, and great deeds of courage.

John F. Kennedy, 35th US President, *Profiles in Courage* (NF)

9 To be courageous . . . requires no exceptional qualifications, no magic formula, no special combination of time, place, and circumstances. It is an opportunity that sooner or later is presented to us all.

Ibid.

10 I wanted you to see what real courage is, instead of getting the idea that courage is a man with a gun in his hand. It's when you know you're licked before you begin, but you begin anyway and you see it through no matter what.

Harper Lee, US author, said by Atticus, *To Kill a Mockingbird* (F)

11 That's all that *brave* means — not thinking about the dangers. Just thinking about what you must do.

Lois Lowry, US author, said by Uncle Henrik, *Number the Stars* (F)

12 You may be the smallest dragonrider ever . . . but you're the bravest.

Anne McCaffrey, US author, said by F'lar, "The Smallest Dragonboy," from *Science Fiction Tales*, ed. by R. Elwood (F)

13 Fortune and bravery often go together.

Scott O'Dell, US author, said by Don Saturino, *Carlota* (F)

14 Real courage, true bravery is doing things in spite of fear, knowing fear.

Maia Wojciechowska, Polish-American author, said by Alfonso Castillo, *Shadow of a Bull* (F)

Death

1 To most the end comes as naturally and simply as sleep.

>   Louisa May Alcott, US author, *Little Women* (F)

2 Down the street his funeral goes
   As sobs and wails diminish.
   He died from drinking straight shellac,
   But he had a lovely finish.

>   Anonymous poem, found in *A Nonny Mouse Writes Again!*, sel. by J. Prelutsky

3 Creatures like to die alone. . . . They like to crawl away where nobody can find them dead.

>   William H. Armstrong, US author, said by the mother, *Sounder* (F)

4 Dying's part of the wheel [of life], right there next to being born. You can't pick out the pieces you like and leave the rest.

>   Natalie Babbitt, US author, said by Tuck, *Tuck Everlasting* (F)

5 Yea, though I walk through the valley of the shadow of death, I will fear no evil: for thou art with me; thy rod and thy staff they comfort me.

>   Bible, Psalms 23:4 (KJV)

6 A brave war chief would prefer death to dishonor.

>   Black Hawk, member of the Sacs tribe, *Farewell, My Nation, Farewell*, found in *My Soul Looks Back, 'Less I Forget*, ed. by D. W. Riley (NF)

7 How you think you *feel* when you dead? Pretty bad, I reckon—near as low as you can get. Think about it. No more breathing fresh air. No more eating salted cashews. No more sweating.

>   Bruce Brooks, US author, said by Dooley, *Everywhere* (F)

8 Don't let us talk about dying; I don't like it. Let us talk about living.

>   Frances Hodgson Burnett, English-American author, said by Mary, *The Secret Garden* (F)

9 At that moment, Liên thought she understood what dying meant. The drop of water had not really gone; it had only changed, like the snowflake, into something else.

>   Helen Coutant, US teacher and writer, *First Snow* (F)

10 [Aunt Jessie's] death, so sudden and unexpected, left us all dazed and jittery. . . . It was as if we'd all been slapped, hard, by a giant hand swooping down from the sky.

>   Sharon Creech, US author, *Chasing Redbird* (F)

11 [F]ew wild animals — regardless of species — ever live out their full life-spans; a violent death almost always intervenes.

Allan W. Eckert, US author, *Incident at Hawk's Hill* (F)

12 When death comes, the rich man has no money, the poor man no debt.

Estonian proverb

13 The reservation doctor reported the cause of [Chief Joseph's] death as "a broken heart."

Russell Freedman, US author, *Indian Chiefs* (NF)

14 The mouse child stared beyond his father's shoulder at the astonishing stillness of the dead.

Russell Hoban, US author, *The Mouse and His Child* (F)

15 I wanted to die quickly, not in little bits struggling for handholds.

Jan Hudson, Canadian author, said by Sweetgrass, *Sweetgrass* (F)

16 Tell all my mourners
To mourn in red —
Cause there ain't no sense
In my bein' dead.

Langston Hughes, US poet, "Wake" from *Selected Poems*

17 [I] thought about what death is and what a loss is — a sharp pain that lessens with time but can never quite heal over. A scar.

Maya Lin, Chinese-American creator of the Vietnam Memorial in Washington, D.C., found in *Maya Lin, Architect and Artist* by M. Malone (NF)

18 No, [it didn't hurt when your grandmother died]. Her heart just stopped beating. She died of old age. Her time for living was simply over.

Lois Lowry, US author, said by Anastasia's father, *Anastasia Krupnik* (F)

19 Around [A.D. 2500] we finally conquered death. Found out that it was a virus. But people still had to be — you know — moved out of the way so new people could be born. So we started doing it by lottery.

Walter Dean Myers, US author, said by Orion Battle, "Things That Go Gleep in the Night" from *Don't Give Up the Ghost*, ed. by D. Gale (F)

20 [A]ll that stuff about happy endings is lies. The only ending in this world is death.

Katherine Paterson, US author, said by Trotter, *The Great Gilly Hopkins* (F)

21 The thing with dying was to try to not die and make death take you with surprise.

Gary Paulsen, US author, thought by Russel Susskit, *Dogsong* (F)

22 Finally I know what *loss* means. The power of the dead is that they leave you with the living.

Richard Peck, US author, thought by Jim Atwater, *Father Figure* (F)

23 When somebody dies alone, you try to fill in the details, maybe to make up for not being there and changing the whole history of the thing.

Ibid.

24 I needed to know that dying and going to heaven didn't involve any regrets or sorrows or worries.

Cynthia Rylant, US author, said by Summer, *Missing May* (F)

25 I would love to believe that when I die I will live again, that some thinking, feeling, remembering part of me will continue.

Carl Sagan, US astronomer and author, in the Mar. 10, 1996 *Parade* magazine (NF) *(He died on Dec. 20, 1996.)*

26 There is no death, only a change of worlds.

Chief Seattle, leader of six Indian tribes in the Pacific Northwest, in an 1854 speech to Gov. Isaac Stevens, found in *The American Reader*, ed. by D. Ravitch (NF)

27 The old man told Joseph that the souls of dead men are reborn to make amends for sins and injustices committed during their previous life-times.

Isaac Bashevis Singer, Polish-American author, *Alone in the Wild Forest* (F)

28 Swing low sweet chariot,
    Comin' for to carry me home,
    I looked over Jordan an' what
        did I see?
    A band of Angels coming after me,
    Comin' for to carry me home.

"Swing Low, Sweet Chariot," words to the spiritual, found in *The Anderson Book of American Folk Tales and Songs*, coll. by A. Durell

29 Just say the report of my death has been grossly exaggerated.

Mark Twain, US author, commenting on rumors that he had died, found in *Mark Twain: America's Humorist, Dreamer, Prophet* by C. Cox (NF)

30 I wish I didn't have to die with egg on my pants and butter on my cap and gravy on my shirt and orange pulp in my ear and banana peel wrapped around my middle.

E. B. White, US author, said by the mouse Stuart, *Stuart Little* (F)

Declaration of Independence

1 We hold these truths to be self-evident, that all men are created equal, that they are endowed by their Creator with certain unalienable* Rights, that among these are Life, Liberty and the pursuit of Happiness.

Declaration of Independence, signed on July 4, 1776, found in *The Faber Book of America*, ed. by Ricks and Vance (NF)   **not to be taken away*

2 That these United Colonies are, and of Right ought to be *Free and Independent States* . . . and that all political connection between them and the State of Great Britain, is and ought to be totally dissolved.

    Ibid.

3 [A]s Free and Independent States, they have full Power to levy War, conclude Peace, contract Alliances, establish Commerce, and to do all other Acts and Things which Independent States may of right do.

    Ibid.

4 And for support of this declaration, with firm reliance on the protection of Divine Providence, we mutually pledge to each other our lives, our fortunes and our sacred honor.

    Ibid.

5 We must indeed all hang together, or most assuredly, we shall all hang separately.

    Benjamin Franklin, Revolutionary statesman, said upon his signing of the Declaration of Independence on July 4, 1776

6 There, I guess King George will be able to read that.

    John Hancock, Revolutionary patriot and statesman, referring to the large size of his signature on the Declaration of Independence

7 This is the object of the Declaration of Independence . . . to place before mankind the common sense of the subject, in terms so plain and firm as to command their assent,* and to justify ourselves in the independent stand we are compelled to take.

    Thomas Jefferson, 3rd US President, in a May 8, 1825 letter to Henry Lee   *agreement*

8 If the American Revolution had produced nothing but the Declaration of Independence, it would have been worthwhile.

    Samuel Eliot Morison, US historian, *The Oxford History of the American People* (NF)

Democracy

1 Responding to challenge is one of democracy's greatest strengths.

    Neil A. Armstrong, US astronaut, in a Sept. 16, 1969 speech to Congress

2 No, we shall have no democracy here. No parliaments. No congressmen. There's but one master on this ship, and that is me.

    Avi, US author, said by Capt. Jaggery, *The True Confessions of Charlotte Doyle* (F)

3 To define democracy in one word, we must use the word "cooperation."

    Dwight D. Eisenhower, 34th US President, in a June 1945 speech in Abilene, KS

4 Democracy benefits by the availability of information.

    Bill Gates, US CEO of Microsoft, in the Jan. 28, 1996 *Parade* magazine (NF)

NELSON MANDELA

8 I have cherished the ideal of a democratic and free society . . . in which persons live together in harmony. It is an ideal which I hope to live for and achieve. But if needs be, it is an ideal for which I am prepared to die.

Nelson Mandela, South African President and former political prisoner, in the Jan. 1992 *Biography Today* (NF)

9 The most important question that can be asked about any society is how much effort do citizens spend exercising their civic responsibility. We can't possibly have a democracy with 200 million Americans and only a handful of citizens.

Ralph Nader, US consumer advocate and author, found in *Contemporary Heroes and Heroines,* ed. by R. B. Browne (NF)

10 One has the right to be wrong in a democracy.

Claude Pepper, US politician, in the May 27, 1946 *Congressional Record* (NF)

11 Democracy is not a static* thing. It is an everlasting march.

Franklin D. Roosevelt, 32nd US President, in an Oct. 1, 1935 speech in Los Angeles, CA   *fixed*

12 The beauty of democracy is that you never can tell when a youngster is born what he is going to do with [his life].

Woodrow Wilson, 28th US President, in a Dec. 10, 1915 speech in Columbus, OH

5 I swear to the Lord
I still can't see
Why Democracy means
Everybody but me.

Langston Hughes, US poet, "The Black Man Speaks" from *Jim Crow's Last Stand*

6 One of the great glories of democracy is the right to protest for right.

Martin Luther King, Jr., US civil rights leader, found in *I Have a Dream: The Life and Words of Martin Luther King, Jr.* by J. Haskins (NF)

7 As I would not be a *slave*, so I would not be a *master*. This expresses my idea of democracy. Whatever differs from this . . . is no democracy.

Abraham Lincoln, 16th US President, on a scrap of paper dated Aug. 1, 1858, found in *Lincoln: A Photobiography* by R. Freedman (NF)

Determination

1 This village has held out against freeze and drought and hail and flood and witches and demons and the Devil himself. We've seen them all, yet we've endured. And we'll do it again.

Bill Brittain, US author, said by Mrs. McCabe, *Dr. Dredd's Wagon of Wonders* (F)

2 It seems I've always known [singing] is what I wanted to do. There was like no choice.

Mariah Carey, US singer, in the Apr. 1996 *Biography Today* (NF)

3 He started to sing as he tackled the thing
That couldn't be done, and he did it.

Edgar A. Guest, English-American journalist and poet, "It Couldn't Be Done" from *The Collected Verses of Edgar A. Guest*

4 There is nothing that cannot be achieved by firm determination.

Japanese proverb

5 He was a determined young pig
and he had a dream; he wanted to fly!

Dick King-Smith, English author, *Pigs Might Fly* (F)

6 From age 11 to age 16 . . . I wanted to be the best swimmer in the world, and there was nothing else.

Diana Nyad, US long-distance swimmer, *Other Shores* (NF)

7 I ran and ran and ran every day, and I acquired this sense of determination, this sense of spirit that I would never, never give up, no matter what else happened.

Wilma Rudolph, US track star, *Wilma* (NF)

8 The stubbornness of [Abel's] character stood him now in good stead. He refused to consider himself defeated.

William Steig, US author and illustrator, *Abel's Island* (F)

9 A voice
I will send
Hear me
The land
All over
A voice
I am sending
Hear me
I will live.

Teton Sioux, North American Indian tribe, found in *The Trees Stand Shining*, sel. by Hettie Jones

10 There was never a time in my youth, no matter how dark and discouraging the days might be, when one resolve did not continually remain with me, and that was a determination to secure an education at any cost.

Booker T. Washington, US educator and author, *Up from Slavery* (NF)

11 If enough people think of a thing and work hard enough at it, I guess it's pretty nearly bound to happen, wind and weather permitting.

Laura Ingalls Wilder, US author, *On the Shores of Silver Lake* (F)

Differences

1 We exist differently, perhaps, you and I, but we both exist. We are both living beings, each in her own way, only we can't touch one another, that's all.

Eleanor Cameron, US author, said by Domi to Nina, *The Court of the Stone Children* (F)

2 What we have to do . . . is find a way to celebrate our diversity and debate our differences without fracturing our communities.

Hillary Rodham Clinton, US lawyer and wife of the 42nd President, in a May 18, 1993 University of PA graduation speech

3 People need to respect each other's concerns and differences. And frankly, there's far more in common than divides us.

David Dinkins, US mayor of New York City, in a 1991 radio interview

4 [The white people] are not our relatives. We don't even know their names. We can't talk with them because they speak a language no one but they understand. They make me uncomfortable with their oddness.

Michael Dorris, Native American author and anthropologist, said by Moss, *Guests* (F)

5 A peaceful world is a world in which differences are tolerated, and are not eliminated by violence.

John Foster Dulles, US politician, *War or Peace* (NF)

6 I'll have [father] explain to you the difference between an honest business transaction and swindling your friends.

John D. Fitzgerald, US author, said by Mamma, *The Great Brain* (F)

7 [Johnny] knew little of the political strife which was turning Boston into two armed camps [in the 1760s]. The Whigs declaring that taxation without representation is tyranny. The Tories believing all differences could be settled with time, patience, and respect for the government.

Esther Forbes, US author, *Johnny Tremain* (F)

8 Many animals could tell the difference between hostile hunters and friendly people by merely looking at them.

Jean Craighead George, US author, *Julie of the Wolves* (F)

9 Because of our work with the chimps, we understand more about humans than we did before. We know we are not as different from the rest of the animal kingdom as we once thought we were.

Jane Goodall, English-American wildlife expert and author, found in *Contemporary Heroes and Heroines*, ed. by R. B. Browne (NF)

10 Maybe the two different worlds [Cherry and I] lived in weren't so different. We saw the same sunset.

S. E. Hinton, US author, said by Ponyboy, *The Outsiders* (F)

15 It made me think about the differences between Cletus and me. About the way he could trust things to be all right. The way I worried about losing everything.

Cynthia Rylant, US author, said by Summer, *Missing May* (F)

16 Day and night cannot dwell together. The Red Man has ever fled the approach of the White Man, as the morning mist flees before the morning sun.

Chief Seattle, leader of six Indian tribes in the Pacific Northwest, from an 1854 speech to Gov. Isaac Stevens, found in *The American Reader*, ed. by D. Ravitch (NF)

17 [S]ome kids don't like a kid who is different. Such as a kid who is allergic to pizza....Or a kid who never watches Saturday morning cartoons. Or a kid who's another color.

Jerry Spinelli, US author, *Maniac Magee* (F)

Disabilities

1 My having one hand was not a big issue when I was a kid. I never gave thought to [it].

Jim Abbott, US professional baseball pitcher, found in *Extraordinary People with Disabilities* by Kent and Quinlan (NF)

2 God gave me this physical impairment to remind me that I'm not the greatest. He is.

Muhammad Ali, US professional boxer, referring to the results of Parkinson's disease, in the May 16, 1988 *Jet* magazine (NF)

11 Our flag is red, white and blue, but our nation is a rainbow — red, yellow, brown, black, and white — we're all precious in God's sight.

Jesse Jackson, US civil rights activist, in a July 16, 1984 speech at the Democratic National Convention

12 There is a big difference between what one hears and [what one] sees.

Japanese proverb

13 The white men were many and we could not hold our own with them. We were like deer. They were like grizzly bears. We had a small country. Their country was large.

Chief Joseph, leader of the Nez Perce, stating his reasons for agreeing to take his tribe to a reservation, found in *Bury My Heart at Wounded Knee* by D. Brown (NF)

14 [My friend] Rufus was solid like a rock. And I was the Jell-O Man. Some pair.

Cynthia Rylant, US author, thought by Pete, *A Fine White Dust* (F)

3 Going blind. Sounds like a fate worse than death, doesn't it? Seems like something which would get a little kid down. . . . Well, I'm here to tell you that it didn't happen that way—at least not to me.

Ray Charles, US singer and composer, *Brother Ray* (NF)

4 [Tiny Tim] hoped the people saw him in the church, because he was a cripple, and it might be pleasant to them to remember, upon Christmas Day, who made lame beggars walk and blind men see.

Charles Dickens, English author, said by Bob Cratchit, *A Christmas Carol* (F)

5 In wheelchair sports, people thought athletes with disabilities were courageous and inspirational. They never give them credit for simply being competitive.

Jean Driscoll, US wheelchair road racer, found in *Women in Sports* by J. Layden (NF)

6 You can't imagine what it's like to come in first in a bunch of handicapped races, then enter some two-legged race and come in last.

Diana Golden, US one-legged World Champion skier, found in *Champions* by B. Littlefield (NF)

7 As a people with disabilities, we've really struggled to be accepted, to blend into society. Now . . . [w]e're reaching a point where we can acknowledge that some of us really are exceptional.

Judy Heumann, US Assistant Secretary of Education, found in *Extraordinary People with Disabilities* by Kent and Quinlan (NF)

8 From the beginning, disability taught me that life could be reinvented. The physical dimensions of life could be created, like poetry; they were not imposed by some celestial landlord.

John Hockenberry, US journalist, referring to his inability to walk due to an automobile accident, found in *Extraordinary People with Disabilities* by Kent and Quinlan (NF)

9 I feel no flattery when people speak of my voice. I'm simply grateful that I found a way to work around my impairment. Once a stutterer, always a stutterer.

James Earl Jones, US actor and the voice of Darth Vader in *Star Wars*, found in *My Soul Looks Back, 'Less I Forget*, ed. by D. W. Riley (NF)

10 I discovered that my physical impairment did not diminish my thinking or the quality of my mind, and it did not impact on my capacity to talk.

Barbara Jordan, member of US Congress and educator, referring to limitations caused by MS, in the Apr. 1996 *Biography Today* (NF)

11 You would think the accident would have narrowed my world, limited me. It did the opposite. I started to pay attention to the world instead of taking it for granted.

I. King Jordan, the first deaf President of Gallaudet University, the only US college for people who are deaf, found in *Extraordinary People with Disabilities* by Kent and Quinlan (NF)

12 The calamity of the blind is immense, irreparable.* But it does not take away our share of the things that count—service, friendship, humor, imagination, wisdom.

Helen Keller, US author and humanitarian, found in *Helen Keller: Humanitarian* by D. Wepman (NF)   *unchangeable*

13 Franklin's illness proved a blessing in disguise, for it gave him strength and courage he had not had before.

Eleanor Roosevelt, US diplomat, author, and wife of the 32nd President, referring to her husband's inability to walk as a result of polio, found in *Eleanor Roosevelt* by R. Freedman (NF)

14 [Tom Cruise's] road was never paved. It was always full of potholes, and he jumped over all of them.

Don Simpson, US movie producer, referring to Cruise's dyslexia, a neurological condition that confuses the way printed words appear on a page, found in *Extraordinary People with Disabilities* by Kent and Quinlan (NF)

15 [My mother] never let me use my deafness as an excuse. We had a positive environment, where if you fail, just try again.

Heather Whitestone, 1995 Miss America, in the Apr. 1995 *Biography Today* (NF)

16 When I was young, my mother taught me never to feel sorry for myself, because handicaps are really things to be used.

Stevie Wonder, US singer and musician, found in *The Story of Stevie Wonder* by J. Haskins (NF)

Dogs

(See also Pets)

1 If you can't decide between a Shepherd, a Setter, or a Poodle, get them all. . . . Adopt a mutt.

ASPCA advertising slogan

2 Soon the old dog was where he most loved to be — the center of attention among some human beings.

Sheila Burnford, US author, *The Incredible Journey: A Tale of Three Animals* (F)

3 Being trusted by a dog, especially a dog that has good reason for not trusting humans, is a nice feeling.

Beverly Cleary, US author, thought by Leigh, *Strider* (F)

4 He who lies down with dogs will rise with fleas.

English proverb

5 It's amazing what a few kind words and a smile can do for a dog.

John R. Erickson, US author, said by Hank, *Hank the Cowdog* (F)

6 [Chester] is not your ordinary cat. (But then, I'm not your ordinary dog, since an ordinary dog wouldn't be writing this book, would he?)

Deborah and James Howe, US authors, said by Harold, *Bunnicula: A Rabbit-Tale of Mystery* (F)

7 In everyone's growing up there should be an all-American, true-blue, one-of-the-family bowwow wonder dog.

William Joyce, US illustrator, from *Speak! Children's Book Illustrators Brag about Their Dogs*, ed. by M. J. Rosen (NF)

8 Dogs have lived so long with humans that they know what's going to happen, sometimes even before their owners do.

Dick King-Smith, English author, *Babe the Gallant Pig* (F)

9 Irish setters were a special breed in themselves, sensitive, intelligent, and proud. . . . Doubt or mistrust in their minds was very hard to overcome.

James Kjelgaard, US author, *Big Red* (F)

10 If you are a dog and your owner suggests that you wear a sweater . . . suggest that he wear a tail.

Fran Lebowitz, US humorist and author, *Social Studies* (NF)

11 The [sled] dogs knew how to run in the dark and see with their heads, with their feet, with their hair and noses. They saw with everything.

Gary Paulsen, US author, *Dogsong* (F)

12 I knew that somewhere in the dogs, in their humor and the way they thought, they had great, old knowledge; they had something we [humans] had lost. And the dogs could teach me.

Gary Paulsen, US author, *Woodsong* (F)

13 Dogs have given up many of their natural ways to cross the boundary between our species and join our families; for this, each dog deserves lifelong care and protection.

Michael J. Rosen, US author, the Introduction to *Speak! Children's Book Illustrators Brag about Their Dogs* (NF)

14 When a dog owns a boy as long as Sam had me, they get to know each other pretty well.

George Selden, US author, said by Tim Farr, *The Genie of Sutton Place* (F)

15 [A]ll dogs know all about the Twilight Barking. It is their way of keeping in touch with distant friends, passing on important news, enjoying a good gossip.

Dodie Smith, English author, *The 101 Dalmatians* (F)

16 [Quentin the pig] had never fancied dogs. Too much tail-wagging and isn't-our-master-marvelous about them.

Mary Stolz, US author, *Quentin Corn* (F)

17 [Prince] loved everything about my mother except her high-heeled shoes. When she dressed up, he would bark at her feet, and occasionally one of her shoes would turn up in a neighbor's flower bed.

Thomas Wharton, US illustrator, from *Speak! Children's Book Illustrators Brag about Their Dogs*, ed. by M. J. Rosen (NF)

Dolphins

(*See* Sea Life)

Dragons

(*See* Monsters and Dragons)

Dreams and Nightmares

1 Dreaming of eating will not satisfy the hungry.

African proverb

2 I have lost my dream! And it was such a beautiful dream! It sang, and shouted, and glittered, and sparkled—and I've lost it! Somebody pulled it away, out of reach, just as I woke up!

Joan Aiken, English author, said by Clem, "Clem's Dream" from *The Last Slice of Rainbow* (F)

3 Facts are the barren branches on which we hang the dear, obscuring foliage of our dreams.

Natalie Babbitt, US author, the Introduction to *Knee-Knock Rise* (F)

4 [Trying to find her way home] was like being in a nightmare, where there is no possible way home and time stretches into infinity.

Eleanor Cameron, US author, *The Court of the Stone Children* (F)

5 In nightmares you may have had the terrifying experience of becoming dinner for a dinosaur.

Daniel Cohen, US author, *Monster Dinosaur* (F)

6 Dreams . . . are very mysterious things. They float around in the night air like little clouds, searching for sleeping people.

Roald Dahl, English author, said by Danny's father, *Danny, the Champion of the World* (F)

7 A dream is a wish your heart makes—
When you're fast asleep. . . .
No matter how your heart is grieving,
If you keep on believing,
The dream that you wish will come true.

Mack David, Al Hoffman, and Jerry Livingston, US composers, music and words to the song "A Dream Is a Wish Your Heart Makes" from Walt Disney's *Cinderella*

8 I wonder if when you dream about somebody they dream about you.

Louise Fitzhugh, US author, said by Harriet, *Harriet the Spy* (F)

9 [My boy] fills the empty space inside himself with foolish dreams that cannot possibly come true.

Russell Hoban, US author, said by a wind-up mouse, *The Mouse and His Child* (F)

10 Hold fast to dreams
For if dreams die
Life is a broken-winged bird
That cannot fly.

Langston Hughes, US poet, "Dreams," found in *The Children's Treasury*, ed. by P. S. Goepfert

11 I have a dream that one day on the red hills of Georgia the sons of former slaves and the sons of former slaveowners will be able to sit down together at the table of brotherhood.

Martin Luther King, Jr., US civil rights leader, in his Aug. 28, 1963 "I Have a Dream" speech in Washington, D.C., found in *The American Reader*, ed. by D. Ravitch (NF)

12 I have a dream my four little children will one day live in a nation where they will not be judged by the color of their skin but by the content of their character.

Ibid.

13 That night Peter . . . ran through his dreams, down echoing halls, across a desert of stones and scorpions, down ice mazes, along a sloping pink, spongy tunnel with dripping walls. This was when he realized he was not being chased by the monster. He was running down its throat.

Ian McEwan, English author, *The Daydreamer* (F)

14 [Peter] ate [a cucumber] that night he had the dream about being caught by cannibals. I'd eat three cucumbers if I could have a dream like that.

L. M. Montgomery, Canadian author, said by Cecily, *Days of Dreams and Laughter: The Story Girl and Other Tales* (F)

15 Not all [people] are blessed with true vision. Some must spend a lifetime searching, building dream upon dream.

Ellen Raskin, US author, written by Noah Figg, *Figgs & Phantoms* (F)

Earth

(See World)

Eating

(See also Food)

1 Eating a mouthful is better than waiting for a helping.

African proverb

2 I can't believe I ate the whole thing!

Alka-Seltzer advertising slogan

3 A diner while dining at Crewe,
    Found quite a large mouse in his stew.
        Said the waiter, "Don't shout,
        And wave it about.
    Or the rest will be wanting one, too."

Anonymous limerick, found in *Laughable Limericks*, comp. by S. and J. Brewton

4 After three years on the farm, I knew better than to be shocked at the idea of eating a creature you knew and were fond of.

Nina Bawden, English author, *Henry* (F)

5 Hunger is a pretty terrible thing. It's like going around all day with a nail in your shoe. You try to put it out of your mind, but you never really quite forget it.

James L. Collier and Christopher Collier, US authors, said by Tim, *My Brother Sam Is Dead* (F)

6 Will you be kind enough to tell me if there are villages in this island where it would be possible to obtain something to eat, without running the danger of being eaten?

Carlo Collodi, Italian author, said by Pinocchio, *The Adventures of Pinocchio* (F)

7 Eat to live, and not live to eat.

Benjamin Franklin, Revolutionary statesman, the 1733 *Poor Richard's Almanack* (NF)

8 "Eat it — it's good for you!"
    That makes me mad.
  How can something good for you
    Taste so bad?

Mary Ann Hoberman, US poet, "Eat It—It's Good for You" from *Fathers, Mothers, Sisters, Brothers*

9 How could [Aldo] eat animals when he liked them so much?

Johanna Hurwitz, US author, *Aldo Peanut Butter* (F)

10 People only eat stupid animals. Like sheep and cows and ducks and chickens. They don't eat clever ones like dogs.

Dick King-Smith, English author, said by the dog Fly to her pups, *Babe the Gallant Pig* (F)

11 Pigs enjoy eating, and they also enjoy lying around most of the day thinking about eating again.

Dick King-Smith, English author, *Babe the Gallant Pig* (F)

12 [A]nyone who had once tasted [the enchanted Turkish Delight] would want more and more of it, and would even, if they were allowed, go on eating it till they killed themselves.

C. S. Lewis, English author, *The Lion, the Witch, and the Wardrobe* (F)

13 All's well that ends with a good meal.

Arnold Lobel, US author and illustrator, the moral in "The Cat and His Visions" from *Fables* (F)

14 How bad could a worm taste? [Billy] had eaten fried liver, salmon loaf, mushrooms, tongue, pig's feet. . . . Heck, he could gag *anything* down for fifty dollars, couldn't he?

Thomas Rockwell, US author, *How To Eat Fried Worms* (F)

15 Then the *Whos*, young and old, would
  sit down to a feast.
And they'd feast! *And they'd feast!*
And they'd FEAST! FEAST! FEAST! FEAST!
They would feast on *Who*-pudding,
  and rare *Who*-roast-beast.
Which was something the Grinch
  couldn't stand in the least!

Dr. Seuss, US author, *How the Grinch Stole Christmas* (F)

16 Silence descended as the Wongs continued their meal, observing the well-learned precept* that talk was not permissible while eating.

Jade Snow Wong, Chinese-American author, *Fifth Chinese Daughter* (NF)   *rule

Education
(See also Learning, School, *and* Teachers)

1 [M]ore people have to start spending as much time in the library as they do on the basketball court. If they took the idea that they could escape poverty through education, I think it would make a more basic and long-lasting change in the way things are done.

Kareem Abdul-Jabbar, US professional basketball player, *Kareem* (NF)

2 [S]ome people, unable to go to school, were more educated and even more intelligent than college professors.

Maya Angelou, US poet and author, *I Know Why the Caged Bird Sings* (NF)

3 A republican government should be based on free and equal education among the people.

Susan B. Anthony, US suffragist and reformer, found in *The Life and Work of Susan B. Anthony* by I. H. Harper (NF)

4 [I]t was . . . important that [the mouse Timothy] have an education. Then when trouble did come along—for surely everyone must anticipate at least a small amount of misfortune—he would be able to reason his way out of it.

Jane Leslie Conly, US author, *Racso and the Rats of NIMH* (F)

5 Getting through [school] isn't a laughing matter. If they drop out, they're going to miss out.

Bill Cosby, US comedian and author, in the Nov. 17, 1977 *Scholastic* magazine (NF)

6 Educate your sons and daughters, send them to school and show them that beside the cartridge box, the ballot box, and the jury box, you have also the knowledge box.

Frederick Douglass, US abolitionist and author, *The Life and Times of Frederick Douglass* (NF)

7 Ignorance is a cure for nothing.

W. E. B. Du Bois, US educator and author, in a Jan. 7, 1905 letter to a student

8 [My father] made it clear to me that I, as a black girl could be anything, do anything and how important it was not to let anything get between me and my education and everything I could be.

Marian Wright Edelman, US lawyer and public official, found in *Marian Wright Edelman* by S. Otfinoski (NF)

9 Getting [a college] degree meant more to me than an NCAA title, being named All-American or winning an Olympic gold medal.

Patrick Ewing, US professional basketball player, found in *My Soul Looks Back, 'Less I Forget,* ed. by D. W. Riley (NF)

10 Big muscles alone won't get you there, you must also know how to read and write to make it in this society.

Jesse Jackson, US civil rights activist, found in *Jesse Jackson* by A. Kosof (NF)

11 Upon the subject of education . . . I can only say that I view it as the most important subject which we, as a people, can be engaged in.

Abraham Lincoln, 16th US President, in a Mar. 9, 1832 recorded speech in Sangamon County, IL

12 Education is very important. It prepares you. . . . It gives you the tools to compete.

> Vilma Martinez, Mexican-American lawyer, found in *Famous Mexican Americans* by Morey and Dunn (NF)

13 [Y]our education and imagination will carry you to places which you won't believe possible.

> Ellison S. Onizuka, Hawaiian astronaut, speaking at a 1980 high school graduation, found in *Famous Asian Americans* by Morey and Dunn (NF)

14 Today, education is perhaps the most important function of state and local governments.

> Supreme Court Decision in *Brown v. Board of Education*, May 17, 1954

15 In these days, it is doubtful that any child may reasonably be expected to succeed in life if he is denied the opportunity of an education. Such an opportunity . . . is a right which must be made available to all on equal terms.

> *Ibid.*

16 Smiley said all a frog wanted was education, and he could do 'most anything — and I believed him.

> Mark Twain, US author, said by Simon Wheeler, "The Celebrated Jumping Frog of Calaveras County" from *The Complete Short Stories by Mark Twain* (F)

17 A mind is a terrible thing to waste.

> United Negro College Fund advertising slogan

18 Better education than wealth.

> Welsh proverb

Equality

(See also Civil Rights, Racism, *and* Women's Rights*)*

1 I believe in the same pay for the same work. Don't you?

> Louisa May Alcott, US author, in an 1874 letter to Maria S. Porter, found in *Great Americans in Their Own Words* (NF)

2 There will never be complete equality until women themselves help to make laws and elect lawmakers.

> Susan B. Anthony, US suffragist and reformer, found in *Herstory*, ed. by Ashby and Ohrn (NF)

3 People are not . . . terribly anxious to be equal . . . but they love the idea of being superior.

> James Baldwin, US author, found in *My Soul Looks Back, 'Less I Forget*, ed. by D. W. Riley (NF)

4 Only equals can be friends.

> Ethiopian proverb

5 That's not right. . . . It's not right for one animal to have it all and the rest of us to have nothing.

> William J. Faulkner, US author, said by Brer Rabbit, "Brer Tiger and the Big Wind" from *The Days When Animals Talked* (F)

6 "We, the people." It is a very eloquent beginning [to the Constitution]. But when that document was completed on the seventeenth of September in 1787, I was not included in that "We, the people."

Barbara Jordan, US member of Congress and educator, in a July 25, 1974 speech to Congress

7 Whenever the white man treats Indians as they treat each other, then we shall have no more wars. We shall be all alike . . . with one sky above us and one country around us, and one government for all.

Chief Joseph, leader of the Nez Perce, found in *Indian Chiefs* by R. Freedman (NF)

8 Life's piano can only produce the melodies of brotherhood when it is recognized that the black keys are as basic, necessary, and beautiful as the white keys.

Martin Luther King, Jr., US civil rights leader, *Where Do We Go From Here?* (NF)

9 Four score and seven years ago our fathers brought forth on this continent, a new nation, conceived in liberty; and dedicated to the proposition that all men are created equal.

Abraham Lincoln, 16th US President, in his Nov. 19, 1863 Gettysburg Address, found in *The Faber Book of America*, ed. by Ricks and Vance (NF)

10 The only way to get equality is for two people to get the same thing at the same time at the same place.

Thurgood Marshall, US lawyer for the NAACP and later Supreme Court Justice, writing the decision in the 1934 Murray case

11 This isn't going to be a good country for any of us to live in until it's a good country for all of us to live in.

Richard Nixon, 37th US President, in the Sept. 29, 1968 issue of *The Observer* (NF)

12 I know, up on top you are seeing great sights,
But down at the bottom we, too, should have some rights.

Dr. Seuss, US author, said by a plain turtle named Mack, *Yertle the Turtle* (F)

13 The doctrine of "separate but equal" has no place [in public education]. . . . Separate facilities are inherently* unequal.

Supreme Court Decision in *Brown v. Board of Education*, May 17, 1954   *basically

14 White is something just like black is something. Everybody born on this earth is something; and nobody, no matter what color, is better than anybody else.

Mildred D. Taylor, US author, said by Mama, *Roll of Thunder, Hear My Cry* (F)

15 It is hereby declared to be the policy of the President that there shall be equal treatment and opportunity for all persons in the armed forces without regard to race, color, religion, or national origin.

Harry S Truman, 33rd US President, in his July 26, 1948 Executive Order 9981 that ended segregation in the US armed forces

16 The year was 2081, and everybody was finally equal.

Kurt Vonnegut, Jr., US author, "Harrison Bergeron" from *Welcome to the Monkey House* (F)

Excellence

1 [Roberto Clemente] played a kind of baseball that none of us had ever seen before—throwing and running and hitting at something close to the level of absolute perfection.

Roger Angell, US sportswriter, found in *Champions* by B. Littlefield (NF)

2 On my honor I will do my best
 To do my duty to God and my country
 and to obey the Scout Law;
 To help other people at all times;
 To keep myself physically strong,
 mentally awake, and morally straight.

The Boy Scout Oath, found in *The Book of Virtues*, ed. by W. J. Bennett

3 The secret of joy in work is contained in one word—*excellence*. To know how to do something well is to enjoy it.

Pearl S. Buck, US author, *The Joy of Children* (NF)

4 Quality, whether it was in a man or dog, just couldn't be hidden.

James Kjelgaard, US author, *Big Red* (F)

5 I want to be worthy of respect because I excel at what I do.

Hilary Lindh, US skier, found in *Women in Sports* by J. Layden (NF)

6 Do whatever you do so well that no man living and no man yet unborn could do it better.

Benjamin Mays, US educator, found in *My Soul Looks Back, 'Less I Forget*, ed. by D. W. Riley (NF)

7 I did my best, as I always had done, in spite of cruelty and injustice.

Anna Sewell, English-American author, said by Black Beauty, *Black Beauty* (F)

8 For most of us, it's not that we don't have the ability [to be great], it's that we don't devote the time. You have to put in the effort and put up with all the frustrations and obstacles.

Dean Keith Simonton, US professor, in the June 16, 1996 *Parade* magazine (NF)

9 The excellence of a man is a benefit to the public.

Turkish proverb

10 If you've anything to do,
 Do it with all your might.
 Don't let trifles* hinder you.
 If you're sure you're right,
 Work away.
 Do it with all your might.

Laura Ingalls Wilder, US author, found in *Laura Ingalls Wilder: A Biography* by W. Anderson (NF) *little things

11 Excellence is the best deterrent* to racism or sexism.

Oprah Winfrey, US actress and TV personality, found in the *Book of Black Heroes, Vol. 2* by T. Igus (NF)   *barrier

Failure

(See Success and Failure)

Fairies and Ghosts

1 [Tinker Bell] can't put [her light] out. That is about the only thing fairies can't do. It just goes out by itself when she falls asleep, same as the stars.

> J. M. Barrie, Scottish author, said by Peter Pan, *Peter Pan* (F)

2 From ghoulies and ghosties and long-legged beasties and things that go bump in the night, Good Lord, deliver us.

> Bill Brittain, US author, prayed by Reverend Terwilliger, *Dr. Dredd's Wagon of Wonders* (F)

3 [A boggart] comes from a . . . sort of invisible creature, that likes to play tricks. Not a ghost. But not human.

> Susan Cooper, US author, said by Emily, *The Boggart* (F)

4 [The faerie] always breakfasted upon [a plate of] light and [a glass of] silence.

> e. e. cummings, US poet, "The Old Man Who Said 'Why'" from *Fairy Tales* (F)

5 I am the Ghost of Christmas Past.
Long Past?
No. Your past.

> Charles Dickens, English author, said by the Ghost of Christmas Past and Scrooge, *A Christmas Carol* (F)

6 Deep down, Thomas didn't believe in ghosts. But when night fell, when he was alone in the dark, he feared he might see one.

> Virginia Hamilton, US author, *The House of Dies Drear* (F)

7 I'm from a long time from now. The year 3003, to be exact. And technically I'm not alive, so I imagine you'd call me a ghost.

> Walter Dean Myers, US author, said by Orion Battle, "Things That Go Gleep in the Night" from *Don't Give Up the Ghost,* ed. by D. Gale (F)

8 [A]s I found out, ghosts have feelings too, and if they are not human, at least they once were.

Richard Peck, US author, said by Alexander, *The Ghost Belonged to Me* (F)

9 Don't you know . . . that everybody's got a Fairyland of their own?

P. L. Travers, Australian-English author, said by Mary Poppins, *Mary Poppins* (F)

10 I knew a ghost once who was afraid of the dark, so he always appeared at noon. He had a terrible time scaring anyone.

Patricia C. Wrede, US author, said by the witch Morwen, *Calling on Dragons* (F)

11 Harlyn had not expected to see a fairy that day in the garden. Buttercups, yes. . . . Yet there it was, flittering about on two fast-beating wings as veined and as transparent as stained glass.

Jane Yolen, US author, "Harlyn's Fairy" from *Twelve Impossible Things Before Breakfast* (F)

12 Now, little old ladies who sleep under trees in a dark wood are almost always fairies in disguise.

Jane Yolen, US author, *Sleeping Ugly* (F)

Fame

1 Fame is a pearl many dive for and only a few bring up. Even when they do, it is not perfect and they sigh for more, and lose better things in struggling for them.

Louisa May Alcott, US author, *Jo's Boys* (F)

2 Fame is a very good thing to have in the house, but cash is more convenient.

Louisa May Alcott, US author, said by Jo, *Little Women* (F)

3 I'm the world champion but I don't feel any different than that fan over there. I'll still walk in the ghettoes, answer questions, kiss babies.

Muhammad Ali, US professional boxer, in the Nov. 11, 1974 *Sports Illustrated* (NF)

4 A celebrity is a person who works hard all his life to become well known, then wears dark glasses to avoid being recognized.

Fred Allen, US radio comedian, found in *The New York Public Library Book of 20th Century American Quotations* ed. by S. Donadio (NF)

**5 Fame is a bee.
It has a song—
It has a sting—
Ah, too, it has a wing.**

Emily Dickinson, US poet, "Fame" from her *Collected Poems*

6 Fame endures longer than life.

Irish proverb

7 Sometimes it's good to be famous. Sometimes it's not.

Ana Quirot, Cuban track and field star, found in *Women in Sports* by J. Layden (NF)

8 What good is fame if it only makes you unhappy?

George Selden, US author, said by Harry Cat, *The Cricket in Times Square* (F)

9 Like other creative geniuses, Einstein was not motivated by a desire for fame. Instead, his obsession with his work was what set him apart.

Dean Keith Simonton, US professor, in the June 16, 1996 *Parade* magazine (NF)

Family

(See also Brothers and Sisters, Fathers, *and* Mothers)

1 We got to stick together like mornin' glories stick on a picket fence.

Patricia Beatty, US author, said by Hannalee's mother, *Be Ever Hopeful, Hannalee* (F)

2 I'm not really dying today. No person ever died that had a family. I'll be around a long time. A thousand years from now a whole township of my offspring will be biting sour apples in the gumwood shade.

Ray Bradbury, US author, said by Grandma, "Good-bye, Grandma" from *Dandelion Wine* (F)

3 It isn't walls and furniture that make a home. It's the family.

Natalie Savage Carlson, US author, said by Armand, *The Family Under the Bridge* (F)

4 I got born in the wrong family.

Helen Cresswell, English author, said by Jack, *Ordinary Jack* (F)

5 Families are pretty crazy when you see them close up.

Paula Fox, US author, said by Elizabeth's grandmother, *Western Wind* (F)

6 Family history can get stale—like those crackers—and sink out of sight.

Ibid.

7 The furthest-back person Grandma and the others talked of—always in tones of awe, I noticed—they would call "The African."

Alex Haley, US author, "My Furthest-Back Person—'The African'" in the July 16, 1972 *The New York Times* Sunday Magazine (NF)

8 When I was growing up, our family was so close it sometimes felt as if we were one person with four parts.

Lee A. Iacocca, US business executive and author, in the Jan. 1992 *Biography Today* (NF)

9 Seem like our family been passed round like a jug of ten-cent whiskey at the tavern table.

Harriet A. Jacobs, US diarist, found in *Letters from a Slave Girl* by M. E. Lyons (F)

10 I felt so alone without my family, like a bare tree in a field of snow.

Sally M. Keehn, US author, said by Regina, *I am Regina* (F)

11 Long before the Americans came to New Mexico, long before there was any such thing here called the United States, there was a Chavez family in this place with sheep. . . . It is even so today.

Joseph Krumgold, US author, thought by Miguel, . . . *And Now Miguel* (F)

12 I wanted to be adopted because I needed someone to be a permanent part of my life.

Charlotte Lopez, Puerto Rican-American who was the 1993 Miss Teen USA, in the Apr. 1994 *Biography Today* (NF)

13 Why aren't we like other [families], with batteries in everything, and toys that work, and jigsaws and card games with all their pieces, and everything in the proper cupboard?

Ian McEwan, English author, said by Peter, *The Daydreamer* (F)

14 An ounce of blood is worth more than a pound of friendship.

Spanish proverb

15 For their part, the Old Ones watched over the living members of the family, for one's obligations to the family did not stop with death.

Laurence Yep, Chinese-American author, said by Moon Shadow, *Dragonwings* (F)

Fathers

(See also Parents)

1 Davy Crockett's father could grin a hailstorm into sunshine, and could look the sun square in the face without sneezing.

Walter Blair, US author, a retelling of "The Amazing Crockett Family" from *Tall Tale America* (F)

2 [N]o father is perfect. Grown-ups are complicated creatures, full of quirks and secrets. Some have quirkier quirks and deeper secrets than others, but all of them . . . have two or three private habits . . . that would make you gasp if you knew about them.

Roald Dahl, English author, said by Danny, *Danny, the Champion of the World* (F)

3 I still—to a very great measure—want to impress my father.

Peter Jennings, Canadian TV news anchor and journalist, in the July 1992 *Biography Today* (NF)

4 [Alexander] Hamilton, whose father had deserted him, looked on [George] Washington as the father he never had. For Washington, who had no children of his own, Hamilton was the son he might have had.

Mollie Keller, US author, *Alexander Hamilton* (NF)

5 Billy Shakespeare accepted the fact . . . that my father was my hero. He protested only slightly when I insisted that the reason my father wasn't President of the United States was that my father didn't want to be.

M. E. Kerr, US author, said by Marijane, "Where Are You Now, William Shakespeare?" from *Me Me Me Me Me* (F)

6 A lot of fathers get up in the morning and go on a business trip. My dad would get up, go away, go up into space.

Susan Lovell, daughter of US astronaut Jim Lovell, in the Jan. 1996 *Biography Today* (NF)

7 I won this for Dad. . . . I won this for Dad.

Edwin Moses, US track star, after winning an Olympic Gold Medal in 1984, in the Feb. 18, 1996 *Parade* magazine (NF) *(Moses's father had died several months before he won the medal.)*

8 It occurs to me that the reason there's nothing familiar about [my father] is that (a) I was nine when he left and so he looks shorter now, and (b) I've never seen a picture of him. He got erased from the family.

Richard Peck, US author, thought by Jim Atwater, *Father Figure* (F)

9 I just can't make myself understand that God and the angels needed my father more than I did.

Eleanor H. Porter, US author, said by Pollyanna, *Pollyanna* (F)

10 I wish my father wouldn't try to fix things anymore, for everything he's mended is more broken than before.

Jack Prelutsky, US poet, "I Wish My Father Wouldn't Try to Fix Things Anymore" from *Something Big Has Happened Here*

11 Papa was tall and somewhat bent over, but he had a kindness that shone about him. There seemed always to be something smiling inside of Papa.

George Selden, US author, *The Cricket in Times Square* (F)

12 My father was a master storyteller. He could tell a fine old story that made me hold my sides with rolling laughter and sent happy tears down my cheeks, or a story of stark reality that made me shiver and be grateful for my own warm, secure surroundings.

Mildred D. Taylor, US author, the Author's Note in *Roll of Thunder, Hear My Cry* (F)

13 As a teenager, I rebelled and wanted to break out of the confines of my strict upbringing. But now . . . I'm becoming more like my father.

Denzel Washington, US actor, in the Nov. 1986 *Essence* magazine (NF)

Fathers **F** 77

Fear

1
Shadows on the wall
Noises down the hall
Life doesn't frighten me at all
Bad dogs barking loud
Big ghosts in a cloud
Life doesn't frighten me at all.

Maya Angelou, US poet and author, "Life Doesn't Frighten Me" from *Still I Rise*

2 I was terrified of car accidents, death, cancer, brain tumors, nuclear war, pregnant women, loud noises, strict teachers, elevators, and scads of other things. But I was not afraid of spiders, snakes, and wasps.

Sharon Creech, US author, said by Salamanca, *Walk Two Moons* (F)

3 I couldn't let fear get the best of my good sense. Pa said that when a man lets his mind get full of something strong like fear or anger, he couldn't think straight.

Cynthia DeFelice, US author, said by Nathan, *Weasel* (F)

4 I felt a thrill of fear as if a bottle had crashed next to me, and the bits of glass were flying toward my face.

Paula Fox, US author, thought by Jessie Bollier, *The Slave Dancer* (F)

5 The king's knights were all cowards who hid under their beds whenever the dragon came in sight, so they were of no use to the king at all.

John Gardner, US author, "Dragon, Dragon" from *Dragon, Dragon and Other Tales* (F)

6 Fear of the law gives safety.

Greek proverb

7 Fear makes you perform beyond what you thought was physically possible.

Sir Edmund Hillary, New Zealand explorer and first person to reach the top of Mt. Everest, in the Sept. 1996 *Biography Today* (NF)

8 I experienced fear on many occasions [when I was mountain climbing]. I often thought, "What the heck am I doing here when I could be on the beach?"

Ibid.

9 I was sweating something fierce, although I was cold. I could feel my palms getting clammy and the perspiration running down my back. I get like that when I'm real scared.

S. E. Hinton, US author, said by Ponyboy, *The Outsiders* (F)

10 Yet fear was in [the wolf cub]. It had come down to him from a heritage he had received directly from his parents; but to them, in turn, it had been passed down through the legacy of the Wild.

Jack London, US author, *White Fang* (F)

11 It was because [the borrowers] were frightened, he thought, that they had grown so small. Each generation had become smaller and smaller, and more and more hidden.

Mary Norton, English author, said by Mrs. May, *The Borrowers* (F)

12 You just have to stand up to your fear and not let it squeeze you white.

Katherine Paterson, US author, thought by Jess, *Bridge to Terabithia* (F)

13 To fear is one thing. To let fear grab you by the tail and swing you around is another.

Katherine Paterson, US author, *Jacob Have I Loved* (F)

14 With the end of fear came a feeling of strength.

Gary Paulsen, US author, *Dogsong* (F)

15 You gain strength, courage, and confidence by every experience in which you really stop to look fear in the face.

Eleanor Roosevelt, US diplomat, author, and wife of the 32nd President, found in *Eleanor Roosevelt* by R. Freedman (NF)

16 [T]he only thing we have to fear is fear itself.

Franklin D. Roosevelt, 32nd US President, in his Mar. 4, 1933 First Inaugural Address

17 When Abby and I were little . . . [our grandfather] Scooter would tell us stories. Not cuddle-your-teddy-bear stories, but screamer stories, tremble stories, sink-your-teeth-into-your-teddy-bear stories.

Jerry Spinelli, US author, said by Crash, *Crash* (F)

18 There have always been five things people fear: war, disease, flood, hunger, and death. And of these, death has always been feared the most.

Maia Wojciechowska, Polish-American author, *Shadow of a Bull* (F)

Fish
(See Sea Life)

Food
(See also Eating)

1 A peanut sat on a
    railroad track,
His heart was all
    a-flutter;
The five-fifteen
    came rushing by—
Toot! Toot!
    peanut butter!

American folk poetry, found in *The Classic Treasury of Silly Poetry*, ed. by J. P. Resnik

2 I scream,
    You scream,
    We all scream
    For ice cream.

Anonymous folk poetry, found in *And the Green Grass Grew All Around*, comp. by A. Schwartz

3 Through the teeth,
    Past the gums,
    Look out stomach,
    Here it comes!
    Ibid.

4 May had a little lamb,
You've heard this tale before;
But did you know
She passed her plate
And had a little more?

Anonymous poem, found in *For Laughing Out Loud*, sel. by J. Prelutsky

5 If Peter Piper picked a
peck of pickled peppers,
Where's the peck of
pickled peppers Peter
Piper picked?

Anonymous tongue twister

6 Give us this day our
daily bread.

Bible, Matthew 6:11 (KJV)

7 We are mountain people so we eat
mountain food. Liver mush and fried cabbage and cranberry beans cooked to nutty
goodness with slabs of thick fatback.

Vera and Bill Cleaver, US authors, said by Mary Call,
Where the Lilies Bloom (F)

8 I don't know what they make [dog food]
out of—hulls, straw, sawdust, anything the
pigs won't eat, and then they throw in a
little grease to give it a so-called flavor.
Tastes like soap and about half the time it
gives me an upset stomach.

John R. Erickson, US author, said by Hank, *Hank the Cowdog* (F)

9 There's cold chicken inside [the lucheon-
basket], coldtonguecoldhamcoldbeefpick-
ledgherkinssaladfrenchrollscresssandwiches
pottedmeatgingerbeerlemonadesodawater.

Kenneth Grahame, English author, said by Rat, *The Wind in the Willows* (F)

10 When I grow up, I'm never gonna eat
another vegetable in my life. . . . [I'm only
gonna eat] what I like. Hamburgers and
French fries.

Barbara Hall, US author, said by Bodean, *Dixie Storms* (F)

11 [The sandwiches] are my specialty.
There's marshmallow and prune, banana
and chocolate, cherry jam and cheese,
peanut butter for the prosaic,* and cream
cheese and date.

Polly Horvath, US author, said by Josephine, *An Occasional Cow* (F)   *ordinary

12 For a raccoon, [peanut but-
ter] is like a hot fudge sundae.

Johanna Hurwitz, US author, said by an exterminator,
Aldo Peanut Butter (F)

13 Meanwhile in the bell tower
Skipper's otter troop
is brewing up a caldron of extra
    hotroot soup.
Only an otter can make it,
it's a very old recipe,
and only an otter would taste it (rather
    him than me).

Brian Jacques, English author and actor, *The Great Redwall Feast* (F)

14 *A*'s are one of our most popular letters. All of them aren't that good. . . . Take the *Z*, for instance—very dry and sawdusty. And the *X*? Why, it tastes like a truckful of stale air. That's why people hardly ever use them.

Norton Juster, US author, said by a salesman, *The Phantom Tollbooth* (F)

15 Betcha can't eat just one.

Lay's potato chips advertising slogan

16 The milk chocolate melts in your mouth—not in your hands.

M&M's advertising slogan

17 [T]here's food for the body and food for the spirit. And [the dog] Shiloh sure enough feeds our spirit.

Phyllis Reynolds Naylor, US author, said by Marty's father, *Shiloh* (F)

18 Nothin' says lovin' like some-thin' from the oven.

Pillsbury advertising slogan

19 And instead of a nice dish of min-nows — they had a roasted grasshopper with lady-bird sauce; which frogs consider a beautiful treat; but *I* think it must have been nasty!

Beatrix Potter, English author, "The Tale of Mr. Jeremy Fisher" from *The Complete Tales of Beatrix Potter* (F)

20 Do you like green eggs and ham?

Dr. Seuss, US author, *Green Eggs and Ham* (F)

21 I get so [hungry] that I imagine the pigeons outside my windows stuffed with sage dressing and browned in gravy. I dream of hot dogs chasing each other over fields of crunchy peanut butter.

Mary Francis Shura, US author, written by Greg, *The Josie Gambit* (F)

22 To tell the truth, I hated chicken and have since I was a kid. Give me a cooked-to-order hamburger, and I am happy.

Dave Thomas, US founder of Wendy's, in the Apr. 1996 *Biography Today* (NF)

23 [A]s it's my birthday, we will begin the wrong way — which I always think is the *right* way — with the Cake!

P. L. Travers, Australian-English author, said by Mr. Wigg, *Mary Poppins* (F)

24 [Mama] put a red pickled plum in the middle of some [rice balls] so they'd resemble the Japanese flag, with its red ball of sun on a field of white.

Yoshiko Uchida, Japanese-American author, said by Rinko, *The Best Bad Thing* (F)

Football

1 Football isn't a contact sport, it's a collision sport. Dancing is a contact sport.

Vince Lombardi, US professional football coach, found in *Sports in America* by J. Michener (NF)

2 I'd never played on a team until high school. [Football] gave me a sense of belonging, a focus, and helped build my confidence.

Howie Long, US football player and sports commentator, in the Nov. 3, 1996 *Parade* magazine (NF)

3 There is nothing more fair
  than to pluck a long forward pass
    from the air
  on a field of grass   except perhaps
  to have thrown the pass.

Lillian Morrison, US poet, "Passing Fair" from *The Sidewalk Racer and Other Poems of Sports and Motion*

4 Football, see, is a violent and emotional game. The more charged up you are, the better you play.

Jerry Spinelli, US author, said by Crash, *Crash* (F)

5 Football isn't for fruitcakes. Football doesn't take any crap from the weather.

Ibid.

6 [I]f I do win a championship, it will probably make me happier than anything else could—right now. But in a few years, it won't make much difference.

Fran Tarkenton, US professional football player, found in *Sport* by D. Schaap (NF)

Freedom

1 Men would rather be
starving and free
than fed in
bonds.*

Pearl S. Buck, US author,
What America Means to Me (NF)
*chains

2 None who have always been free can understand the terrible fascinating power of the hope of freedom to those who are not free.

Ibid.

3 Sir, it's worth dying to be free.

James L. Collier and Christopher Collier, US authors, said by Sam, *My Brother Sam Is Dead* (F)

4 I bet [the birds] sing so pretty because [they're] free.

Frederick Douglass, US abolitionist and author, found in *Frederick Douglass Fights for Freedom* by M. Davidson (NF)

5 That on the 1st day of January, in the year of our Lord 1863, all persons held as slaves within any state . . . shall be then, thenceforward, and forever free.

Emancipation Proclamation, issued by President Lincoln on Jan. 1, 1863 (*It was not until ratification of the 13th Amendment on Dec. 2, 1865—after Lincoln's death— that slaves legally became free.*)

6 Is life so dear, or peace so sweet, as to be purchased at the price of chains and slavery? . . . I know not what course others may take, but as for me . . . give me liberty or give me death!

Patrick Henry, Revolutionary leader, in a Mar. 23, 1775 speech before the second Virginia Convention, found in *The American Reader*, ed. by D. Ravitch (NF)

7 Freedom! The word tastes like Christmas when I say it aloud. Like a juicy orange or a cup of sweetened milk.

Harriet A. Jacobs, US diarist, found in *Letters from a Slave Girl* by M. E. Lyons (F)

8 You might as well expect the rivers to run backward as that any man who was born free should be contented penned up and denied liberty to go where he pleases.

Chief Joseph, leader of the Nez Perce tribe, found in *500 Nations* by A. M. Josephy, Jr. (NF)

9 [W]hen we let [freedom] ring from every village and hamlet, from every state and city, we will be able to speed up that day when all of God's children . . . will be able to join hands and to sing in the words of the Negro spiritual, "Free at last, free at last, thank God Almighty, we are free at last!"

Martin Luther King, Jr., US civil rights leader, in his Aug. 28, 1963 "I Have a Dream" speech in Washington, D.C., found in *The American Reader*, ed. by D. Ravitch (NF)

10 Alone, no one wins freedom.

Ursula K. Le Guin, US author, said by Ged, *The Tombs of Atuan* (F)

11 [P]roclaim liberty through all the land unto all the inhabitants thereof.

Liberty Bell inscription from the Bible, Leviticus 25:10, found in *Celebrating America*, comp. by L. Whipple (NF)

12 In *giving* freedom to the slave, we *assure* freedom to the *free*.

Abraham Lincoln, 16th US President, in his Dec. 1, 1862 annual address to Congress, found in *Lincoln: A Photobiography* by R. Freedman (NF)

13 A country's freedom cannot be bought by any amount of gold.

Philippine proverb

14 And today the great Yertle, the
       Marvelous he,
   Is King of the Mud. That is all he can
       see.
   And the turtles of course . . . all the
       turtles are free
   As turtles and, maybe, all creatures
       should be.

Dr. Seuss, US author, *Yertle the Turtle* (F)

15 My country 'tis of thee
   Sweet land of liberty;
       Of thee I sing.
   Land where my fathers died
   Land of the pilgrims' pride
   From every mountainside
       Let freedom ring.

Samuel F. Smith, US clergyman, words from the song "America," written in 1832, found in *The American Reader*, ed. by D. Ravitch (NF)

16 A hungry man is not a free man.

Adlai Stevenson, US politician, in a Sept. 6, 1952 campaign speech

17 There were two things I had a right to, liberty and death. If I could not have one, I would have the other, for no man should take me alive.

Harriet Tubman, US abolitionist and liberator of 300–400 slaves, found in *Herstory*, ed. by Ashley and Ohrn (NF)

18 Most of the verses of the plantation songs had some reference to freedom [in them].

Booker T. Washington, US educator and author, *Up from Slavery* (NF)

19 Liberty, when it begins to take root, is a plant rapid in growth.

George Washington, 1st US President, in a Mar. 2, 1788 letter to James Madison

Friendship

1 Little friends might prove great friends.

Aesop, Greek writer, the moral in the fable "A Lion and a Mouse," found in *The Children's Treasury*, ed. by P. S. Goepfert (F)

2 Tell me quick before I faint,
Is we friends, or is we ain't?

Anonymous folk poem, found in *And the Green Grass Grew All Around*, comp. by A. Schwartz

3 I have no heart, you know, so I am careful to help all those who may need a friend, even if it happens to be only a mouse.

L. Frank Baum, US author, said by Tin Woodman, *The Wonderful Wizard of Oz* (F)

4 Greater love has no one than this, that one lay down his life for his friends.

Bible, John 15:13 (NIV)

5 [H]e that proclaims many friends declares that he has none.

John Christopher, English author, said by a Vagrant, *The White Mountains* (F)

6 Friends have ways of speaking without words.

Alice Dalgliesh, US author, *The Courage of Sarah Noble* (F)

7 There are friends, I think, we can't imagine living without. People who are sisters to us, or brothers.

Julie Reece Deaver, US author and illustrator, thought by Morgan, *Say Goodnight, Gracie* (F)

8 The only way to have a friend is to be one.

Ralph Waldo Emerson, US poet and writer, *Friendship*

9 [L]ike the Good Book says, we should honor our father and mother, but I, personally, think we should honor our friends, too.

Louise Fitzhugh, US author, said by Jessie May, *The Long Secret* (F)

10 The river was like that to me. A comfortable buddy sharing a lazy day.

Eddy Harris, US author, *Mississippi Solo* (NF)

11 I've stood by you without batting an eye in earthquakes, fire and flood—in poker games, dynamite outrages, police raids, train robberies, and cyclones.

O. Henry, US author, said by Bill to Sam, *The Ransom of Red Chief* (F)

12 Well, I don't suppose anyone ever is completely self-winding. That's what friends are for.

Russell Hoban, US author, said by the frog, *The Mouse and His Child* (F)

13 I loved my friend.
He went away from me.
There's nothing more to say.
The poem ends,
Soft as it began—
I loved my friend.

Langston Hughes, US poet, "Poem" found in *Valentine's Day: Stories and Poems*, ed by C. F. Bauer

14 Buster and Ben are best friends. In their hearts they are brothers, although, in fact, Buster is a purebred Doberman pincher and Ben is a mutt. . . . Each day is a new adventure, and they share it side by side.

Trina Schart Hyman, US illustrator, from *Speak! Children's Book Illustrators Brag about Their Dogs*, ed. by M. J. Rosen (NF)

15 Love your friend with his faults.

Italian proverb

16 I get by with a little help from my friends.

John Lennon, English musician and composer, words to the song "With a Little Help from My Friends," written with P. McCartney

17 [A friend is] one who has the same enemies you have.

Abraham Lincoln, 16th US President, in a June 30, 1862 letter to William H. Seward

18 Probably one of the most important things in life, and also one of the most difficult things to find, is friendship. I mean *true* friendship.

Ann M. Martin, US author, found in *Ann M. Martin: The Story of the Author of the Baby-sitters Club* by M. Becker R. (NF)

19 I wish Pooh were here. It's so much more friendly with two.

A. A. Milne, English author, said by Piglet, "Surrounded by Water" from *Winnie-the-Pooh* (F)

20 It's harder to make friends [when you get older] because you end up asking more from everybody.

Walter Dean Myers, US author, said by Stuff, *Fast Sam, Cool Clyde, and Stuff* (F)

21 Make new friends, but keep the old;
Those are silver, these are gold.

"New Friends and Old Friends," anonymous poem, found in *The Book of Virtues*, ed. by W. J. Bennett

22 Men have no more time to understand anything. They buy things all ready made at the shops. But there is not a shop anywhere where one can buy friendship.

Antoine de Saint-Exupéry, French author and illustrator, said by the fox, *The Little Prince* (F)

23 I've discovered a way to stay friends forever—
There's really nothing to it.
I simply tell you what to do
And you do it!

Shel Silverstein, US poet and illustrator, "Friendship" from *A Light in the Attic*

24 [Amos and Boris] became the closest possible friends. They told each other about their lives, their ambitions. They shared their deepest secrets.

William Steig, US author, *Amos and Boris* (F)

25 Friends gotta trust each other . . . 'cause ain't nothin' like a true friend.

Mildred D. Taylor, US author, said by T. J., *Roll of Thunder, Hear My Cry* (F)

26 A friend can tell you things you don't want to tell yourself.

Frances Ward Weller, US author, *Boat Song* (F)

27 No pig ever had truer friends, and [Wilbur] realized that friendship is one of the most satisfying things in the world.

E. B. White, US author, *Charlotte's Web* (F)

Future

1 Heck, we was going to live forever. Can you picture what it felt like to find that out?

Natalie Babbitt, US author, said by Jesse Tuck, *Tuck Everlasting* (F)

2 Ghost of the Future! . . . I fear you more than any specter* I have seen.

Charles Dickens, English author, said by Scrooge, *A Christmas Carol* (F)   *ghost

3 I never think of the future. It comes soon enough.

Albert Einstein, German-American physicist, in a 1930 interview

4 [In 1903] *The New York Times* commented that a man-carrying airplane would eventually be built—but only if mathematicians and engineers worked steadily for the next one million to ten million years.

Russell Freedman, US author, *The Wright Brothers* (NF)

5 What if everything died off [from nuclear radiation] except people? People wrapped in special space suits, eating imitation food. No more touching. Even if people wanted to touch. . . . How long could humans last that way?

Karen Hesse, US author, thought by Nyle, *Phoenix Rising* (F)

6 The future is impartial, and Fortune smiles on whom she will.

Russell Hoban, US author, said by the frog, *The Mouse and His Child* (F)

7 I felt like I was holding the future like summer berries in my hands.

Jan Hudson, Canadian author, said by Sweetgrass, *Sweetgrass* (F)

8 Learn the future by looking at the past.

Indian proverb

9 I like dreams of the future better than the history of the past.

Thomas Jefferson, 3rd US President, in an Aug. 1, 1816 letter to John Adams

10 After [their kiss], no future seemed possible unless they could spend it together, forever. Romeo and his Juliet, Juliet and her Romeo.

Geraldine McCaughrean, English author, the retelling of *Romeo and Juliet* from *The Random House Book of Stories from the Ballet* (F)

11 It becomes clearer and clearer that the future world will be a shabby and dangerous place to live in—yes, even for Americans to live in—if it is ruled by force in the hands of a few.

Franklin D. Roosevelt, 32nd US President, in his Jan. 4, 1940 State of the Union message

12 To me, it appears likely that in the coming decades we will have information on at least hundreds of other planetary systems close to us in the vast Milky Way Galaxy.

Carl Sagan, US astronomer and author, in the June 9, 1996 *Parade* magazine (NF)

13 A large animal needs a large area. If you protect that area, you're also protecting thousands of other plants and animals. You're saving all these species that future generations will want—you're saving the world for your children and your children's children.

George Schaller, US naturalist and field biologist, in the Feb. 2, 1997 *Parade* magazine (NF)

14 The future depends entirely on what each of us does every day.

Gloria Steinem, US author and women's rights activist, in the Mar. 9, 1992 *Time* magazine (NF)

15 The oceans are the frontier that coming generations will explore and cultivate.

Philip Sterling, US author, *Sea and Earth: The Life of Rachel Carson* (NF)

Ghosts

(See Fairies and Ghosts*)*

Goals

1 What we need are positive, realistic goals and the willingness to work. Hard work and practical goals.

Kareem Abdul-Jabbar, US professional basketball player, *Kareem* (NF)

2 It's fun to set goals, reach goals, and reset them.

Bonnie Blair, US speed skater, in the Apr. 1994 *Biography Today* (NF)

3 Having achieved what I thought was an ultimate ambition, I found, as I think is often the case, that there remained something more.

John Christopher, English author, thought by Will Parker, *The White Mountains* (F)

4 We simply desire that we shall be recognized as men; that we have no obstructions placed in our way; that the same laws that govern white men shall direct colored men . . . that we be dealt with . . . in equality and justice.

Colored People's Convention, written in Nov. 1865 after all slaves had been freed by the Emancipation Proclamation, found in *Black Voices from Reconstruction: 1865-1877* by J. D. Smith (NF)

5 I know what I want. A full belly, a contented heart, and a place in this world.

Karen Cushman, US author, said by Alyce, *The Midwife's Apprentice* (F)

6 [When I was a slave,] I set out with high hope, and a fixed purpose, at whatever cost or trouble, to learn how to read.

Frederick Douglass, US abolitionist and author, *Escape from Slavery*, ed. by M. McCurdy (NF)

7 My desire is to do everything within my power to further free the people from drudgery* and create the largest possible measures of happiness and prosperity.

Thomas Edison, US inventor, found in *The Thomas A. Edison Album* by L. F. Frost (NF)   *unpleasant work*

8 "Live for others!" That's my motto in life.

Kenneth Grahame, English author, said by Toad, *The Wind in the Willows* (F)

9 Mama exhorted* her children at every opportunity to "jump at de sun." We might not land on the sun, but at least we would get off the ground.

Zora Neale Hurston, US anthropologist and author, *Dust Tracks on the Road* (NF)   *urged

10 I always had something to shoot for each year: to jump one inch further.

Jackie Joyner-Kersee, US track star, found in *My Soul Looks Back, 'Less I Forget*, ed. by D. W. Riley (NF)

11 The goal will not be reached if the right distance is not traveled.

Tibetan proverb

12 I hope I shall always possess firmness and virtue enough to maintain (what I consider the most enviable of all titles) the character of an "Honest Man."

George Washington, 1st US President, in an Aug. 28, 1788 letter to Alexander Hamilton

13 You can make a difference if you come together with one goal in mind — and if you don't care what people think about you.

Jody Williams, US creator of the International Campaign to Ban Landmines, said upon receiving the news that she had won the 1997 Nobel Peace Prize

14 I still want what I've always wanted . . . to be the best person I can be.

Oprah Winfrey, US actress and TV personality, found in *Oprah Winfrey* by S. Otfinoski (NF)

God

(See also Religion)

1 People see God every day, they just don't recognize Him.

Pearl Bailey, US singer and author, in the Nov. 26, 1967 issue of *The New York Times* (NF)

2 God is our refuge and strength, an ever present help in trouble.

Bible, Psalms 46:1 (NIV)

3 I've been looking for you, God. I looked in the temple. I looked in church. And today, I looked for you when I wanted to confess. But you weren't there. . . . Why do I only feel you when I'm alone?

Judy Blume, US author, said by Margaret, *Are You There, God? It's Me, Margaret* (F)

4 Sarah thought of the Lord as a kind old man like her grandfather. Her mother said no one knew how [God] looked, but Sarah was sure *she* knew.

Alice Dalgliesh, US author, *The Courage of Sarah Noble* (F)

5 God bless us, every one!

Charles Dickens, English author, said by Tiny Tim, *A Christmas Carol* (F)

6 O God, save me! God, deliver me! Let me be free! Is there a God? Why am I a slave?

Frederick Douglass, US abolitionist and author, *Escape from Slavery*, ed. by M. McCurdy (NF)

7 I guess . . . that people made up God to make themselves feel better. After all, when you think about space, I mean *all that space* out there, it is pretty ghastly.

Louise Fitzhugh, US author, said by Janie, *The Long Secret* (F)

8 A caterpillar does not ask himself, "Let's see, shall I spin myself into a cocoon and turn into a butterfly? Or is it more fun to be a caterpillar?" He just does what he does and cannot do otherwise. God had decided He wouldn't get much pleasure from humans who acted like caterpillars.

Ruth Bell Graham, US author, *One Wintry Night* (F)

9 I believe in a God who knows how complicated human life is, how difficult it is to be a good person at all times, and who expects not a perfect life but an honest effort at a good one.

Harold S. Kushner, US rabbi and author, in the Sept. 8, 1996 *Parade* magazine (NF)

10 Mother says we should never try to make bargains with God. That isn't the way God works.

Madeleine L'Engle, US author, said by Vicky, *The Twenty-four Days Before Christmas* (F)

11 I always figured God had eyebrows just like Pop's, and when somebody lied or stole or punched a person in the face, God's eyebrows went right up like Pop's.

Cynthia Rylant, US author, thought by Pete, *A Fine White Dust* (F)

12 Pray to God but continue to row to the shore.

Russian proverb

13 Your God loves your people and hates mine. . . . He has forsaken His red children —if they really are His. Our God, the Great Spirit, seems also to have forsaken us.

Chief Seattle, leader of six Indian tribes in the Pacific Northwest, in an 1854 speech to Gov. Isaac Stevens, found in *The American Reader*, ed. by D. Ravitch (NF)

14 [God] can hear everybody at the same time, because He is the good heavenly Father, and not a mere mortal like you and me.

Johanna Spyri, Swiss author, said by Mrs. Sesemann, *Heidi* (F)

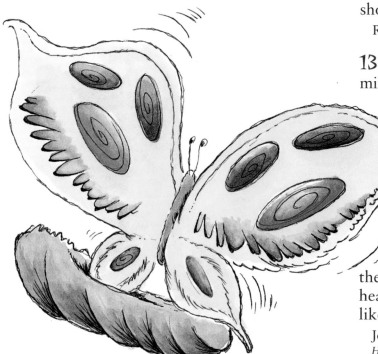

15 To service the poor purely for the love of God.

Mother Teresa, Yugoslavian missionary to India, a statement of her mission in 87 countries

16 [Papa] says God is just as much out in the park or the open fields as He is inside our dark, musty Japanese church. That's what I think, too.

Yoshiko Uchida, Japanese-American author, thought by Rinko, *The Best Bad Thing* (F)

17 What God has intended for you goes far beyond anything you can imagine.

Oprah Winfrey, US actress and TV personality, found in *My Soul Looks Back, 'Less I Forget*, ed. by D. W. Riley (NF)

Good and Bad

1 [People are] all you said. And worse, some of them; but some are better than you told me. If I can't have the good without the bad, I'll take it all together.

Lloyd Alexander, US author, said by Lionel to the wizard, *The Cat Who Wished To Be a Man* (F)

2 Ah, no one knows who makes evil storms. . . . We only know that they come. When they come we must live through them as bravely as we can, and after they are gone, we must feel again how wonderful life is.

Pearl S. Buck, US author, said by Kino's father, *The Big Wave* (F)

3 But I suppose there *might* be good in things, even if we don't see it.

Frances Hodgson Burnett, English-American author, said by Sara, *A Little Princess* (F)

4 [N]othing bad could ever happen to me and [my brother] Daniel. Ever. I wanted to think we were like the boulders down by the river — unmovable, strong, eternal.

Pam Conrad, US author, said by Julia Creath, *My Daniel* (F)

5 And the world will still be imperfect because men are imperfect . . . and there will still be pain and disease and famine, anger and hate. But if you work and care and are watchful . . . then in the long run the worse will never, ever triumph over the better.

Susan Cooper, US author, said by Merriman, *Silver on the Tree* (F)

6 In [Phoebe's] world, no one was ordinary. People were either perfect — like her father — or, more often, they were lunatics or axe murderers.

Sharon Creech, US author, said by Salamanca, *Walk Two Moons* (F)

7 Mama always said things seem better in the morning.

Cynthia DeFelice, US author, said by Nathan, *Weasel* (F)

8 Where there's no good within, no good comes out.

Dutch proverb

9 [I]n spite of everything I still believe that people are really good at heart. I simply can't build my hopes on a foundation of confusion, misery, and death.

Anne Frank, Dutch diarist, *Anne Frank: The Diary of a Young Girl*, July 15, 1944 entry (NF)

10 [D]o you ever feel that sometimes when unexpected things happen, they were meant to, and that it works out for the best in the end?

James Herriot, English veterinarian and author, said by Mr. Dakin, *Blossom Comes Home* (F)

11 Things gotta get better, I figured. They couldn't get worse. I was wrong.

S. E. Hinton, US author, said by Ponyboy, *The Outsiders* (F)

12 Can you know excellence if you've never seen it? Can you know good if you have seen only bad?

E. L. Konigsburg, US author and illustrator, said by Mr. Singh, *The View from Saturday* (F)

13 [In the book *Pollyanna*,] goodness triumphs; I like that, even though it rarely seems to happen in real life these days.

Lois Lowry, US author, the Afterword to *Pollyanna* by E. H. Porter (F)

14 [If Macbeth] can never pray again or say "Amen," it will mean that he is cut off from all goodness for ever and ever.

Bernard Miles, English actor and author, the retelling of *Macbeth* from *Favorite Tales from Shakespeare* (F)

15 The game was to just find something about everything to be glad about—no matter what 'twas. . . . You see, when you're hunting for the glad things, you sort of forget the other kind.

Eleanor H. Porter, US author, said by Pollyanna, *Pollyanna* (F)

16 Pa says you have to look at a situation and measure the good against the bad and then do what you think is right, no matter what other people do.

Carolyn Reeder, US author, said by Meg, *Shades of Gray* (F)

17 Nobody can make you feel bad about yourself unless you let them.

Eleanor Roosevelt, US diplomat, author, and wife of the 32nd President, found in *America's Most Influential First Ladies* by C. S. Anthony (NF)

18 [P]eople don't say what's good about themselves. They tell their faults. Not big ones, see, little ones. Expecting nobody'll believe them, of course.

Mary Stolz, US author, said by Emily, *Quentin Corn* (F)

19 Mama always says bad things happen in threes.

Yoshiko Uchida, Japanese-American author, thought by Rinko, *The Best Bad Thing* (F)

Government

1 As the happiness of the people is the sole end of government, so the consent of the people is the only foundation of it.

John Adams, 2nd US President, proclamation adopted by the Council of Massachusetts Bay in 1774

2 I find, although the colonies have differed in religion, laws, customs, and manners, yet in the great essentials of society and government they are all alike.

John Adams, 2nd US President, in a July 10, 1776 letter to his wife Abigail

3 Government is best which governs least.

American proverb

4 A simple and a proper function of government is just to make it easy for us to do good and difficult for us to do wrong.

Jimmy Carter, 39th US President, in his July 15, 1976 acceptance speech at the Democratic National Convention

5 The only people who should be in government are those who care more about people than they do about power.

Millicent Fenwick, US politician, in a 1980 interview

6 But with all the imperfections of our present government, it is without comparison the best existing, or that ever did exist.

Thomas Jefferson, 3rd US President, in a Mar. 15, 1787 letter to Edward Carrington

7 I believe this government can not endure permanently half slave and half free.

Abraham Lincoln, 16th US President, in his June 16, 1858 acceptance speech in Springfield, IL

8 The government is us; we are the government, you and I.

Theodore Roosevelt, 26th US President, in a Sept. 9, 1902 speech in Asheville, NC

9 Secrecy and a free, democratic government don't mix.

Harry S Truman, 33rd US President, found in *Plain Speaking* by M. Miller (NF)

10 Whenever you have an efficient government, you have a dictatorship.

Harry S Truman, 33rd US President, in a 1959 lecture at Columbia University

11 No matter what the system [of government], if it is not based on truth, on morality, on honesty, it hasn't a chance.

Lech Walesa, Poland's first democratically elected President, found in *Contemporary Heroes and Heroines*, ed. by R. B. Browne (NF)

12 The very idea of the power and the right of the people to establish government presupposes* the duty of every individual to obey the established government.

George Washington, 1st US President, in his Sept. 17, 1796 Farewell Address   *presumes*

13 The firm basis of government is justice, not pity.

Woodrow Wilson, 28th US President, in his Mar. 4, 1913 Inaugural Address

Grandparents

1 Be good to Grandma, little chaps,
Whatever else you do.
And then she'll grow to be—perhaps—
More tolerant of you.

Anonymous poem, found in *A Nonny Mouse Writes Again!*, sel. by J. Prelutsky

2 [Grandma] had stuffed turkeys, chickens, squabs, gentlemen, and boys. She had washed ceilings, walls, invalids, and children. She had laid linoleum, repaired bicycles, wound clocks, stoked furnaces, swabbed iodine on ten thousand grievous wounds.

Ray Bradbury, US author, "Good-by, Grandma" from *Dandelion Wine* (F)

3 My grandfather was a giant of a man. When he walked, the earth shook. When he laughed, the birds fell out of the trees. His hair caught fire from the sun. His eyes were patches of sky.

Eth Clifford, US author, said by Grandma Goldina, *The Remembering Box* (F)

4 If you want to know where I come by the passionate commitment I have to bringing people together without regard to race, it all started with my grandfather.

Bill Clinton, 42nd US President, in the July 1992 *Biography Today* (NF)

5 I saw [my grandmother] as my liberator and my model. Her stories were parables from which to glean* *Truth*.

Judith Ortiz Cofer, Puerto Rican author, found in *Latino Voices*, ed. by F. R. Aparicio (NF)   *collect

6 [Their grandmother] was round and soft, like an overstuffed bed, and she smelled faintly like mothballs, false teeth, and lilacs.

Pam Conrad, US author, *My Daniel* (F)

7 My grandparents Hiddle were . . . full up to the tops of their heads with goodness and sweetness, and mixed in with all that goodness and sweetness was a large dash of peculiarity. This combination made them interesting to know, but you could never predict what they would do or say.

Sharon Creech, US author, said by Salamanca, *Walk Two Moons* (F)

8 Grandfather was well known for being stubborn in his ideas. For instance . . . [y]ou had to go to sleep facing east so that you would be ready to greet the sun when it returned.

Michael Dorris, Native American author and anthropologist, thought by Moss, *Guests* (F)

9 Hug [your] grandparents and say, "I want to thank you for what you've done to make me and my life possible."

Alex Haley, US author, in the Feb. 4, 1985 *Jet* magazine (NF)

10 I don't hate grandmother. . . . But I hate it that she's so old. It makes my heart hurt.

Lois Lowry, US author, said by Anastasia, *Anastasia Krupnik* (F)

11 [My grandfather] Izzy has always had strong opinions on everything. . . . Food, weather, and health are usually the only safe subjects for conversation.

Norma Fox Mazer, US author, thought by Rachel, *After the Rain* (F)

12 Grampa Hec says that he stopped counting birthdays at 99, but . . . it's hard to tell when he's telling one of his stories and when he's telling what is really so.

Robert McCloskey, US author, said by Homer, *Centerburg Tales* (F)

13 What are grandmothers good for?
Well, mine is good for me.

David McCord, US poet, "Grandmothers," found in *Poems for Grandmothers*, sel. by M. C. Livingston

14 It took me a long time to get used to the reality that my grandmother had passed away. Wherever I was, in the house, in the garden, out on the fields, her face always appeared so clearly to me.

Huynh Quang Nhuong, South Vietnamese author, *The Land I Lost* (NF)

15 [My sister and I] both grew up thinking [our grandfather's] bed was the safest place in the world, like a boat in a sea full of crocs. . . . It was a place where you could say things out loud that you might only think anywhere else.

Jerry Spinelli, US author, thought by Crash, *Crash* (F)

16 [My grandmother] taught me early on about doing the right thing, working hard, doing a job well, and having fun.

Dave Thomas, US founder of Wendy's, in the Apr. 1996 *Biography Today* (NF)

17 My great-great-great-grandmother walked as a slave from Virginia to Eatonton, Georgia. . . . It is in memory of this walk that I chose to keep and to embrace my "maiden" name, Walker.

Alice Walker, US author, *In Search of Our Mothers' Gardens* (NF)

Greatness

(See Excellence)

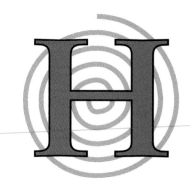

Handicaps

(See Disabilities)

Happiness

1 A cheerful heart is good medicine, but a crushed spirit dries up the bones.

Bible, Proverbs 17:22 (NIV)

2 Poor Earthworm . . . he hates to be happy. He is only happy when he is gloomy. Now isn't that odd?

Roald Dahl, English author, said by Ladybug, *James and the Giant Peach* (F)

3 I am light as a feather, I am as happy as an angel, I am as merry as a schoolboy. I am as giddy as a drunken man. A merry Christmas to everybody! A happy New Year to all the world!

Charles Dickens, English author, said by Scrooge after realizing he wasn't dead, *A Christmas Carol* (F)

4 Gran had said you can't pursue* happiness. It can strike in the middle of trouble, and it can disappear for no apparent reason, even when you think you ought to be happy.

Paula Fox, US author, thought by Elizabeth, *Western Wind* (F)

5 [W]hoever is happy will make others happy too. He who has courage and faith will never perish in misery.

Anne Frank, Dutch diarist, *Anne Frank: The Diary of a Young Girl*, Mar. 7, 1944 entry (NF)

6 Happiness begins where ambition ends.

Hungarian proverb

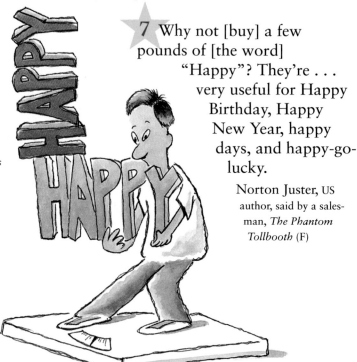

7 Why not [buy] a few pounds of [the word] "Happy"? They're . . . very useful for Happy Birthday, Happy New Year, happy days, and happy-go-lucky.

Norton Juster, US author, said by a salesman, *The Phantom Tollbooth* (F)

*search for

8 When one door of happiness closes, another opens; but often we look so long at the closed door that we do not see the one which has been opened to us.

Helen Keller, US author and humanitarian, *We Bereaved* (NF)

9 [The Parsee] smiled one smile that ran all around his face two times.

Rudyard Kipling, English-American journalist and author, "How the Rhinoceros Got His Skin" from *Just So Stories* (F)

10 Happiness is excitement that has found a settling down place, but there is always a little corner that keeps flapping around.

E. L. Konigsburg, US author and illustrator, *From the Mixed Up Files of Mrs. Basil E. Frankweiler* (F)

11 And instead of the deadly silence the whole place rang with the sounds of happy roarings, brayings, yelpings, barkings, squealings, cooings, neighings, stampings, shouts, hurrahs, songs and laughter.

C. S. Lewis, English author, *The Lion, the Witch, and the Wardrobe* (F)

12 And everyone lived happily ever after—or at least as happily as is possible in this mortal world.

Phyllis McGinley, US author, *The Plain Princess* (F)

13 Nobody can be uncheered with a balloon.

A. A. Milne, English author, "Eeyore Has a Birthday" from *Winnie-the-Pooh* (F)

14 Suddenly everybody was happy. It was like seeing a rainbow when it was still raining.

Walter Dean Myers, US author, said by Stuff, *Fast Sam, Cool Clyde, and Stuff* (F)

15 I felt the way popcorn kernels must feel when they're sizzling.

Sylvia Peck, US author, said by Molly, *Seal Child* (F)

16 [T]hat princess held happiness in both her hands. Then, just like that, she threw it out.

Barbara Ann Porte, US author, said by Alice, "What the Princess Discarded," found in *Birthday Surprises*, ed. by J. Hurwitz (F)

17 If anyone were to ask me what I want out of life I would say—the opportunity for doing something useful, for in no other way, I am convinced, can true happiness be attained.

Eleanor Roosevelt, US diplomat, author, and wife of the 32nd President, found in *Eleanor Roosevelt* by R. Freedman (NF)

18 If [Hector] had had a tail, it would have been wagging.

Gary Soto, Mexican-American author, *Summer on Wheels* (F)

19 Why had [Derek] wanted to be rich, or to feel rich? Was he an unhappy mouse before? Didn't he see the King himself often looking sad? Was anyone completely happy?

William Steig, US author, *The Real Thief* (F)

20 [The night the Velveteen Rabbit became Real] he was almost too happy to sleep, and so much love stirred in his little saw-dust heart that it almost burst.

Margery Williams, English-American author, *The Velveteen Rabbit* (F)

21 Happy days are here again,
The skies above are clear again.
Let us sing a song of cheer again,
Happy days are here again!

Jack Yellen, US songwriter, words to the song "Happy Days Are Here Again," used in Democratic Party campaigns since Franklin Roosevelt, found in *The American Reader*, ed. by D. Ravitch (NF)

Health

(See Sickness)

Heroes

(See Also Tall Tale Heroes)

1 If I patterned my life after anyone, it was [Jackie Robinson's], not because he was the first black baseball player in the major leagues but because he was my hero.

Kareem Abdul-Jabbar, US professional basketball player, *Kareem* (NF)

2 So David triumphed over [Goliath] with a sling and a stone; without a sword in his hand he struck down [the giant] and killed him.

Bible, 1 Samuel 17:50 (NIV)

3 Heroes and heroines serve as models and leaders of people and nations because they reflect the feelings, dreams, fantasies, and needs of individuals and of society itself.

Ray B. Browne, US author and editor, the Introduction to *Contemporary Heroes and Heroines* (NF)

4 I began to feel like some sort of hero. Maybe I'm not so medium after all.

Beverly Cleary, US author, said by Leigh Botts, *Dear Mr. Henshaw* (F)

5 Heroes are creatures of adversity — war, fire, accident, or disaster.

Jane Leslie Conly, US author, said by the rat Nicodemus, *Racso and the Rats of NIMH* (F)

6 There's a thin line between heroism and stupidity, and I try to stay on the south side of it.

John R. Erickson, US author, said by Hank, *Hank the Cowdog* (F)

7 That colossal-osal, gigantic-antic, Super-Duper, that same Super-Duper who defied the elements . . . yes, who was tougher than steel, he stooped down and said . . ."Ouch!"

Robert McCloskey, US author, "The Case of the Cosmic Comic" from *Homer Price* (F)

8 We can't all be heroes because somebody has to sit on the curb and clap as they go by [in a parade].

Attributed to Will Rogers, US humorist and author

9 Superman, disguised as Clark Kent, mild-mannered reporter for a great metropolitan newspaper, fights a never-ending battle for truth, justice, and the American way.

Superman introduction to the old radio series

History

1 The histories of the poor and the powerless are as important as those of their conquerors, their colonizers, their kings and queens.

Johnnetta B. Cole, US educator, found in *Words to Make My Dream Children Live*, ed. by D. Mullane (NF)

2 The history of free men really is never written by chance but choice — their choice.

Dwight D. Eisenhower, 34th US President, in an Oct. 9, 1956 speech in Pittsburgh, PA

3 This tale is a work of the imagination, but the most surprising part of it is true. Some royal households in past centuries *did* keep whipping boys to suffer the punishments due a misbehaving prince. History is alive with lunacies and injustices.

Sid Fleischman, US author, the Note at the end of *The Whipping Boy* (F)

4 History, in general, only informs us what bad government is.

Thomas Jefferson, 3rd US President, in a June 11, 1807 letter to John Norvell

5 America was named after a man who discovered no part of the New World. History is like that, very chancy.

Samuel Eliot Morison, US historian, *The Oxford History of the American People* (NF)

6 [A]ll big things in human history have been arrived at slowly and through many compromises.

Eleanor Roosevelt, US diplomat, author, and wife of the 32nd President, found in *Eleanor and Franklin* by J. P. Lash (NF)

7 Sometimes great people don't make it into the history books. A lot of women achieved remarkable things but went unrecognized.

Dean Keith Simonton, US professor, in the June 16, 1996 *Parade* magazine (NF)

8 If history could be unwound and [Derek the mouse] were there again, he would consider the consequences and he wouldn't steal.

William Steig, US author, *The Real Thief* (F)

9 [I]n the South where I was born, I learned a history not then written in books but one passed from generation to generation . . . a history of great-grandparents and of slavery and of the days following slavery.

Mildred D. Taylor, US author, the Author's Note in *Roll of Thunder, Hear My Cry* (F)

10 Men make history and not the other way around. In periods where there is no leadership, society stands still. Progress occurs when courageous, skillful leaders seize the opportunity to change things for the better.

Harry S Truman, 33rd US President, in the Feb. 22, 1959 issue of *This Week* magazine (NF)

Home

1 Home is where the heart is.
American proverb

2 The ache for home lives in all of us, the safe place where we can go as we are and not be questioned.

Maya Angelou, US poet and author, *All God's Children Need Traveling Shoes* (NF)

3 [T]here is no place like home.

L. Frank Baum, US author, said by Dorothy, *The Wonderful Wizard of Oz* (F)

4 Seems to me home is where I am loved and safe and needed.

Karen Cushman, US author, written by Lucy, *The Ballad of Lucy Whipple* (F)

5 Home was the place I never saw because I saw it all the time, too up close to see it well.

Michael Dorris, Native American author and anthropologist, thought by Moss, *Guests* (F)

6 "Not home" was the last spot a person would want to stay, no matter how interesting or exciting it might seem for a while.
Ibid.

7 E. T. phone home.

E.T., the famous line from the movie, *E. T. The Extra-Terrestrial*, 1982

8 I came upon the [six-foot hemlock] last summer and dug and burned it out until I made a snug cave in the tree that I now call home.

Jean Craighead George, US author, said by Sam, *My Side of the Mountain* (F)

9 Papa always said you should never be ashamed of your home or your town. When you are, then you're getting too big for your britches.

Barbara Hall, US author, said by Dutch, *Dixie Storms* (F)

10 O give me a home where the
    buffalo roam
Where the deer and the antelope play
Where seldom is heard a discouraging
    word
And the skies are not cloudy all day.

Attributed to Brewster Higley, US doctor, the words to the song "Home on the Range," written in 1873, found in *The American Reader*, ed. by D. Ravitch (NF)

11 *Home* was . . . the most beautiful word in the English language.

Phyllis Reynolds Naylor, US author, thought by the cat Polo, *The Great Escape* (F)

12 Mid pleasure and palaces tho we may
    roam,
Be it ever so humble, there's no place
    like home.

John Howard Payne, US actor and writer, words to the song "Home, Sweet Home," written in 1823, found in *The American Reader*, ed. by D. Ravitch (NF)

13 I'd *like* a home — just a common one, ya know, with a mother in it.

Eleanor H. Porter, US author, said by the orphan Jimmy Bean, *Pollyanna* (F)

14 You can roam all over the world, but after all, it's what the people at home think of you that really counts.

Will Rogers, US humorist and author, found in *Will Rogers: Quotable Cowboy* by C. L. Bennett (NF)

15 Home is all the words that call you in for dinner, over to help, into a hug, out of a dream.

Michael J. Rosen, US author, *Home: A Collaboration of 30 Distinguished Authors and Illustrators of Children's Books to Aid the Homeless* (NF)

16 [A]n address is where you stay at night, where you walk right in the front door without knocking, where everybody talks to each other and uses the same toaster.

Jerry Spinelli, US author, *Maniac Magee* (F)

 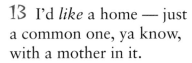

Honesty

(See Lies and Lying and Truth)

Hope

1 For those who don't expect miracles, but hope for them anyway.

Lloyd Alexander, US author, the Dedication in *The Wizard in the Tree* (F)

2 But those who hope in the Lord will renew their strength. They will soar on wings like eagles; they will run and not grow weary, they will walk and not be faint.

Bible, Isaiah 40:31 (NIV)

3 At the gates of my Master's realm in the stygian* depths of Hades, certain words appear in letters as black as sin. They read: *ALL HOPE ABANDON, YE WHO ENTER HERE!*

Bill Brittain, US author, said by Dredd, *Dr. Dredd's Wagon of Wonders* (F)   *dark and gloomy

4 The hope is always here, always alive, but only your fierce caring can fan it into a fire to warm the world.

Susan Cooper, US author, said by Merriman, *Silver on the Tree* (F)

5 You must go forward, ever forward. Never stop hoping, never give up.

Arnica Esterl, German author, *Okino and the Whales* (F)

6 I am going to preach a gospel not of despair but of hope — hope for the individual, for society, and for the world.

Billy Graham, US evangelist, found in *Contemporary Heroes and Heroines*, ed. by R. B. Browne (NF)

7 Hard hopes hurt when they finally break apart.

Barbara Hall, US author, thought by Dutch, *Dixie Storms* (F)

8 Keep hope alive.

Jesse Jackson, US civil rights activist, in his July 18, 1988 speech at the Democratic National Convention

9 The highest hopes may lead to the greatest disappointments.

Arnold Lobel, US author and illustrator, the moral in "The Frogs at the Rainbow's Edge" from *Fables* (F)

10 Hope is the last thing to die.

Mexican proverb

11 Well, that is another hope gone. My life is a perfect graveyard of buried hopes.

L. M. Montgomery, Canadian author, said by Anne, *Anne of Green Gables* (F)

12 It matters little where we pass the remnant* of our days. They will not be many. The Indian's night promises to be dark. Not a single star of hope hovers above his horizon.

Chief Seattle, leader of six Indian tribes in the Pacific Northwest, in an 1854 speech to Gov. Isaac Stevens, found in *The American Reader*, ed. by D. Ravitch (NF)   *remainder

13 "While there's life, there's hope!" as my father used to say.

J. R. R. Tolkien, English author, said by Bilbo Baggins, *The Hobbit* (F)

Horses

1 Horses have always served me for kin.* The first time one looked back into my eyes, I knew that I was no longer alone on this earth, orphan or not. . . . I felt among family with 'em, and forlorn as a ghost when they'd gone.

Paul Fleischman, US author, said by Shem Suggs, *Bull Run* (F)
*relatives

2 It's a willing horse they saddle the most.

Jamaican proverb

3 The only other person 'cept me, who tried [to ride my horse] was Curley Joe. Widow Maker tossed him into the top of Pike's Peak.

Robert D. San Souci, US author, said by Pecos Bill, a retelling of "Slue-Foot Sue and Pecos Bill" from *Larger Than Life* (F)

4 We call them dumb* animals, and so they are, for they cannot tell us how they feel, but they do not suffer less because they have no words.

Anna Sewell, English-American author, said by an unnamed lady, *Black Beauty* (F)   *unable to speak

5 [W]hen his harness is once on, [a horse] may neither jump for joy nor lie down for weariness.

Anna Sewell, English-American author, *Black Beauty* (F)

6 Things like confidence matter to horses, and they let you know if you don't have enough of it.

Zilpha Keatley Snyder, US author, *The Changeling* (F)

7 It takes all the dignity out of a horse to make him do tricks.

John Steinbeck, US author, said by Jody's father, *The Red Pony* (F)

8 [Children] knew instinctively that a man on a horse is spiritually as well as physically bigger than a man on foot.

John Steinbeck, US author, *The Red Pony* (F)

9 I use enchanted fertilizer to help it grow, but the hay itself is nothing special. Winged horses eat pretty much the same things as regular horses, plus a little birdseed.

Patricia C. Wrede, US author, said by Farmer MacDonald, *Calling on Dragons* (F)

Imagination

1 Make-believe was so real to [Peter Pan] that during a meal of it you could see him getting rounder.

J. M. Barrie, Scottish author, *Peter Pan* (F)

2 [T]he most beautiful world is always entered through the imagination. If you wish to be something you are not . . . you shut your eyes, and for one dreamy moment you are that which you long to be.

Helen Keller, US author and humanitarian, found in *Helen Keller: Humanitarian* by D. Wepman (NF)

3 Imagination prepares us for what's going to happen.

Robert Lipsyte, US author, said by Gary, "Future Tense" from *Sixteen* (F)

4 [The dog] Buck possessed a quality that made for greatness—imagination. He fought by instinct, but he could fight by his head as well.

Jack London, US author, *The Call of the Wild* (F)

5 [Peter] could have been setting his school on fire or feeding his sister to an alligator and escaping in a hot-air balloon, but all [grown-ups] saw was a boy staring at the blue sky without blinking, a boy who did not hear you when you called his name.

Ian McEwan, English author, *The Daydreamer* (F)

6 They've no imagination. A tail isn't a tail to *them*, it's just a Little Bit Extra at the back.

A. A. Milne, English author, said by Eeyore, "Eeyore Loses a Tail" from *Winnie-the-Pooh* (F)

7 I have never, ever lost an imaginary basketball game. When I'm depressed I sometimes miss imaginary shots, though.

Walter Dean Myers, US author, said by Stuff, *Fast Sam, Cool Clyde, and Stuff* (F)

8 When I was a kid, my fantasy life was my salvation. . . . It saved me by taking me from where I was to where I wanted to be.

Rosie O'Donnell, US actress, in the July 13, 1997 *Parade* magazine (NF)

9 When you have an overactive imagination, no one believes anything you say, even if it's true. If King Kong reached in my window and squished me to death, my father would think I squished myself.

Barbara Parks, US author, said by Howard, *The Kid in the Red Jacket* (F)

⭐ **10** A fertile* imagination is the jumping-off point. Think of life without new ideas, without daydreams, without painting, without fiction. Think of life without dreams.

Justine Rendal, US author, said by Conner, a computer program, *A Very Personal Computer* (F)
active

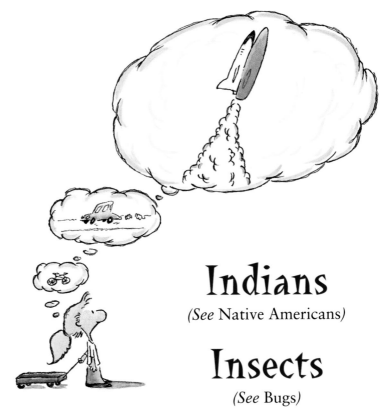

11 I always say nothing you can imagine is totally *impossible*. It might be *unlikely,* but that's as far as I'll go.

Emily Rodda, Australian author, said by Sandy, *The Pigs Are Flying* (F)

12 [Mike's new sneakers] were so gorgeous. . . . I could see myself jumping over backboards, defenders sobbing like babies, spectators gasping at moves no human had ever made before.

Jerry Spinelli, US author, thought by Crash, *Crash* (F)

13 I got more thrill out of flying before I had ever been in the air at all—while lying in bed thinking how exciting it would be to fly.

Orville Wright, US inventor, found in *The Wright Brothers* by R. Freedman (NF)

Indians
(See Native Americans*)*

Insects
(See Bugs*)*

Intelligence

1 Since we humans have the better brain, isn't it our responsibility to protect our fellow creatures from, oddly enough, ourselves?

Joy Adamson, Austrian wildlife conservationist and author, found in *The Beacon Book of Quotations by Women*, comp. by R. Maggio (NF)

2 Ashes to ashes
Dust to dust
Oil those brains
Before they rust.

Anonymous poem, found in *A Nonny Mouse Writes Again!*, sel. by J. Prelutsky

3 Mirror, mirror, in my hand, who is the most fantastically intellectually gifted being in the land?

Claire Boiko, US playwright, said by Think-Tank in the play *The Book That Saved the Earth* (F)

4 Intelligence consists of recognizing opportunity.

Chinese proverb

5 Just because you don't know everything don't mean you know nothing.

Karen Cushman, US author, said by Will Russet, *The Midwife's Apprentice* (F)

6 Genius is 1% inspiration and 99% perspiration.

Thomas Edison, US inventor, found in *The Thomas A. Edison Album* by L. F. Frost (NF)

7 [Jemmy] realized that he'd lost his taste for ignorance.

Sid Fleischman, US author, *The Whipping Boy* (F)

8 Brain against brute force — and brain came out on the top — as it's bound to do.

Kenneth Grahame, English author, said by Toad, *The Wind in the Willows* (F)

9 How can human beings read the same books I do and still be so thick*?

Deborah and James Howe, US authors, said by Chester the cat, *Bunnicula: A Rabbit-Tale of Mystery* (F)   *stupid

10 Do not call for Black power or green power. Call for brain power.

Barbara Jordan, US member of Congress and educator, *Barbara Jordan* (NF)

11 [Big Red] could do anything because a dog with his brains could be taught anything. He . . . he was almost human.

James Kjelgaard, US author, *Big Red* (F)

12 The trouble with being a daydreamer who doesn't say much is that the teachers at school, especially the ones who don't know you very well, are likely to think you are stupid.

Ian McEwan, English author, thought by Peter, *The Daydreamer* (F)

13 [T]o say that a dog is not smart because it is not as smart as a man is to say that snow is not smart. Dogs are not men. And as dogs, if they are allowed to be dogs, they are often smarter than men.

Gary Paulsen, US author, said by Oogruk, *Dogsong* (F)

14 Why is it every time I'm around a girl, my I.Q. drops a quick fifty points?

Richard Peck, US author, thought by Jim Atwater, *Father Figure* (F)

15 No one can become wise without experience, no one can become a scholar without studying.

Isaac Bashevis Singer, Polish-American author, said by an old man, "A Tale of Three Wishes" from *Stories for Children* (F)

16 How was anyone to guess that this playful creature [Pongo] owned one of the keenest brains in Dogdom?

Dodie Smith, English author, *The 101 Dalmatians* (F)

17 It's all very well . . . to be smarter than most, but a person shouldn't *show* it.

Mary Stolz, US author, said by Mrs. Benway, *Quentin Corn* (F)

18 The Duke thinks you are not so wise as he thinks you think you are.

James Thurber, US author, said by the Goluz to the Prince, *The 13 Clocks* (F)

Inventions and Inventors

1 Television is the result of [Vladimir] Zworykin's dream of extending human vision. . . . He wanted humans to be able to see sights that were too far away, too small, too restricted, too dangerous for the average person to see.

Nathan Aaseng, US author, *American Profiles: 20th Century Inventors* (NF)

2 The grass you are standing on . . . is made of a new kind of soft, minty sugar that I've just invented! I call it swudge! Try a blade! Please do! It's delectable!

Roald Dahl, English author, said by Willy Wonka, *Charlie and the Chocolate Factory* (F)

3 I'm proud of the fact that I never invented weapons to kill.

Thomas Edison, US inventor, in the June 8, 1915 issue of *The New York Times* (NF)

4 Everything, everything, everything is being invented or improved all the time by somebody somewhere — whether by teams of scientists in huge factories and laboratories, or by lonely men sitting and just thinking in tiny workshops without many tools.

Ian Fleming, English writer, *Chitty Chitty Bang Bang: The Magical Car* (F)

5 [An inventor is someone who has] the ability to see a right idea in spite of the fact that others do not, and to cling to it in the face of discouragement and self-mistrust.

Bette Nesmith Graham, US inventor of Liquid Paper correction fluid, found in *Women Inventors & Their Discoveries* by Vare and Ptacek (NF)

6 I thought we should make a doll like [my daughter's] paper dolls, but three-dimensional. A doll with breasts and a narrow waist and painted fingernails. When I told my people [at Mattel] what I wanted to do, they looked at me like I was asking the impossible.

Ruth Handler, US inventor of the Barbie doll, found in *Women Inventors & Their Discoveries* by Vare and Ptacek (NF)

7 May not work at all. You never can tell about an invention until you test it.

Clifford B. Hicks, US author, said by Alvin Fernald, *The Marvelous Inventions of Alvin Fernald* (F)

8 [I]t's a scientific fact: Inventors are frequently musical, and musicians are often inventive.

Barbara Anne Porte, US author, "What the Princess Discarded," found in *Birthday Surprises*, ed. by J. Hurwitz (F)

9 Benjamin Franklin believed that useful inventions should contribute to the public good, not to the bank account of the inventor.

Robert R. Potter, US author, *Benjamin Franklin* (NF)

10 So I quickly invented my Super-Axe-Hacker
which whacked off four Truffula Trees
at one smacker.

Dr. Seuss, US author, *The Lorax* (F)

11 I've done it, I've done it!
Guess what I've done!
Invented a light that plugs into the sun.
The sun is bright enough,
The bulb is strong enough,
But, oh, there's only one thing wrong . . .
The cord ain't long enough.

Shel Silverstein, US poet and illustrator, "Invention" from *Where the Sidewalk Ends*

12 [Orville and Wilbur] are equal in their inventions, neither claiming any superiority above the other, nor accepting any honor to the neglect of the other.

Milton Wright, Orville and Wilbur's father, found in *The Wright Brothers* by R. Freedman (NF)

Justice and Injustice

1 [W]e have to believe . . . justice will prevail over injustice, tolerance over intolerance and progress over reaction.

> Hillary Rodham Clinton, US lawyer and wife of the 42nd President, in a May 18, 1993 University of PA graduation speech

2 Growing up, I could see all the injustices and I would think, "If only I could do something about it."

> Jessie Lopez De La Cruz, US union organizer for migrant workers, found in *Herstory,* ed. by Ashby and Ohrn (NF)

3 I hope *one* thing only, and that is that this hatred of the Jews will be a passing thing. . . . For anti-Semitism is unjust!

> Anne Frank, Dutch diarist, *Anne Frank: The Diary of a Young Girl,* May 22, 1944 entry (NF)

4 [J]ustice too long delayed is justice denied.

> Martin Luther King, Jr., US civil rights leader, *Letter from Birmingham City Jail* (NF)

5 Injustice anywhere is a threat to justice everywhere.

> *Ibid.*

6 [W]e refuse to believe that the bank of justice is bankrupt. We refuse to believe that there are insufficient funds in the great vaults of opportunity of this nation.

> Martin Luther King, Jr., US civil rights leader, in his Aug. 28, 1963 "I Have a Dream" speech in Washington, D.C., found in *The American Reader,* ed. by D. Ravitch (NF)

7 There is justice in the world, but it is blind.

> Lithuanian proverb

8 Keep on going—keep on insisting— keep on fighting injustice.

> Mary Church Terrell, US women's rights activist, found in the *Book of Black Heroes, Vol. 2* by T. Igus (NF)

9 The council-tent is our Congress, and anybody can speak who has anything to say, women and all. . . . If women could go into [your] Congress, I think justice would soon be done to the Indians.

> Sarah Winnemucca, daughter of the Paiute Indian Chief, Winnemucca II, found in *Herstory,* ed. by Ashby and Ohrn (NF)

10 [I]t wasn't fair that Wendy only did the housework in Neverland and that Peter Pan and the boys got to fight Captain Hook.

> Jane Yolen, US author, thought by Darla, "Lost Girls" from *Twelve Impossible Things Before Breakfast* (F)

Kindness

1 No act of kindness, no matter how small, is ever wasted.

> Aesop, Greek writer, the moral in the fable "The Lion and the Mouse" (F)

2 The Tin Woodman knew very well he had no heart, and therefore he took great care never to be cruel or unkind to anything.

> L. Frank Baum, US author, *The Wonderful Wizard of Oz* (F)

3 It was getting danged hard to hate [the Northerners]—they were treating me so tenderly. Pap would have said they were killing me with kindness, or at least killing my hate.

> Patricia Beatty, US author, thought by Hannalee, *Be Ever Hopeful, Hannalee* (F)

4 Kindness must be the highest virtue—don't let me forget that ever.

> Joan W. Blos, US author, written by Catherine Cabot Hall, *A Gathering of Days* (F)

5 Anyone who is kind wants to know when people have been made happy. They care for that more than for being thanked.

> Frances Hodgson Burnett, English-American author, said by Sara, *A Little Princess* (F)

6 Noah, Nadia, and Ethan found kindness in others and learned how to look for it in themselves.

> E. L. Konigsburg, US author and illustrator, said by Mr. Singh, *The View from Saturday* (F)

7 One can pay back the loan of gold, but one dies forever in the debt to those who are kind.

> Malayan proverb

8 Kindness comes with no price.

> Laurence Yep, Chinese-American author, said by Auntie Lily, "Waters of God" from *Tongues of Jade* (F)

Language

(See also Talking *and* Words*)*

1 Language alone is man's way of communicating with his fellow man, and it is language alone which separates him from the lower animals.

Maya Angelou, US poet and author, *I Know Why the Caged Bird Sings* (NF)

2 How is it that animals understand things I do not know, but it is certain that they do understand. Perhaps there is a language which is not made of words and everything in that world understands it.

Frances Hodgson Burnett, English-American author, said by Sara, *A Little Princess* (F)

3 [He] who knows the language is at home everywhere.

Dutch proverb

4 It never occurred to Mr. and Mrs. Neal that their cats could talk. Not only could they talk, but they spoke the English language. What other language would they know . . . having been with the Neals since they were ten weeks old?

Phyllis Reynolds Naylor, US author, *The Great Escape* (F)

5 Slang is a language that rolls up its sleeves, spits on its hands, and goes to work.

Carl Sandburg, US poet and biographer, in the Feb. 13, 1959 issue of *The New York Times* (NF)

6 [B]arks are only a small part of a dog's language. A wagging tail can mean so many things. . . . Then there are the snufflings and sniffings, the pricking of ears—all meaning different things. And many, many words are expressed by a dog's eyes.

Dodie Smith, English author, *The 101 Dalmatians* (F)

7 Language grows out of life, out of its needs and experiences.

Anne Sullivan, US disabilities teacher, in a July 1894 speech

8 The Prince and Princess spoke in a silent language with their eyes.

James Thurber, US author, *The 13 Clocks* (F)

Laughter

1 An onion can make people cry, but there's no vegetable that can make them laugh.

Anonymous saying

2 [W]hen the first baby laughed for the first time, its laugh broke into a thousand pieces, and they all went skipping about, and that was the beginning of fairies.

J. M. Barrie, Scottish author, said by Peter Pan, *Peter Pan* (F)

3 We've laughed until my cheeks are tight.
We've laughed until my stomach's sore.
If we could only stop we might
Remember what we're laughing for.

"Bursting," anonymous poem, found in *For Laughing Out Loud*, sel. by J. Prelutsky

4 Th' more they laugh th' better for 'em!
. . . Good healthy child laughin's better than pills any day o' th' year.

Frances Hodgson Burnett, English-American author, said by Mrs. Sowerby, *The Secret Garden* (F)

5 [T]here is nothing in the world so irresistibly contagious as laughter and good humor.

Charles Dickens, English author, *A Christmas Carol* (F)

6 I got dizzy from laughing, lost my breath from laughing. My stomach hurt from laughing. Tears ran from my eyes. Everything was funny.

Michael Dorris, Native American author and anthropologist, thought by Moss, *Guests* (F)

7 I am especially glad of the divine gift of laughter; it has made the world human and loveable, despite all its pain and wrong.

W. E. B. Du Bois, US educator and author, found in *My Soul Looks Back, 'Less I Forget*, ed. by D. W. Riley (NF)

8 Laughter is the best way to release tensions and fear.

Dick Gregory, US comedian and social activist, found in *Contemporary Heroes and Heroines*, ed. by R. B. Browne (NF)

9 No one has ever suffered loss because of laughter.

Japanese proverb

10 But when it came to laughing, my father had to sit up. It wasn't a big laugh, the kind there is after a joke. It was a deep one, covered up, and the only part to see was what escaped.

Joseph Krumgold, US author, thought by Andy, *Onion John* (F)

11 He had a broad face and a little round belly
That shook, when he laughed, like a bowl full of jelly.

Clement Clarke Moore, US professor, "A Visit from St. Nicholas," found in *The Children's Treasury*, ed. by P. S. Goepfert

12 I do believe dogs *do* laugh in a panting sort of way. I'm sure old Towser did. And there was no doubt of his broad grin.

Bill Peet, US illustrator and author, *Bill Peet: An Autobiography* (NF)

13 Laughter's like a seedling,
waiting patiently to sprout.
All it takes is just a push
to make it pop right out.

David Saltzman, US author and illustrator, *The Jester Has Lost His Jingle* (F)

 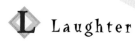

14 So when you're feeling lonely
    or sad
    or bad
    or blue
    remember where laughter's hiding . . .
    It's hiding inside
      of
      YOU!
    Ibid.

15 [Gabilan] bit Jody in the pants and stomped on Jody's feet. Now and then his ears went back and he aimed a tremendous kick at the boy. Every time he did one of these bad things, [the pony] settled back and seemed to laugh to himself.

John Steinbeck, US author, *The Red Pony* (F)

16 Laughing, [Quentin the pig] thought, was just about the best part of being human.

Mary Stolz, US author, *Quentin Corn* (F)

17 Remember laughter. You'll need it even in the blessed isles of Ever After.

James Thurber, US author, said by the Goluz to the Prince and Princess, *The 13 Clocks* (F)

18 [I]f I laugh . . . I become so filled with Laughing Gas that I simply can't keep on the ground. Even if I smile it happens. The first funny thought, and I'm up like a balloon.

P. L. Travers, Australian-English author, said by Mr. Wigg, *Mary Poppins* (F)

Learning

(See also Education, Schools, *and* Teachers)

1 Learning is important! . . . I can't spend my whole life lying around in the sewers eating garbage.

Jane Leslie Conly, US author, said by the rat Racso, *Racso and the Rats of NIMH* (F)

2 If thou'rt to learn . . . patience and care are better teachers than a bad temper.

Marguerite de Angeli, English author and illustrator, said by Brother Matthew, *The Door in the Wall* (F)

3 *Ganas** suggests a powerful urge to get ahead, a willingness to sacrifice and to work hard. *Ganas* conquers all. "*Ganas* Is All I Need" is a motto I give my students. I tell them that once they have *ganas*, learning is easy.

Jaime Escalante, Mexican-American teacher, found in *Famous Hispanic Americans* by Morey and Dunn (NF)

desire to succeed

4 [Harriet] never minded admitting she didn't know something. So what, she thought, I could always learn.

Louise Fitzhugh, US author, *Harriet the Spy* (F)

5 Already [Martin] had learned a number of lessons that a farm kitten needs to know. Cows have big feet that could easily squash you, sows get angry if you go too near their piglets, broody hens are bad-tempered birds, and collie dogs chase cats.

Dick King-Smith, English author, *Martin's Mice* (F)

6 I think you should learn, of course, and some days you must learn a great deal. But you should also have days when you allow what is already in you to swell up inside of you until it touches everything.

E. L. Konigsburg, US author, said by Mrs. Frankweiler, *From the Mixed-up Files of Mrs. Basil E. Frankweiler* (F)

7 You know, you can learn to do practically anything if you really want to hard enough.

Janet Taylor Lisle, US author, said by Sara-Kate, *Afternoon of the Elves* (F)

8 [H]e learned the most important rule of survival, which was that feeling sorry for yourself didn't work.

Gary Paulsen, US author, *Hatchet* (F)

9 Learning is wealth that can't be stolen.
Philippine proverb

10 Few [are] too young, and none too old, to make the attempt to learn.

Booker T. Washington, US educator and author, *Up from Slavery* (NF)

11 Learn to do a thing so thoroughly that no one can improve upon what has been done.
Ibid.

Libraries

1 When an old man dies, it is as if a library has been burned to the ground.
African proverb

2 The dim, dusty room . . . the cozy chairs, the globes, and best of all, the wilderness of books in which [Jo] could wander where she liked, made the library a region of bliss to her.

Louisa May Alcott, US author, *Little Women* (F)

3 In the 25th century. . . we Earthlings . . . taught the Macronites the difference between sandwiches and books . . . and we established a model library in their capital city of Macronopolis.

Claire Boiko, US playwright, said by Historian in the play *The Book That Saved the Earth* (F)

4 With our diplomas [from eighth grade], Mr. Dorman handed each of us a small buff card, our first adult library card, a symbol marking the end of childhood.

Beverly Cleary, US author, *A Girl from Yamhill: A Memoir* (NF)

5 [When I was in my early teens,] I started with the first book on the bottom shelf and went through the lot, one by one. I didn't read a few books. I read the [Detroit Public] library.

Thomas Edison, US inventor, found in *The Thomas A. Edison Album* by L. F. Frost (NF)

6 Any kid who grows up twenty years from now will be able to go to a library and browse the world's knowledge on a computer.

Bill Gates, US CEO of Microsoft, in the Jan. 28, 1996 *Parade* magazine (NF)

7 I went to the library, opened up an encyclopedia, and looked up *ballet*. . . . And I went "Wow! I can do this! I can go to New York. I can do this for a living. I can actually grow up to be what I want to be!"

Lourdes Lopez, Cuban-American ballet dancer, found in *Famous Hispanic Americans* by Morey and Dunn (NF)

10 Whenever I felt bad, . . . I went [to the library]. In fact, I went there when I felt good too. I was there every day. I got mad one time at Christmas when I found out the library was closed.

Jerry Spinelli, US author, said by April Mendez, *The Library Card* (F)

Lies and Lying

1 Liars are not believed even when they tell the truth.

Aesop, Greek writer, the moral in the fable "The Shepherd Boy and the Wolf" (F)

2 A lie comes back sooner or later.

African proverb

3 Cross my heart and hope to die,
Cut me in half if I told a lie.

Anonymous folk poetry, found in *And the Green Grass Grew All Around*, comp. by A. Schwartz

4 Liar, liar, pants on fire,
Tongue as long as a telephone wire.
Ibid.

8 There will be rats coming in [to the library] to practice reading, and some to do research.

Robert C. O'Brien, US author, said by Nicodemus, *Mrs. Frisby and the Rats of NIMH* (F)

9 [M]y most prized possession was my library card from the Oakland Public Library.

Bill Russell, US professional basketball player, *Second Wind* (NF)

5 That's one of the troubles with a lie. You've got to keep adding to it to make it believable to people.

Bertrand R. Brinley, US author, *The Mad Scientists' Club* (F)

6 At this third lie, his nose grew to such an extraordinary length that poor Pinocchio could not move in any direction.

Carlo Collodi, Italian author, *The Adventures of Pinocchio* (F)

7 Little lies that make people feel better are not bad, like thanking someone for a meal they made even if you hated it, or telling a sick person they look better when they don't.

Louise Fitzhugh, US author, said by Ole Golly, *Harriet the Spy* (F)

8 I lie to myself all the time. But I never believe me.

S. E. Hinton, US author, said by Ponyboy, *The Outsiders* (F)

9 A good many lies, there's at least two sides to them and you can take a point of view. But this was a flat lie. You couldn't get around it.

Joseph Krumgold, US author, thought by Andy, *Onion John* (F)

10 Anastasia wasn't crazy about telling lies, even to herself; she did it, sometimes, but it always gave her a stomachache.

Lois Lowry, US author, *Anastasia Krupnik* (F)

11 There's nothing hurts a man so much as being thought a liar.

Guy de Maupassant, French author, "The Piece of String" found in *The Book of Virtues*, ed. by W. J. Bennett (F)

12 Now, to keep a man in the hardest bondage, to crush his body by excessive labor and his soul by absolute ignorance, to whip him . . . and after that . . . to tell us that you are our TRIED friends, is more than a lie, it is a cruel insult and nothing short of it.

New Orleans *Tribune,* the first black daily newspaper in the US, found in *Black Voices from Reconstruction: 1865-1877* by J. D. Smith (NF)

13 Even Hitler or—or Jack the Ripper—sometimes said things that were true. It's *impossible* to lie all the time.

Thomas Rockwell, US author, said by Billy, *How to Eat Fried Worms* (F)

14 Repetition does not transform* a lie into a truth.

Franklin D. Roosevelt, 32nd US President, in an Oct. 26, 1939 radio speech   *change*

15 Stop telling such outlandish tales. Stop turning minnows into whales.

Dr. Seuss, US author, *And to Think That I Saw It on Mulberry Street* (F)

16 Sure, over the years [Mongoose and Weasel] had told their share of lies, both of them. Who didn't? But never had they lied to each other. Till now. And it hurt.

Jerry Spinelli, US author, "Mongoose" from *The Library Card* (F)

17 Elves cannot lie. A lie stinks on our skin, like rotten meat. Anyone could smell it.

Ann Turner, US author, said by the elf Nata, *Elfsong* (F)

Life

1 Life has its ups and downs.

American proverb

2 Life's got to be lived, no matter how long or short. You got to take what comes. We just go along, like everybody else, one day at a time.

Natalie Babbitt, US author, said by Mae Tuck, *Tuck Everlasting* (F)

3 I am come that they may have life, and that they might have it more abundantly.

Bible, John 10:10 (KJV)

4 [A]nd remember, as we used to say, that life is like a pudding: it takes both the salt and the sugar to make a really good one.

Joan W. Blos, US author, written by Catherine Hall Onesti, *A Gathering of Days* (F)

5 Folks keep growing from one person into another all their lives.

Carol Ryrie Brink, US author, said by Caddie Woodlawn, *Caddie Woodlawn* (F)

6 Live not for battles won.
Live not for the-end-of-the-song.
Live in the along.

Gwendolyn Brooks, US poet, "Speech to the Young," from *Disembark*

7 There are no shortcuts to life; hard work is the only way to go. Strive to be the best you can be and remember that when you try your best, you can't ask any more from yourself and people can't ask any more from you.

Michael Chang, Chinese-American professional tennis player, found in *Famous Asian Americans* by Morey and Dunn (NF)

8 I also came to understand that we cannot expect flowers to bloom continuously in life.

Beverly Cleary, US author, *A Girl from Yamhill: A Memoir* (NF)

9 Life is a bowl of spaghetti . . . every now and then you get a meatball.

Sharon Creech, US author, embroidered on a sampler, *Chasing Redbird* (F)

10 Knowing what you have to lose, but risking the loss anyway. That's what [life is] all about.

Julie Reece Deaver, US author and illustrator, thought by Morgan, *Say Goodnight, Gracie* (F)

11 That it will never come again
Is what makes life so sweet.

Emily Dickinson, US poet, from *The Complete Poems of Emily Dickinson*

12 [L]ife is such a fragile thing and . . . painful though it might be, death is a part of life. Realizing this, accepting it, is a part of growing up. But it was never easy to accept, not for anyone.

Allan W. Eckert, US author, *Incident at Hawk's Hill* (F)

13 Never think life is not worth living or that you cannot make a difference. Never give up.

Marian Wright Edelman, US lawyer and public official, found in *Marian Wright Edelman* by S. Otfinoski (NF)

14 Life is all getting used to what you're not used to.

Paula Fox, US author, said by Elizabeth's grandmother, *Western Wind* (F)

15 Rat race is a perfect name for it. We're always going and going and going, and never asking where. . . . It seems like we're always searching for something to satisfy us, and never finding it.

S. E. Hinton, US author, said by Cherry, *The Outsiders* (F)

16 Slake knew that life was some persistent weed that grew in gravel in broken sidewalks, in fetid* alleys, and would have no more difficulty doing so [in the subway] than anywhere else he knew.

Felice Holman, US author, *Slake's Limbo* (F)

*bad smelling

17 Life is like the baseball season, where even the best team loses at least a third of its games and even the worst team has its days of brilliance. The goal is not to win every game but to win more than you lose, and if you do that often enough, in the end you may find you have won it all.

Harold S. Kushner, US rabbi and author, in the Sept. 8, 1996 *Parade* magazine (NF)

18 There were times when it seemed to [Peter] that all he had ever done in his life, and all he was ever going to do, was wake up, get up, and go to school.

Ian McEwan, English author, *The Daydreamer* (F)

19 Life ain't supposed to be nothing, 'cept maybe tough.

Katherine Paterson, US author, said by Trotter, *The Great Gilly Hopkins* (F)

20 [Life is] an unbearable gift sometimes. Unbearably beautiful and unbearably painful, but always a gift.

Justine Rendal, US author, said by Conner, a computer program, *A Very Personal Computer* (F)

21 A life is not important except in the impact it has on others.

Jackie Robinson, US professional baseball player, found in *Jackie Robinson: Baseball Great* by R. Scott (NF)

22 Who ever told you that life is fair? Certainly not a navvy,* nor an upstairs maid, nor a poor man trying to feed his family.

Jane Yolen, US author, said by the oldest Wendy, "Lost Girls" from *Twelve Impossible Things Before Breakfast* (F)

*a laborer

Likes and Dislikes

1 [The crocodile] liked my arm so much . . . that it has followed me ever since . . . licking its lips for the rest of me.

J. M. Barrie, Scottish author, said by Capt. Hook, *Peter Pan* (F)

2 I like long hair, tuna fish, the smell of rain and things that are pink. I hate pimples, baked potatoes, when my mother's mad, and religious holidays.

Judy Blume, US author, written by Margaret, *Are You There, God? It's Me, Margaret* (F)

3 [When I was young,] I not only liked the pictures and the stories [in library books] but the feel and the smell of the books themselves.

Judy Blume, US author, in the Jan. 1992 *Biography Today* (NF)

4 Research tells us that fourteen out of any ten individuals like chocolate.

Sandra Boynton, US author and artist, *Chocolate: The Consuming Passion* (NF)

5 If there is anything I dislike, it was a good story that ended up as a dream. Authors of such stories, including Lewis Carroll, were cheating, I felt, because they could not think of another conclusion.

Beverly Cleary, US author, *A Girl from Yamhill: A Memoir* (NF)

6 I happen to be a kind of inquisitive* guy and when I see things I don't like, I start thinking why do they have to be like this and how can I improve them.

Walt Disney, US cartoonist and movie producer, found in *The Man Behind the Magic* by K. and R. Greene (NF) *curious*

7 [M]ostly I don't like . . . nothing. You know, *nothing*. I don't like it when there's nothing to hear, nothing to taste, nothing to touch, especially when there's nothing to see.

Michael Dorris, Native American author and anthropologist, said by Star Boy, *Morning Girl* (F)

8 If you don't like somebody, walk away, Ole Golly said, but don't try to make them like you.

Louise Fitzhugh, US author, said by Harriet, *Harriet the Spy* (F)

9 When one has not what one likes, one must like what one has.

French proverb

10 I never met a man I didn't like.

Will Rogers, US humorist, found in *Will Rogers: Quotable Cowboy* by C. L. Bennett (NF)

Loss

(See Winning and Losing*)*

Love

1 [L]ove is like a virus. It can happen to anybody at any time.

> Maya Angelou, US poet and author, found in *My Soul Looks Back, 'Less I Forget*, ed. by D. W. Riley (NF)

2 I love you, I love you,
I love you, I do.
But don't get excited,
I love monkeys, too.

> Anonymous folk poetry, found in *And The Green Grass Grew All Around*, comp. by A. Schwartz

3 I know you little, I love you lots,
My love for you would fill ten pots,
Fifteen buckets, sixteen cans,
Three teacups, and four dishpans.

> Anonymous poem, found in *A Nonny Mouse Writes Again!*, sel. by J. Prelutsky

4 Everyone loved [the Good Witch of the South], but her greatest sorrow was that she could find no one to love in return, since all the men were much too stupid and ugly to mate with one so beautiful and wise.

> L. Frank Baum, US author, *The Wonderful Wizard of Oz* (F)

5 Love is patient, love is kind. It does not envy, it does not boast, it is not proud.

> Bible, I Corinthians 13:4 (NIV)

6 All is fair in love and war.

> English proverb

7 If you would be loved, love and be lovable.

> Benjamin Franklin, Revolutionary statesman, the 1755 *Poor Richard's Almanack* (NF)

8 When a man will lay down his life for a friend, well, then there ain't no greater love in this here world than that.

> Bette Greene, US author, said by Ruth, *Summer of My German Soldier* (F)

9 It seemed impossible to me that love could evaporate like dew on a summer lawn. If love didn't stick around, then what did?

> Barbara Hall, US author, thought by Dutch, *Dixie Storms* (F)

10 I've decided to stick with love. Hate is too great a burden to bear.

> Martin Luther King, Jr., US civil rights leader, found in *My Soul Looks Back, 'Less I Forget*, ed. by D. W. Riley (NF)

11 [Y]ou don't have to be perfect to be worth loving.

> Harold S. Kushner, US rabbi and author, in the Sept. 8, 1996 *Parade* magazine (NF)

12 All You Need Is Love

> John Lennon, English musician and composer, song title

13 She loves you, yeh, yeh, yeh,
And with a love like that you know you should be glad.

> John Lennon, English musician and composer, words to the song "She Loves You," written with P. McCartney

14 The love between [Ivan and Princess Nadeshda] was instant—like a lightning strike.

Geraldine McCaughrean, English author, the retelling of *The Firebird* from *The Random House Book of Stories from the Ballet* (F)

15 When every story ends,
when spring does not renew,
when all the clocks have stopped,
then I'll stop loving you.

Eve Merriam, US poet, "When," found in *Valentine Day: Stories and Poems*, ed. by C. F. Bauer

16 That's just how true love happens. It isn't a thing you decide. It suddenly gets you in its power and you can't escape.

Bernard Miles, English actor and author, the retelling of *Twelfth Night* from *Favorite Tales from Shakespeare* (F)

17 [S]ometimes something does happen between people and animals. There seems to be a bond that overcomes all fear, prejudice, everything objectionable. I suppose you might call it a perfect love.

Walt Morey, US author, said by Mark's mother, *Gentle Ben* (F)

18 Do you think love, real love, is ever a mistake?

Sylvia Peck, US author, said by Ruby, *Seal Child* (F)

19 I know now that you can't expect anything from anybody. If somebody loves you, it's because he wants to. And it's never because it's what he's supposed to do.

Cynthia Rylant, US author, thought by Pete, *A Fine White Dust* (F)

20 You cannot touch love . . . but you [can] feel the sweetness that it pours into everything.

Anne Sullivan, US disabilities teacher, found in *The Story of My Life* by H. Keller (NF)

21 Tell me why the stars do shine.
Tell me why the ivy twines.
Tell me why the sky's so blue,
And I will tell you just why I love you.

"Tell Me Why," anonymous song, found in *Gonna Sing My Head Off!*, col. and arr. by K. Krull

22 It is not how much we do, but how much love we put into the doing.

Mother Teresa, Yugoslavian missionary in India, found in *Contemporary Heroes and Heroines*, ed. by R. B. Browne (NF)

23 Love, I felt more than ever, is stronger than death and the fear of death.

Ivan Turgenev, Russian author, "The Sparrow" (F)

Magic

1 Magic can't work miracles.

Lloyd Alexander, US author, said by the wizard Arbican, *The Wizard in the Tree* (F)

2 It works! I can make any plastic toy I like come alive, come real! It's real magic.

Lynne Reid Banks, US author, said by Omri, *The Indian in the Cupboard* (F)

3 All you have to do is to knock the heels together three times and command the shoes to carry you wherever you wish to go.

L. Frank Baum, US author, said by the Good Witch of the South to Dorothy, *The Wonderful Wizard of Oz* (F)

4 Somehow, something always happens . . . just before things get to the very worst. It is as if the Magic did it. . . . The worst thing never *quite* comes.

Frances Hodgson Burnett, English-American author, said by Sara, *A Little Princess* (F)

5 I am sure there is Magic in everything, only we have not sense enough to get hold of it and make it do things for us—like electricity and horses and steam.

Frances Hodgson Burnett, English-American author, said by Colin, *The Secret Garden* (F)

6 The Big Friendly Giant makes his magic powers out of the dreams that children dream when they are asleep.

Roald Dahl, English author, said by Danny's father, *Danny, the Champion of the World* (F)

7 Then she felt the magic, the African mystery. Say she rose just as free as a bird. As light as a feather.

Virginia Hamilton, US author, the retelling of "The People Could Fly" from *The People Could Fly: American Black Folktales* (F)

8 If you should ever feel tempted to try a piece of magic on your own, remember that stopping a spell is just as important as starting one (sometimes *more* important, as the unfortunate apprentice found out.)

John Hosier, the retelling of "The Sorcerer's Apprentice" from *The Sorcerer's Apprentice and Other Stories* (F)

9 [T]hree is the number . . . that is at the root of all magic.

Mollie Hunter, Scottish author, said by Howdy, *The Mermaid Summer* (F)

10 [The White Witch] has made a magic so that it is always winter in Narnia—always winter, but it never gets to Christmas.

C. S. Lewis, English author, *The Lion, the Witch, and the Wardrobe* (F)

11 [E]ven without being believed, magic can begin to change things. It moves invisibly through the air, dissolving the usual ways of seeing, allowing new ways to creep in, secretly, quietly, like a stray cat sliding through the bushes.

Janet Taylor Lisle, US author, *Afternoon of the Elves* (F)

12 [When Princess Odette and Prince Siegfried plunged to their deaths in the lake,] all von Rothbart's magic burst inside him, scalding, freezing, poisonous, deadly. He fell dead on the spot.

Geraldine McCaughrean, English author, the retelling of *Swan Lake* from *The Random House Book of Stories from the Ballet* (F)

13 [The old rulers of Damar] were . . . magicians. They could call the lightning down on the heads of their enemies, that sort of thing—useful stuff for founding an empire.

Robin McKinley, US author, said by Dedham, *The Blue Sword* (F)

14 I asked [the genie] Dooley why he just didn't do it all by magic, and he said there was no point in doing by magic what you could do by hand.

George Selden, US author, said by Tim Farr, *The Genie of Sutton Place* (F)

15 You have a magic carpet
That will whiz you through the air,
To Spain or Maine or Africa
If you just tell it where.
So will you let it take you
Where you've never been before,
Or will you buy some drapes to match
And use it
On your
Floor?

Shel Silverstein, US poet and illustrator, "Magic Carpet" from *A Light in the Attic*

16 There is little or no magic about [hobbits], except the ordinary everyday sort which helps them to disappear quietly and quickly when large stupid folk like you and me come blundering along, making a noise like elephants.

J. R. R. Tolkien, English author, *The Hobbit* (F)

17 Books spoke of magic as if it were a kind of sweet spice in an autumn pie—something to savor and delight in—something almost cozy.

Ann Turner, US author, thought by Mandy, *Elfsong* (F)

18 [I]t's like [the ants] have magic or something. And I don't. You know—magic! Ugga-bugga-abracadabra-zam-booie!

Jane Yolen, US author, said by Harlyn, "Harlyn's Fairy" from *Twelve Impossible Things Before Breakfast* (F)

Manners

1 [W]hen it is possible, we should show courtesy to everyone, if we wish it to be extended to us in our hour of need.

Carlo Collodi, Italian author, said by Cricket, *The Adventures of Pinocchio* (F)

2 [A]ll the people politely thanked the faerie [for taking their troubles from them] . . . and they dusted their clothes and straightened their neckties and all flew away.

e. e. cummings, US poet, "The Old Man Who Said 'Why'" from *Fairy Tales* (F)

3 Good manners are very important, particularly in the morning.

Louise Fitzhugh, US author, said by Ole Golly, *Harriet the Spy* (F)

4 Better good manners than good looks.

Irish proverb

5 [T]here came down to the beach . . . one Rhinoceros with a horn on his nose, two piggy eyes, and few manners.

Rudyard Kipling, English-American journalist and author, "How the Rhinoceros Got His Skin" from *Just So Stories* (F)

6 It is sometimes necessary to use unnecessary words like "thank you" and "please" just to make life prettier.

E. L. Konigsburg, US author, said by Ampara, "In the Village of Weavers" from *Throwing Shadows* (F)

7 I believe in courtesy. It is the way we avoid hurting people's feelings.

E. L. Konigsburg, US author, said by Mrs. Olinski, *The View from Saturday* (F)

8 Indians take great stock in politeness. Should you meet one, speak to him just the same as to the minister back home.

Elizabeth George Speare, US author, said by Matt's father, *The Sign of the Beaver* (F)

9 A child should always say what's true And speak when he is spoken to, And behave mannerly at table: At least as far as he is able.

Robert Louis Stevenson, English poet, "Whole Duty of Children" from *A Child's Garden of Verses*

10 Alice and Ella and Peter and Mary and Laura did not say a word at the table, for they knew that children should be seen and not heard.

Laura Ingalls Wilder, US author, *Little House in the Big Woods* (F)

11 Kazul [the dragon] won't eat you once you've been properly introduced. . . . Dragons are very polite.

Patricia C. Wrede, US author, said by Queen Cimorene, *Calling on Dragons* (F)

12 [Princess Miserella] was the meanest, wickedest, and most worthless princess around. She liked stepping on dogs. She kicked kittens. She threw pies into the cook's face. And she never—not even once—said thank you or please.

Jane Yolen, US author, *Sleeping Ugly* (F)

Math
(See Arithmetic*)*

Mice and Rats

1 A mouse in her room woke Miss Dowd;
  She was frightened and screamed very
      loud,
    Then a happy thought hit her—
    To scare off the critter,
  She sat up in bed and meowed.

Anonymous limerick found in *Laughable Limericks*, comp. by S. and J. Brewton

2 I dare say it is rather hard to be a rat. Nobody likes you. . . . But nobody asked this rat if he wanted to be a rat when he was made. Nobody said, "Wouldn't you rather be a sparrow?"

Frances Hodgson Burnett, English-American author, said by Sara, *A Little Princess* (F)

3 [Mice are] pretty skilled at keeping out of sight, dodging attacks, scuttling for safety. Wouldn't you be, in a world full of cats and hawks thirty times your size looking for supper?

Peter Dickinson, English author, *Time and the Clock Mice, Etcetera* (F)

4 All around the rats were closing in, large as dogs and smiling strangely; smiling like people.

Elizabeth Enright, US author, "Nancy" from *The Moment Before the Rain* (F)

5 [T]he rats feed and breed by the hundreds [near the brewery]. Grow big as street cats. And short-tempered! They'll swarm all over you and hang on by their teeth.

Sid Fleischman, US author, said by Jemmy, *The Whipping Boy* (F)

6 [The large rat] smelled of darkness, of stale and moldy things, and garbage.

Russell Hoban, US author, *The Mouse and His Child* (F)

7 Under the big table . . . hordes of mice formed huge battalions, awaiting orders from the terrible, seven-headed Mouse King. Where would it all end?

E. T. A. Hoffmann, German author, *Nutcracker* (F)

8 A mouse a day . . . keeps the vet away.

Dick King-Smith, English author, said by the mother of the cat Martin, *Martin's Mice* (F)

9 The rat that has but one hole is soon caught.

Spanish proverb

10 The rat had no morals, no conscience, no scruples, no consideration, no decency, no milk of rodent kindness, no compunctions,* no higher feeling, no friendliness, no anything.

E. B. White, US author, *Charlotte's Web* (F)   *remorse

Money

(*See* Wealth and Poverty)

Monsters and Dragons

1 Dragons had suddenly started breeding quicker than wasps, and the whole country was full of them. Put your Sunday roast in the oven, and half an hour later a dozen dragons . . . would be battering at your window like bulldozers.

Joan Aiken, English author, "Think of a Word" from *The Last Slice of Rainbow* (F)

2 [I]f we hatch [these eggs], we'll have creatures that have been extinct for over a hundred million years.

Isaac Asimov, US author, said by the son to his father, "A Statue for Father" (F)

3 Young Frankenstein's robot invention
  Caused trouble too awful to mention.
    Its actions were ghoulish,
    Which proves it is foolish
  To monkey with Nature's intention.

Berton Braley, "Young Frankenstein," found in *Laughable Limericks*, comp. by S. and J. Brewton

4 But what if they're not all dead. . . . What if there are still one or two dragons wandering around the sand hills, eating buffalo, squashing soddies.*

Pam Conrad, US author, said by Julia Creath, *My Daniel* (F)

*prairie homes

5 [W]hat a terrible country [Loompaland] is! Nothing but thick jungles infested by the most dangerous beasts in the entire world — hornswogglers and snozzwangers and those terrible wicked whangdoodles.

Roald Dahl, English author, said by Willy Wonka, *Charlie and the Chocolate Factory* (F)

6 Opening his mouth as if for a yawn, the dragon swallowed the middle son in a single gulp and put the horse in the freezer to eat another day.

John Gardner, US author, "Dragon, Dragon" from *Dragon, Dragon and Other Tales* (F)

7 The question is always the same with a dragon: will he talk with you or will he eat you?

Ursula K. Le Guin, US author, said by Arha's prisoner, *The Tombs of Atuan* (F)

8 Call the Ghouls, and the Boggles, and Ogres, and the Minotaurs. Call the Cruels, the Hags, the Spectres, and the people of the Toadstools. We will fight.

C. S. Lewis, English author, said by the White Witch, *The Lion, the Witch, and the Wardrobe* (F)

9 If you don't believe in dragons,
It is curiously true
That the dragons you disparage*
Choose to not believe in you.

Jack Prelutsky, US poet, "If You Don't Believe in Dragons" from *The Dragons Are Singing Tonight*   *make fun of*

10 Some dragons would just go stomping along, eyes glowing, smoke twirling from their nostrils, never giving a thought to being secret, to keeping out of sight.

Sarah Sargent, US author, *Weird Henry Berg* (F)

11 My armour is like tenfold shields, my teeth are swords, my claws spears, the shock of my tail a thunderbolt, my wings a hurricane, and my breath death!

J. R. R. Tolkien, English author, said by the dragon Smaug, *The Hobbit* (F)

12 [T]he Dragon King is one creature you stay friends with, since he can cause earthquakes as well as floods and droughts.

Laurence Yep, Chinese-American author, said by Moon Shadow, *Dragonwings* (F)

13 The monster wasn't much, as monsters go. A couple of horns, a snubbed snout, nine stubby talons . . . and a tail with three barbs, all quite worn.

Jane Yolen, US author, "Phoenix Farm" from *Twelve Impossible Things Before Breakfast* (F)

Moon and Stars

1 I was sure the moon would be a hospitable* host. It had been awaiting its first visitors for a long time.

Neil A. Armstrong, US astronaut, explaining his feelings about being the first person to land on the moon on July 21, 1969, found in *Eyewitness to History*, ed. by J. Carey (NF)

friendly

2 Stars are beautiful, but they may not take an active part in anything; they must just look on for ever. It is a punishment put on them for something they did so long ago that no star now knows what it is.

J. M. Barrie, Scottish author, *Peter Pan* (F)

3 [O]ne star in particular was so bright that [Robert] wondered if it were really the Star of Bethlehem.

Pearl S. Buck, US author, "Christmas Day in the Morning," in the Dec. 23, 1955 *Collier's* magazine (F)

4 Who knows if the moon's
a balloon, coming out of a keen city in the sky—filled with pretty people?

e. e. cummings, US poet, "who knows if the moon" from *Tulips and Chimneys*, ed. by G. J. Firmage

5 The night I flew over the Pacific was a night of stars. They seemed to rise from the sea and hang outside my cockpit window, near enough to touch.

Amelia Earhart, US aviation pioneer, found in *Sky Pioneer* by C. Szabo (NF)

6 I am lost. . . . There is no North Star to guide me.

Jean Craighead George, US author, said by Miyax, *Julie of the Wolves* (F)

7 The Indians believed the stars were children of the sun. In the morning before the sun left for work, he would put his children to bed. Then in the evening, when he came home, he would wake all his children up and set them in the sky to watch over the world while he slept.

Natalie Kinsey-Warnock, US author, *The Canadian Geese Quilt* (F)

8 All men have the stars, but they are not the same things for different people. For some, who are travelers, the stars are guides. For others they are no more than little lights in the sky.

Antoine de Saint-Exupéry, French author and illustrator, said by the Little Prince, *The Little Prince* (F)

9 Here am I
Behold me
It said as it rose,
I am the moon
Behold me.

Teton Sioux, North American Indian tribe, found in *The Trees Stand Shining*, sel. by Hettie Jones

10 The night wind
rips a cloud sheet
into rags,
then rubs, rubs
the October moon
until it shines
like a brass doorknob.

Judith Thurman, US poet, "Rags," found in *The Sky Is Full of Song*, sel. by L. B. Hopkins

11 [The children] saw that [Mary Poppins] was sticking the Gingerbread Stars to the sky. As each one was placed in position it began to twinkle furiously, sending out rays of sparkling golden light.

P. L. Travers, Australian-English author, *Mary Poppins* (F)

Mothers

(See also Parents*)*

1 To describe my mother would be to write about a hurricane in its perfect power.

Maya Angelou, US poet and author, *I Know Why the Caged Bird Sings* (NF)

2 Not only had [Peter Pan] no mother, but he had not the slightest desire to have one. He thought them very overrated persons.

J. M. Barrie, Scottish author, *Peter Pan* (F)

Mother was of royal African blood. . . . Throughout all her bitter years of slavery, she had managed to preserve a queenlike dignity.

Mary McLeod Bethune, US educator and author, found in *My Soul Looks Back, 'Less I Forget*, ed. by D. W. Riley (NF)

4 My mother is always telling me about when she was a girl. It's supposed to make me feel that she understands everything.

Judy Blume, US author, said by Margaret, *Are You There, God? It's Me, Margaret* (F)

5 My mother . . . taught me about family and hard work and sacrifice. She held steady through tragedy after tragedy. And she held our family . . . together through tough times.

Bill Clinton, 42nd US President, in the July 1992 *Biography Today* (NF)

6 Had it not been for [my mother's] faith in me at a critical time in my experiences, I should very likely never have become an inventor.

Thomas Edison, US inventor, found in *The Thomas A. Edison Album* by L. F. Frost (NF)

7 [Old man Vane's] mother died when he was very young and he always said that it was the hardest thing in the world, growing up without a mother.

Louise Fitzhugh, US author, said by Mr. Rocque, *Sport* (F)

8 In the eyes of its mother every beetle is a gazelle.

Moroccan proverb

9 For money, [Mama] will tell your fortune, find lost articles, see through walls, and call up the departed. She can read tea leaves, a pack of cards, your palm, a crystal ball.

Richard Peck, US author, said by Blossom Culp, "The Special Powers of Blossom Culp" found in *Birthday Surprises*, ed. by J. Hurwitz (F)

10 I thought [my mother] must have had some kind of magic to be able to do all the things she did, to work so hard and never complain and to make us all feel happy.

Jackie Robinson, US professional baseball player, found in *Jackie Robinson: Baseball Great* by R. Scott (NF)

11 The doctors told me I would never walk, but my mother told me I would, so I believed my mother.

Wilma Rudolph, US track star, *Wilma* (NF)

12 He listened. As some people listened for bird calls, Sonseray listened for mothers. All about him he heard them: directing, snapping, soothing, threatening, promising, yessing, noing, wait'll-we-get-homing.

Jerry Spinelli, US author, "Sonseray" from *The Library Card* (F)

13 And so our mothers and grand-mothers have, more often than not anony-mously, handed on the creative spark, the seed of the flower they themselves never hoped to see.

Alice Walker, US author, *In Search of Our Mothers' Gardens* (NF)

14 My mom is my inspiration. She worked with me every day. She never let me use my deafness as an excuse.

Heather Whitestone, 1995 Miss America, in the Apr. 1995 *Biography Today* (NF)

Music

(*See also* Singing)

1 Music was my refuge. I could crawl into the space between the notes and curl my back to loneliness.

Maya Angelou, US poet and author, *Gather Together in My Name* (NF)

2 Ten tom-toms,
Timpani, too,
Ten tall tubas
And an old kazoo.

Ten trombones —
Give them a hand!
The sitting-standing-
marching-running
Big Brass Band.

Anonymous poem, found in *A Nonny Mouse Writes Again!*, sel. by J. Prelutsky

3 [Sounder's bark] filled up the night and made music as though the branches of all the trees were being pulled across silver strings.

William H. Armstrong, US author, *Sounder* (F)

4 It's strange how some songs with memories tied to them went to a person's heart and stayed there.

Patricia Beatty, US author, thought by Hannalee, *Be Ever Hopeful, Hannalee* (F)

5 I was born with music inside me. . . . Music was one of my parts. Like my ribs, my liver, my kidney, my heart. Like my blood.

Ray Charles, US singer and composer, *Brother Ray* (NF)

6 The [Latino] rhythm has become part of the "Heartbeat of America."

Willie Colón, Puerto Rican composer, found in *Latino Voices*, ed. by F. R. Aparicio (NF)

7 The Old-Green-Grasshopper became a member of the New York Symphony Orchestra, where his playing was greatly admired.

Roald Dahl, English author, *James and the Giant Peach* (F)

8 [E]ven after [a big bell] is silent you can put your hand on the metal and feel the last tingle of vibrations, as though it were still singing to itself, private music of its own which we can't hear.

Peter Dickinson, English author, *Time and the Clock Mice, Etcetera* (F)

9 The loud, throbbing music took hold of Chip's body and made even his bones vibrate. . . . It was like climbing aboard a high-speed train and having it jerk him off his feet and never slow down.

Fred D'Ignazio, US author, "The Case of the Computer Bully" from *Chip Mitchell* (F)

10 Every tune [sung by slaves] was a testimony against slavery, and a prayer to God for deliverance from chains.

Frederick Douglass, US abolitionist and author, *Narrative of the Life of Frederick Douglass* (NF)

11 Through music you learn not to care about the color of someone's skin.

Vince Gill, US country singer and songwriter, in the Apr. 7, 1996 *Parade* magazine (NF)

12 No matter how hard times are, people still want music.

Irene Hunt, US author, said by Howie, *No Promises in the Wind* (F)

13 He who sings drives away sorrow.
Italian proverb

14 I feel everyone has a song inside. It's a matter of whether it can be brought out.

June Kuramoto, Japanese-American musician and composer, found in *Famous Asian Americans* by Morey and Dunn (NF)

15 [T]here are two kinds of music — good music and bad music. Good music is music that I like to hear. Bad music is music I don't want to hear.

Fran Lebowitz, US humorist and author, *Metropolitan Life* (NF)

16 Bach takes you to a very quiet place within yourself, to the inner core, a place where you are calm and at peace.

Yo-Yo Ma, Chinese-American cellist, in the July 1992 *Biography Today* (NF)

17 I have yet to find something that beats the power of being in love, or the power of music at its most magical.

Ibid.

18 We hear all the music that's in the wind, so much music that it itches my foot to start tapping. Just like a fiddle.

Robert Newton Peck, US author, said by Rob's father, *A Day No Pigs Would Die* (F)

19 Oh, such a moaning sound will weave round those cliffs. You'd like to pretend it was nothing more than wind and scrub oak, but it's the seals singing of their own, all the same.

Sylvia Peck, US author, said by Ruby, *Seal Child* (F)

20 And for a few minutes, while [Chester Cricket's] song lasted, Times Square was as still as a meadow at evening, with the sun streaming in on the people there and the wind moving among them as if they were only tall blades of grass.

George Selden, US author, *The Cricket in Times Square* (F)

21 It's got polka in it, a little bit of country, a little bit of jazz. Fuse all those types of music together, and I think that's where you get Tejano.

Selena, US singer, in the Jan. 1996 *Biography Today* (NF)

22 Elves hear all the songs of the world, and animals, birds, and other creatures hear pieces of the songs of the world. Humans hear none of the notes, only the slightest, faintest traces of their whispers. Which they call wind. Which they call water.

Ann Turner, US author, *Elfsong* (F)

Names

1 Sticks and stones will break my bones,
But names will never hurt me.

Anonymous folk poetry, found in *And the Green Grass Grew All Around*, comp. by A. Schwartz

2 It'd be nice to have a new name, to start with, one that's not all worn out from being called too much.

Natalie Babbitt, US author, said by Winnie Foster, *Tuck Everlasting* (F)

3 I have fallen in love with American names,
The sharp names that never get fat.
The snakeskin-titles of mining-claims,
The plumed war-bonnet of Medicine Hat,
Tucson and Deadwood and Lost Mule Flat.

Stephen Vincent Benét, US poet, "American Names," found in *The Faber Book of America*, ed. by Ricks and Vance (NF)

4 *Must* a name mean something?

Lewis Carroll, English author, said by Alice, *Through the Looking Glass* (F)

5 [His aunts] never called [James] by his real name, but always referred to him as "you disgusting little beast" or "you filthy nuisance" or "you miserable creature."

Roald Dahl, English author, *James and the Giant Peach* (F)

6 Names are strange and special gifts. There are names you give to yourself and names you show to the world, names that stay for a short while and names that remain with you forever, names that come from things you do and names that you receive as presents from other people.

Michael Dorris, Native American author and anthropologist, said by Morning Girl, *Morning Girl* (F)

7 They always seem to have names like [Skye Pennington] don't they? Rich, beautiful girls are never named Elsie Pip or Mary Smith.

M. E. Kerr, US author, said by Buddy Boyle, *Gentlehands* (F)

8 Shepherds usually give their dogs short names, like Gyp or Moss—it's so much quicker and easier than shouting "Bartholomew" or "Wilhelmina!"

Dick King-Smith, English author, *Babe the Gallant Pig* (F)

9 We don't have a nickname for [James]. You have to know a person pretty well before you can give him a nickname. Like, if we knew him better, we could decide if he was a Jamie or a Jim or a Jimmy.

Ann M. Martin, US author, thought by Jonno, *Inside Out* (F)

10 I read in a book once that a rose by any other name would smell as sweet, but I've never been able to believe it. I don't believe a rose would be as nice if it was called a thistle or a skunk cabbage.

L. M. Montgomery, Canadian author, said by Anne, *Anne of Green Gables* (F)

11 Never name any of my dogs. Dogs one, two, three, and four is all. When I want 'em, I whistle; when I don't, I give 'em a kick. "Git," "Scram," "Out," and "Dammit"; *that's* my dogs' names.

Phyllis Reynolds Naylor, US author, said by Judd, *Shiloh* (F)

12 [E]ven their names—[Homily, Pod and Arrietty] were never quite right. They imagined they had their own names— quite different from human names—but with half an ear you could tell they were borrowed.

Mary Norton, English author, said by Mrs. May, *The Borrowers* (F)

13 Everyone in our tribe had two names, the real one which was secret and was seldom used, and one which was common, for if people used your secret name it becomes worn out and loses its magic.

Scott O'Dell, US author, said by Won-a-pa-lei (Karana), *Island of the Blue Dolphins* (F)

15 [N]ames that had been suggested and rejected for the . . . seven dwarfs in *Snow White* . . . were Scrappy, Hoppy, Dirty, Dumpy, Hungry, Thrifty, Weepy, Doleful, Awful, Grabby, Flabby, Shifty, Helpful, Crabby, Daffy, Puffy, Chesty, Busy, Biggy, Graspy, and Snoopy. I'm glad that Disney decided not to use the name Snoopy.

Charles Schultz, US cartoonist and creator of "Peanuts," *Charles Brown, Snoopy, and Me* (NF)

16 There are some people who don't look at home in their names. Not their real names, nor the names they invent for themselves.

George Selden, US author, said by Tim Farr, *The Genie of Sutton Place* (F)

17 Inside his house, a kid gets one name, but on the other side of the door, it's whatever the rest of the world wants to call him.

Jerry Spinelli, US author, *Maniac Magee* (F)

14 My parents came from Canton, China. . . . They named me Bong Way Wong, but my brothers and sisters called me Billy.

Allen Say, Japanese author, said by Billy, *El Chino* (F)

18 [Y]ou do know my name, though you don't remember that I belong to it. I am Gandalf, and Gandalf means me!

J. R. R. Tolkien, English author, said by the wizard Gandalf, *The Hobbit* (F)

19 I always think it's too bad we can't choose our own names and are stuck with the ones our parents give us when we're too small and dumb to know any better.

Yoshiko Uchida, Japanese-American author, thought by Rinko, *The Best Bad Thing* (F)

20 We [Chinese] feel that a man should be able to change his name as he changes, the way a hermit crab can throw away his shell when it's too small and find another one.

Laurence Yep, Chinese-American author, said by Moon Shadow, *Dragonwings* (F)

Native Americans

1 America does not seem to remember that it derived its wealth, its values, its food, much of its medicine, and a large part of its "dream" from Native America.

Paula Gunn Allen, Laguna-Pueblo/Sioux author and scholar, *The Sacred Hoop* (NF)

2 It occurred to Omri for the first time that his idea of Indians, taken entirely from Western films, had been somehow false.

Lynne Reid Banks, US author, *The Indian in the Cupboard* (F)

3 I want people to see American Indians as a part of modern America. Too many people think we are a dead culture. But that's not true.

Ben Nighthorse Campbell, Native American US senator, in the June 2, 1996 *Parade* magazine (NF)

4 Pa said white men called the Indians savages because that made it easier to hate them, and hating them made it easier to drive them off or kill them and take their land. He said that as long as folks thought of the Shawnees as savages, they didn't have to think of them as people.

Cynthia DeFelice, US author, said by Nathan, *Weasel* (F)

5 Few of us . . . will soon forget the wail of mingled grief, rage, and horror which came from the camp 400 or 500 yards from us when the Indians returned to it and recognized their slaughtered warriors, women, and children.

Col. Gibbon, US military officer in charge of the attack on the sleeping Nez Perce camp on Aug. 9, 1877, found in *Indian Chiefs* by R. Freedman (NF)

CHIEF JOSEPH

6 Our chiefs are killed. . . . The old men are dead. . . . The little children are freezing to death. My people, some of them have run away to the hills and have no blankets, no food. . . . My heart is sick and sad. From where the sun now stands, I will fight no more forever.

Chief Joseph, leader of the Nez Perce, stating his reasons for surrendering on Oct. 5, 1877, found in *Indian Chiefs* by R. Freedman (NF)

7 [F]aithlessness on [the white man's] part in the matter of treaties, and gross swindling* of the Indians . . . are at the bottom of this Indian trouble.

Alvin M. Josephy, Jr., US author, reported in the *New York Herald* newspaper in June 1870, following Chief Red Cloud's charges against the government for its broken promises to the Indians, found in *500 Nations* (NF)   *lies and deceit*

8 In 1492 there were six million native people residing in what is now the US. They spoke 2000 languages, and had been part of thriving civilizations long before the coming of Columbus. This rich culture of the native people, nonetheless, was demolished methodically* and ruthlessly within a historically short period.

Wilma Mankiller, Chief of the Cherokee Nation of Oklahoma, in the Apr. 1994 *Biography Today* (NF)

in a planned way

9 Being Indian is an attitude, a state of mind, a way of being in harmony with all things and all beings.

Brooke Medicine-Eagle, Sioux/Nez Perce writer and ceremonial leader, found in *Shamanic Voices* by J. Halifax (NF)

10 When you first came we were many, and you were few; now you are many, and we are getting very few, and we are poor.

Red Cloud, Chief of the Oglala Sioux, in a July 16, 1870 speech in New York City

11 Every time the government moved the Indians, they gave 'em the same treaty: "You shall have this land as long as the grass grows and the water flows." But finally they settled the whole Indian problem. They put the Indians on land where the grass won't grow, and the water won't flow.

Will Rogers, US humorist and author, found in *As Long as the Rivers Flow* by Allen and Smith (NF)

12 The buffaloes are gone.
And those who saw the buffaloes are gone.

Carl Sandburg, US poet and biographer, "Buffalo Dusk," found in *Rainbows Are Made*, sel. by L. B. Hopkins

13 Every hillside, every valley, every plain and grove, has been hallowed* by some sad or happy event in days long vanished. Even the rocks . . . thrill with memories of stirring events connected with the lives of my people.

Chief Seattle, leader of six Indian tribes in the Pacific Northwest, from an 1854 speech to Gov. Isaac Stevens, found in *The American Reader*, ed. by D. Ravitch (NF)

greatly honored

14 What law have I broken? Is it wrong for me to love my own? Is it wicked in me because my skin is red; because I am a Sioux . . . because I would die for my people and my country?

Sitting Bull, Chief of the Sioux, found in *American Quotations* by Carruth and Ehrlich (NF)

15 What treaty that the whites ever made with red men have they kept? Not one.

Ibid.

16 Where today are the Pequot? Where are the Narragansett, the Mohican, the Pokanet, and the many other once powerful tribes of our people? They have vanished before the avarice* and the oppression of the White Man, as snow before a summer sun.

Tecumseh, Shawnee leader, found in *Bury My Heart at Wounded Knee* by D. Brown (NF)   *greed

Nature

(See also Pollution, Trees, *and* Weather*)*

1 The sea can swallow ships, and it can spit out whales upon the beach like watermelon seeds. It will take what it wants, and it will keep what it has taken, and you may not take away from it what it does not wish to give.

Natalie Babbitt, US author, the Prologue in *The Eyes of Amaryllis* (F)

2 That river—it was full of good and evil together. It would water the fields when it was curbed, but then if an inch were allowed it, it crashed through like a roaring dragon.

Pearl S. Buck, US author, *The Old Demon* (F)

3 Those who dwell . . . among the beauties and mysteries of the earth are never alone or weary of life.

Rachel Carson, US environmentalist and author, *The Sense of Wonder* (NF)

4 The boughs of no two trees ever have the same arrangement. Nature always produces *individuals*; She never produces *classes*.

Lydia Maria Child, US suffragist and author, found in *The Beacon Book of Quotations*, comp. by R. Maggio (NF)

5 The richest thing [in the world] is the earth, for out of the earth come all the riches of the world.

Parker Fillmore, said by the Shepherd, "Clever Manka" from *Womenfolk and Fairy Tales*, ed. by R. Minard (F)

6 As a babe . . . I was warmed by the sun, rocked by the winds, and sheltered by the trees.

Geronimo, Apache leader, found in *As Long as the Rivers Flow* by Allen and Smith (NF)

7 A river is a magic thing. A magic, moving, living part of the very earth itself— for it is from the soil, both from its depth and from its surface, that a river has its beginning.

Laura Gilpin, US photographer and author, *The Rio Grande* (NF)

8 From winter's white
   to summer's gold,
   from spring to autumn, we uphold
   these bounties
   Mother Nature brings.
   Respect her earth and living things.

   Brian Jacques, English author and actor, part of the
   Redwall grace, *The Great Redwall Feast* (F)

9 There is no sea here. But the land
rolls a little like the sea.

   Patricia MacLachlan, US author, said by Sarah, *Sarah,
   Plain and Tall* (F)

10 [T]he river was very lazy that day, and
hardly seemed to mind if it didn't get there
at all.

   A. A. Milne, English author, "Eeyore Joins a Game" from
   The House at Pooh Corner (F)

11 A flower touches everyone's heart.

   Georgia O'Keeffe, US painter, found in *Painting: Great
   Lives* by S. Glubok (NF)

12 The nation behaves well if it treats the
natural resources as assets which it must
turn over to the next generation increased
. . . in value.

   Theodore Roosevelt, 26th US President, in an Aug. 29,
   1910 speech

13 How can man own land? Land same as
air. Land for all people to live on. For
beaver and deer. Does deer own land?

   Elizabeth George Speare, US author, said by Attean, *The
   Sign of the Beaver* (F)

14 [The sun] casts his most beautiful
beams across the [mountains] so that they
will not forget that he is coming again in
the morning.

   Johanna Spyri, Swiss author, said by Grandfather,
   Heidi (F)

15 To me the sea is a continual miracle,
   The fishes that swim — the rocks — the
      motion of the waves — the ships with
      men in them,
   What stranger miracles are there?

   Walt Whitman, US poet, "Miracles", found in *The
   Anthology of American Poetry*, ed. by G. Gesner

Nightmares
(See Dreams and Nightmares)

Noise
(See Sounds)

Occupations

1 It's just a job. Grass grows, birds fly, waves pound on the sand. I beat up people.

Muhammad Ali, US professional boxer, in the Apr. 6, 1977 issue of *The New York Times* (NF)

2 I take photographs because there are things nobody would see unless I photographed them.

Diane Arbus, US photographer, found in *Herstory*, ed. by Ashby and Ohrn (NF)

3 Farming's a piece of fun for you. It's a life sentence for me.

Nina Bawden, English author, said by Mrs. Jones, *Henry* (F)

4 I used to think I'd be an undertaker when I grew up—my Uncle Warren is one and he's rich—but now I've changed my mind. Undertaking is a dying business, if you know what I mean.

Tom Birdseye, US author, said by Gordon, *Tarantula Shoes* (F)

5 I love the life of a Senator, even on its bad days. It's the greatest elective job in the world.

Bill Bradley, professional basketball player and US senator, in the Jan. 7, 1996 *Parade* magazine (NF)

6 I'm not a *medical* doctor. I'm a paleontologist. My patients have all been dead for 50 million years or so.

Oliver Butterworth, US author, said by Dr. Ziemer, *The Enormous Egg* (F)

SAY AH.

7 When I get to be a nurse, none of my patients are going to die. I'm going to make it real clear — *no dying!*

Betsy Byars, US author, said by Carlie, *The Pinballs* (F)

8 It dawned on me that by becoming a biologist, I had given myself something to write about.

Rachel Carson, US biologist and writer, found in *Rachel Carson* by M. Jezer (NF)

9 There is one good thing about being president [of the US]—nobody can tell you when to sit down.

Dwight D. Eisenhower, 34th US President, in the Aug. 9, 1953 "Sayings of the Week" in the *Observer* (NF)

10 My name is Harold. I come to writing purely by chance. My full-time occupation is dog.

Deborah and James Howe, US authors, *Bunnicula: A Rabbit-Tale of Mystery* (F)

11 I've been working on the railroad,
All the live-long day,
I've been working on the railroad,
Just to pass the time away.

"I've Been Working on the Railroad," anonymous song, found in *Gonna Sing My Head Off!*, coll. and arr. by K. Krull

12 Now I find teaching extraordinarily satisfying. I'm teaching young people who will move into local, state, and federal positions of power.

Barbara Jordan, US member of Congress and educator, found in *Herstory*, ed. by Ashby and Ohrn (NF)

13 If it falls your lot to be a street sweeper, . . . sweep streets so well that all the host of Heaven and earth will have to pause and say, "Here lived a great sweeper, who swept his job well."

Martin Luther King, Jr., US civil rights leader, in a Dec. 10, 1956 speech in Montgomery, AL

14 If I didn't start painting, I would have raised chickens.

Grandma Moses, US painter, *Grandma Moses: My Life's Story* (NF)

15 Maybe witchcraft's [Judith's] career. I mean, don't knock it till you've tried it.

Phyllis Reynolds Naylor, US author, said by Marjorie, *Witch's Sister* (F)

16 When I was traveling in space, I thought about how lucky I was to be up there and how so many people would want to have the job I have. Viewing the earth from space is very special.

Ellen Ochoa, Mexican-American astronaut, found in *Famous Hispanic Americans* by Morey and Dunn (NF)

17 There's no higher calling than animal husbandry, and making things live and grow. We farmers are stewards. Our lot is to tend all of God's good living things, and I say there's nothing finer.

Robert Newton Peck, US author, said by Ben Turner, *A Day No Pigs Would Die* (F)

18 He is a wild moose, and he lives here of his own free will; he is the headwaiter.

Daniel Manus Pinkwater, US author and illustrator, said by Mr. Breton, *Blue Moose and Return of the Moose* (F)

19 Moppet and Mittens have grown up into good rat-catchers. . . . They charge so much a dozen, and earn their living very comfortably.

Beatrix Potter, English author, "The Tale of Samuel Whiskers" from *The Complete Tales of Beatrix Potter* (F)

20 Personally, I have always felt that the best doctor in the world is the veterinarian. He can't ask his patients what is the matter—he's got to just know.

Will Rogers, US humorist and author, found in *Will Rogers: Quotable Cowboy* by C. L. Bennett (NF)

21 Cartooning is hard work sometimes, but at least one has the satisfaction of knowing he has made others laugh.

Charles Schultz, US cartoonist and creator of "Peanuts," *Charles Brown, Snoopy, and Me* (NF)

22 Television is the most fun. Music is the most rewarding, and film is the most interesting.

Will Smith, US actor and rapper, in the Sept. 1994 *Biography Today* (NF)

23 A bullfighter must have courage, skill, and grace. And of these courage is the most important.

Maia Wojciechowska, Polish-American author, said by an old man, *Shadow of a Bull* (F)

Parents

(See also both Fathers *and* Mothers)

1 There's always someone worse off than you. . . . It's sad you have no papa, but a mama you have. There are boys who don't have both, you know.

Judie Angell, US author, said by Mr. Meyer, "I Saw What I Saw," from *Within Reach*, ed. by D. Gallo (F)

2 Children, obey your parents in the Lord, for this is right.

Bible, Ephesians 6:10 (NIV)

3 I hated it when [my parents] had a fight in front of me. Why didn't they know how much I hated it! Didn't they know how awful they sounded?

Judy Blume, US author, said by Margaret, *Are You There, God? It's Me, Margaret* (F)

4 Good parents, happy marriages, good children, fine funerals.

Chinese proverb

5 I wanted, desperately, for my mother and father to have some fun, to have friends, to go to movies—anything. They seemed to have given up happiness.

Beverly Cleary, US author, *A Girl from Yamhill: A Memoir* (NF)

6 The truth is that parents are not really interested in justice. They just want quiet.

Bill Cosby, US comedian and author, *Fatherhood* (NF)

7 Wilbur and Orville believed that their mechanical aptitude came from their mother . . . who enjoyed working with her hands. . . . Their father had trouble driving a nail straight.

Russell Freedman, US author, *The Wright Brothers* (NF)

8 My parents warned me about the traps [in life] . . . the drugs, and the drink, the streets that could catch you if you got careless.

Michael Jordan, US professional basketball player, in the Jan. 1992 *Biography Today* (NF)

9 Are anybody's parents typical?

Madeleine L'Engle, US author, *Two-Part Invention* (F)

10 [Nine-year-old Pippi Longstocking] had no mother and no father, and that was, of course, very nice because there was no one to tell her to go to bed just when she was having the most fun.

Astrid Lindgren, Swedish author, *Pippi Longstocking* (F)

11 A child's conduct will reflect the ways of his parents.

Arnold Lobel, US author and illustrator, the moral in "The Bad Kangaroo" from *Fables* (F)

12 They both wanted—her mother and her father—wanted and wanted, and she had to choose [between them].

Norma Fox Mazer, US author, *Taking Terri Mueller* (F)

13 Children aren't happy with nothing
    to ignore,
And that's what parents were
    created for.

Ogden Nash, US poet, "The Parent," found in *Custard and Company*, sel. by Q. Blake

15 Gilly gave [Trotter] the 300-watt smile that she had designed especially for melting the hearts of foster parents.

Katherine Paterson, US author, *The Great Gilly Hopkins* (F)

16 Sometimes I wish we could turn the day upside down so that [parents'] main time at home would be in the morning before breakfast—before they get all worn out. I'll tell you, at the end of a day it doesn't take much to crush a parent.

Jerry Spinelli, US author, thought by Crash, *Crash* (F)

17 We [parents] are always too busy for our children; we never give them the time or interest they deserve. We lavish gifts on them; but the most precious gift—our personal association, which means so much to them—we give grudgingly.*

Mark Twain, US author, found in *Mark Twain: A Biography* by A. B. Paine (NF)   *unwillingly

Patriotism
(*See* America and Americans)

Peace
(*See also* War)

1 Here lies John Adams, who took upon himself the responsibility of the peace with France in the year 1800.

John Adams's tombstone inscription (*Adams died on July 4, 1826.*)

14 To me what's really important is how a room *feels*, not where the bed is. Parents don't always understand stuff like this. To them the most important thing about a room is how it looks.

Barbara Parks, US author, said by Howard, *The Kid in the Red Jacket* (F)

2 When life is so tiresome, there ain't no peace like the greatest peace—the peace of the Lord's hand holding you.

William H. Armstrong, US author, sung by the mother, *Sounder* (F)

3 Blessed are the peacemakers; for they shall be called the children of God.

Bible, Matthew 5:9 (KJV)

4 To work for better understanding among people, one does not have to be a former president sitting at a fancy conference room table. Peace can be made in the neighbor-hoods, the living rooms, the playing fields, and the classrooms of our country.

Jimmy Carter, 39th US President, found in *Jimmy Carter* by C. Lazo (NF)

5 You cannot have peace longer than your neighbor chooses.

Danish proverb

6 I want to make a treaty that will last, so that both [the Apache and the white man] can travel over the country and have no trouble.

Delshay, a member of the Tonto Apaches, in an 1871 report to the US Secretary of the Interior

7 I say we are going to have peace even if we have to fight for it.

Dwight D. Eisenhower, 34th US President, in a June 10, 1945 speech in Germany

8 The mere absence of war is not peace.

John F. Kennedy, 35th US President, in his Jan. 14, 1963 State of the Union speech

9 Peace is a daily, a weekly, a monthly process, gradually changing opinions, slowly eroding old barriers, quietly build-ing new structures.

John F. Kennedy, 35th US President, in a Sept. 20, 1963 speech to the United Nations General Assembly

10 I was, and still am, convinced that the women of the world, united without any regard for national or racial dimensions,* can become a most powerful force for international peace and brotherhood.

Coretta Scott King, US civil rights activist and wife of Dr. Martin Luther King, Jr., found in the *Book of Black Heroes, Vol. 2* by T. Igus (NF)   *differences

11 I have always believed that we cannot have peace in the world until *all of us* understand how wars start.

Jean F. Merrill, US author, the Introduction to *The Pushcart War* (F)

12 [P]eace has to be watched and guarded. Its enemies are always ready to break it, for the forces of evil never sleep.

Bernard Miles, English actor and author, the retelling of *Macbeth* from *Favorite Tales from Shakespeare* (F)

13 It isn't enough to talk about peace. One must believe in it. And it isn't enough to believe in it. One must work for it.

Eleanor Roosevelt, US diplomat, author, and wife of the 32nd President, in a Nov. 11, 1951 *Voice of America* radio broadcast

14 To be at peace with God and man, that is well-being indeed.

Johanna Spyri, Swiss author, said by Grandfather, *Heidi* (F)

15 To be prepared for war is one of the most effectual* means of preserving peace.

George Washington, 1st US President, in a Jan. 8, 1790 speech to Congress   *practical

Pets

(See also Animals, Cats, *and* Dogs*)*

1 The main reason I had been willing to even consider becoming an adult was so I could have as many pets as I wanted.

Betsy Byars, US author, *The Moon and I: A Memoir* (NF)

2 All I've *got* at home is two dogs and four cats and six bunny rabbits and two parakeets and three canaries and a green parrot and a turtle and a bowl of goldfish and a cage of white mice and a silly old hamster! I want a *squirrel*!

Roald Dahl, English author, said by Veruca, *Charlie and the Chocolate Factory* (F)

3 Pets are the hobby of my brother Bert.
He used to go to school with a mouse in his shirt.

Ted Hughes, English poet, "My Brother Bert" from *Meet My Folks*

4 I'd much rather be your pet than your breakfast, which is what I would have been if you'd been an ordinary cat.

Dick King-Smith, English author, said by the mouse Drusilla to Martin, *Martin's Mice* (F)

5 [Archibald Peregrine Edmund Spring-Russell] wanted to be sure that any animal he parted with would be properly looked after, and though he didn't intend to ask money for his creatures, he thought that getting something for nothing was not a good idea.

Dick King-Smith, English author, *Mr. Ape* (F)

6 [Mom] has this thing about pets not belonging in the city, and birds not belonging in cages anywhere.

Anne Lindbergh, US author, thought by Owen, *Travel Far, Pay No Fare* (F)

7 With fists full of hay, the children coaxed [the buffalo called Old Shaggysides] inside the corral, where he lived out his old age in comfort and ease as a pet of the family.

Walter L. Maughan, US author, *Old Shaggysides* (F)

8 In short, it is against the law to have a tame moose.

Daniel Manus Pinkwater, US author and illustrator, said by Mr. Bobwicz, *Blue Moose and Return of the Moose* (F)

9 You were supposed to bring home an ordinary chicken to eat . . . not a 266-pound chicken to keep as a pet.

Daniel Manus Pinkwater, US author and illustrator, said by Arthur's mother, *The Hoboken Chicken Emergency* (F)

10 Like many other much-loved humans, [Mr. and Mrs. Dearly] believed that they owned their dogs, instead of realizing that their dogs owned them.

Dodie Smith, English author, *The 101 Dalmatians* (F)

11 They say [Maniac Magee] kept an eight-inch cockroach on a leash and that rats stood guard over him while he slept.

Jerry Spinelli, US author, *Maniac Magee* (F)

12 Mother doesn't want a dog.
She's making a mistake.
Because, more than a dog, I think
She will not want this snake.

Judith Viorst, US poet, "Mother Doesn't Want a Dog," found in *The Random House Book of Poetry,* sel. by J. Prelutsky

Pollution

(See also World*)*

1 We live in an environment whose principal product is garbage.

Russell Baker, US journalist, in the Feb. 22, 1968 issue of *The New York Times* (NF)

2 For the first time in the history of the world, every human being is now subjected to contact with dangerous chemicals, from the moment of conception until death.

Rachel Carson, US environmentalist and author, *Silent Spring* (NF)

3 We have been massively intervening in the environment without being aware of many of the harmful consequences of our acts. . . . We are, in effect, conducting a huge experiment *on ourselves.*

Barry Commoner, US biologist and educator, *Science and Survival* (NF)

4 None of us can do all the things that will save the planet, but each of us can do some of them, and all of that will add up and be better than nothing.

Paula Danziger, US author, said by Jil!, *Earth to Matthew* (F)

5 [Americans] use over 80 billion aluminum soda cans every year. . . . Imagine throwing all of the cans out. What a waste! Now imagine [recycling] them all and using them again. Much better.

EarthWorks Group, *50 Simple Things Kids Can Do to Save the Earth* (NF)

6 Every day Americans throw out an average of 4 pounds (1.8 kg) of garbage each. If you piled everyone's trash together, it would weigh more than 438,000 tons (398,000 metric tons).

Evan and Janet Hadingham, US authors, *Garbage!* (NF)

7 Imagine a world where humans would
   Do their best for the planet's good:
   Water pure and forests fair—
   No pollution to kill the air.
   Can we change our ways much faster
   And avoid complete disaster?

   James Marsh, English author and illustrator, "Future Ark"
   from *Bizarre Birds & Beasts: Animal Verses*

8 As a people we have developed a life-
   style that is draining the earth of its price-
   less and irreplaceable resources without
   any regard for the future.

   Margaret Mead, US anthropologist, "The Energy Crisis—
   Why Our World Will Never Again Be the Same" (NF)

9 One person's trash is another's living
   space.

   National Academy of Sciences, the slogan in its 1995
   "Waste Management and Control" campaign

10 "Once-ler!" he cried with a cruffulous
      croak.
   "Once-ler! You're making such
      smogulous smoke!
   My poor Swomee-Swams . . . why, they
      can't sing a note!
   No one can sing who has smog in his
      throat."

   Dr. Seuss, US author, *The Lorax (F)*

11 Industrial vomit . . . fills our skies and
   seas.

   Alvin Toffler, US author, *Future Shock* (NF)

Possible and Impossible

1 It is easy to propose impossible remedies.

   Aesop, Greek writer, the moral in the fable "Belling the
   Cat," found in *The Children's Treasury*, ed. by P. S.
   Goepfert (F)

2 [A]ll things are possible with God.

   Bible, Mark 10:27 (NIV)

3 The young do not know
enough to be prudent,*
and therefore they
attempt the impossible
—and achieve it.

   Pearl S. Buck, US author, *The Goddess Abides* (F)

   careful, cautious

4 There's no use trying . . . one can't
believe impossible things.

   Lewis Carroll, English author, said by Alice, *Through the
   Looking Glass* (F)

5 Why, sometimes I've believed as many as
six impossible things before breakfast.

   Lewis Carroll, English author, said by the White Queen,
   Through the Looking Glass (F)

6 The only way of finding the limits of the
possible is by going beyond them into the
impossible.

   Arthur C. Clark, English science-fiction author, *The Lost
   Worlds* (F)

7 Nothing's impossible I have found,
for when my chin is on the ground,
I pick myself up,
dust myself off,
start all over again.

Julie Reece Deaver, US author and illustrator, words to a song from the movie *Swing Time*, found in *Say Goodnight, Gracie* (F)

8 It's kind of fun to do the impossible.

Walt Disney, US cartoonist and movie producer, found in *The Man Behind the Magic* by K. and R. Greene (NF)

9 It *was* impossible, and still you did it. . . . Aren't you wonderful!

Giggy Lezra, US author, said by the lady in blue, *The Cat, The Horse, and the Miracle* (F)

10 [Marco] thought all animals could talk. Just because he hadn't heard them didn't mean it couldn't happen.

Ann M. Martin, US author, "No Such Thing," found in *Birthday Surprises*, ed. by J. Hurwitz (F)

11 It was the oddest thing, to climb out of your body, just step out of it and leave it lying on the carpet like a shirt you had just taken off.

Ian McEwan, English author, *The Daydreamer* (F)

12 You must do the thing you think you cannot do.

Eleanor Roosevelt, US diplomat, author, and wife of the 32nd President, the Foreword to *Eleanor Roosevelt* by R. Freedman (NF)

13 The difficult we do immediately. The impossible takes a little longer.

US Army Corps of Engineers, its motto during World War II

Poverty

(See Wealth and Poverty)

Prejudice

(See Racism)

The Presidency

1 [The office of Vice President is] the most insignificant office that ever the invention of man contrived.*

John Adams, Vice President to George Washington and then the 2nd US President, in a Dec. 19, 1793 letter to his wife Abigail

*created

2 I pray Heaven to bestow the best Blessings on this House and all that shall hereafter inhabit it. May none but honest and wise men ever rule beneath this roof.

John Adams, 2nd US President, in his personal journal, Nov. 2, 1800 entry, the second night in the brand new presidential mansion, later known as the White House

3 No man who ever held the office of President would congratulate a friend on obtaining it.

> John Adams, 2nd US President, written after the election of his son, John Quincy Adams, as the 6th US President in 1824

4 Although I was surrounded by people eager to help me, my vivid impression of the Presidency remains the loneliness in which the most difficult decisions had to be made.

> Jimmy Carter, 39th US President, found in *Jimmy Carter* by C. Lazo (NF)

5 I think the President is the only person who can change the direction or attitude of our nation.

> Jimmy Carter, 39th US President, in the June 21, 1976 issue of the *Encore American & Worldwide News* (NF)

6 [A] halo descends on all the murdered Presidents, and on Lincoln most of all.

> Alistair Cooke, English-American writer and TV commentator, *America* (NF)

7 No easy problems ever come to the President of the United States. If they are easy to solve, somebody else has solved them.

> Dwight D. Eisenhower, 34th US President, repeated by John F. Kennedy in the Apr. 8, 1962 *Parade* magazine (NF)

8 To me the Presidency and the Vice Presidency were not prizes to be won but a duty to be done.

> Gerald R. Ford, Vice President to Richard Nixon and then the 38th US President, *A Time To Heal* (NF)

9 I can with truth say mine is a situation of dignified slavery.

> Andrew Jackson, 7th US President, referring to his duties as President, in a Nov. 30, 1829 letter to Robert J. Chester

10 A President's hardest task is not to do what is right, but to know what is right.

> Lyndon B. Johnson, 36th US President, in his Jan. 4, 1865 State of the Union speech

11 I know I've got a heart big enough to be President. I know I've got guts enough to be President. But I wonder whether I've got the intelligence and ability to be President—I wonder if any man does.

> Lyndon B. Johnson, 36th US President, *A Very Personal Presidency* (NF)

12 Certainly in the next 50 years we shall see a woman president, perhaps sooner than you think. A woman can and should be able to do any political job that a man can do.

> Richard M. Nixon, 37th US President, in an Apr. 16, 1969 speech to the League of Women Voters in Washington, D.C.

13 No President who performs his duties faithfully and conscientiously* can have any leisure.

> James K. Polk, 11th US President, in a Sept. 1, 1847 diary entry
>
> *carefully

14 In my opinion, eight years as President is enough and sometimes too much for any man. . . . There is a lure in power. It can get into a man's blood just as gambling and lust for money have been known to do.

Harry S Truman, 33rd US President, in an Apr. 16, 1950 memorandum

15 The President of the United States is two people: he's the President and he's a human being.

Harry S Truman, 33rd US President, in a Nov. 14, 1959 speech to the National Association of Broadcasters

16 [Tom Sawyer and Joe Harper] said they would rather be outlaws a year in Sherwood Forest than President of the United States forever.

Mark Twain, US author, *The Adventures of Tom Sawyer* (F)

17 [Being President is like] entering upon an unexplored field, enveloped* on every side with clouds and darkness.

George Washington, 1st US President, said before leaving his Mt. Vernon home to become the first president, found in *George Washington* by R. Bruns (NF)   *closed in

Pride

1 I'm the greatest!

Muhammad Ali, US professional boxer, his slogan, found in *Words to Make My Dream Children Live*, ed. by D. Mullane (NF)

2 Pride goeth before destruction, and a haughty spirit before a fall.

Bible, Proverbs 16:18 (KJV)

3 Say It Loud: I'm Black and I'm Proud

James Brown, US singer and songwriter, 1979 song title

4 The nation is proud that an American woman should be the first woman in history to fly an airplane alone across the Atlantic Ocean.

Herbert Hoover, 31st US President, said about Amelia Earhart, found in *Sky Pioneer* by C. Szabo (NF)

5 It is the high and mighty who have the longest distance to fall.

Arnold Lobel, US author and illustrator, the moral in "King Lion and the Beetle" from *Fables* (F)

6 Pride swells with flattery.

Serbo-Croatian proverb

7 The rabbit looked down and he saw a big bear.
  "*I'm* best of the beasts," said the bear. "And so there!"

Dr. Seuss, US author, "The Big Brag" from *Yertle the Turtle and Other Stories* (F)

8 Raúl [Castro] was determined to show everyone that being poor did not mean being dumb, and being Mexican was something to be proud of.

Warren H. Wheelock and J. O. Maynes, Jr., US authors, *Hispanic Heroes of the U.S.A.* (NF)

Problems and Solutions

(See also Trouble)

1 Our success in space led us to hope that this strength can be used in the next decade in the solution of many of our planet's problems.

Neil A. Armstrong, US astronaut, in a Sept. 16, 1969 speech to Congress

2 [As a teenager I] had a lot of tensions and problems. . . . I was a good girl, had to do well, please everyone. That was my role in life.

Judy Blume, US author, in the Jan. 1992 *Biography Today* (NF)

3 Drugs take you further than you
    want to go,
  Keep you there longer than you
    want to stay,
  And cost you more than you
    can ever pay.

  Chester Brewer, Jr., US professional baseball player,
  found in *Words To Make My Dream Children Live*, ed. by D.
  Mullane (NF)

4 Everybody is just walking along con-
cerned with his own problems, his own
life, his own worries. And we're all expecting other people to tune into our own
agenda. "Look at my worry. Worry with
me. Step into my life. Care about my
problems. Care about me."

  Sharon Creech, US author, said by Salamanca's grandmother, *Walk Two Moons* (F)

5 The problem is, the problem is . . . well,
the problem is that there is no problem!

  Roald Dahl, English author, said by Earthworm, *James
  and the Giant Peach* (F)

6 Our problem is that we don't think
it's fair that you don't like us just
because we're not like you were when
you were our age.

  Jamie Gilson, US author, said by Hobie Hanson to
  Mr. Bobb, *Sticks and Stones and Skeleton Bones* (F)

7 [When we were growing up,] we knew
about problems, heard about them, saw
them, even lived through some hard ones
ourselves, but our community wrapped
itself around us, put itself between us and
the hard knocks, to cushion the blows.

  Eloise Greenfield and Lessie Jones Little, US
  authors, *Childtimes* (NF)

8 Gordy's life was as cracked as the old
platter I was drying, and Mother had no
glue to fix it with.

  Mary Downing Hahn, US author, thought by Margaret,
  Stepping on the Cracks (F)

9 [W]hen an obstacle came in [Thomas
Edison's] path, he either passed around it
or turned it into his advantage.

  Francis Jehl, a member of Edison's staff, found in *The
  Thomas A. Edison Album* by L. F. Frost (NF)

10 If you run into a wall, don't turn
around and give up. Figure out how to
climb it, go through it, or
work around it.

  Michael Jordan, US pro-
  fessional basketball player,
  *I Can't Accept Not
  Trying* (NF)

11 A lot of
us have problems and
sometimes it's hard to get around
them. Some things you just can't
do anything about. And when that happens
you feel bad and you feel little. Not little,
but alone.

  Walter Dean Myers, US author, said by Clyde, *Fast Sam,
  Cool Clyde, and Stuff* (F)

12 Everyone has different problems, but
everyone has some kind of problem.

  Justine Rendal, US author, said by Conner, a computer
  program, *A Very Personal Computer* (F)

Rabbits

1 Even the hare's hair hides the hare's ears.
Anonymous tongue twister

2 If you run after two rabbits, you won't catch either one.
Armenian proverb

3 A rabbit, I concluded, is cute to look at, but is generally useless, especially as a companion to dogs.
Deborah and James Howe, US authors, said by Harold the dog, *Bunnicula: A Rabbit-Tale of Mystery* (F)

4 As soon as [Rabbit] woke up, he felt important, as if everything depended upon him.
A. A. Milne, English author, "Rabbit's Busy Day" from *The House at Pooh Corner* (F)

5 I don't think we want to live in a place where we can't go out to get meat for the table without the rabbits shootin' back.
Joan Lowery Nixon, US author, said by Claude, *If You Say So, Claude* (F)

6 "So you see," bragged the rabbit, "it's perfectly true
   That my ears are the best, so I'm better than you!"
Dr. Seuss, US author, "The Big Brag" from *Yertle the Turtle and Other Stories* (F)

7 [I]n the beginning [the Velveteen Rabbit] was really splendid. He was fat and bunchy, as a rabbit should be.
Margery Williams, English-American author, *The Velveteen Rabbit* (F)

Racism

(See also Civil Rights*)*

1 As long as you keep a person down, some part of you has to be down there to hold him down so it means you cannot soar as you otherwise might.

Marian Anderson, US opera singer, found in *Herstory*, ed. by Ashby and Ohrn (NF)

2 Prejudice is like a hair across your cheek. You can't see it, you can't find it with your fingers, but you keep brushing at it because the feel of it is irritating.

Marian Anderson, US opera singer, found in *My Soul Looks Back, 'Less I Forget*, ed. by D. W. Riley (NF)

3 Racism can't be overcome. . . . There will always be people who don't like you because you're Black, Hispanic, Jewish. You have to figure out how to deal with it.

Arthur Ashe, US professional tennis player, in the July 1991 *Sports Illustrated* (NF)

4 Racism is not an excuse to not do the best you can.

Ibid.

5 Being black is the greatest burden I've had to bear.

Arthur Ashe, US professional tennis player, found in *Words to Make My Dream Children Live*, ed. by D. Mullane (NF)

6 Surely the day will come when color means nothing more than skin tone . . . when understanding breeds love and brotherhood.

Josephine Baker, US singer, found in *Words to Make My Dream Children Live*, ed. by D. Mullane (NF)

7 God does not show favoritism but accepts men from every nation who fear him and do what is right.

Bible, Acts 10:43 (NIV)

8 For racism to die, a totally different America must be born.

Stokely Carmichael, US civil rights activist, found in *Words to Make My Dream Children Live*, ed. by D. Mullane (NF)

9 Racism is so universal in this country, so widespread and deep-seated, that it is invisible because it is so normal.

Shirley Chisholm, US politician, *Unbought and Unbossed* (NF)

10 "Jim Crow" was not a person—it was another name for segregation, the way that whites kept black people away from white people.

Jeri Ferris, US author, *What I Had Was Singing* (NF)

11 [In 1939] the racial lines were firmly, but strangely, drawn [in Washington, D.C.]. A black artist could perform at the National Theater, for example, but no blacks could be in the audience.

Ibid.

12 I started noticing racism as a teenager. . . . We were treated differently and it was a bitter and hurtful experience. I was treated badly because I was poor, Mexican American, and a girl.

Dolores Huerta, Mexican-American Vice President of the United Farm Workers, found in *Famous Mexican-Americans* by Morey and Dunn (NF)

13 If people are informed, they will do the right thing. It's when they are not informed that they become hostages to prejudice.

Charlayne Hunter-Gault, US journalist, found in *Women's Words: The Columbia Book of Quotations by Women* by M. Biggs (NF)

14 Let us discard all these things [about one race being inferior], and unite as one people throughout this land until we shall once more stand up declaring that all men are created equal.

Abraham Lincoln, 16th US President, in a July 10, 1858 speech in Chicago, IL

15 We have poverty which enslaves and racial prejudice which does the same.

Eleanor Roosevelt, US diplomat, author, and wife of the 32nd President, found in *Eleanor Roosevelt* by R. Freedman (NF)

16 The struggle is to keep the prejudice from turning into bigotry* and hatred. Bigotry . . . is mankind's biggest enemy.

Bill Russell, US professional basketball player, *Second Wind* (NF)   *intolerance

17 [A]t first, color [of a person's skin] doesn't mean very much to little children, black or white. Only as they grow older and absorb poisons from adults does color begin to blind them.

Roy Wilkins, US civil rights activist and author, found in *My Soul Looks Back, 'Less I Forget*, ed. by D. W. Riley (NF)

Rain
(See Weather)

Reading
(See also Books)

1 Read the best books, and they will improve your [writing] style.

Louisa May Alcott, US author, in an Oct. 24, 1878 letter to John Preston True, found in *Great Americans in Their Own Words* (NF)

2 For me, reading books and writing them are tied together. The words of other writers teach me and refresh me and inspire me.

Betsy Byars, US author, *The Moon and I: A Memoir* (NF)

3 [I]t was unlawful, as well as unsafe, to teach a slave to read.

Frederick Douglass, US abolitionist and author, *Escape from Slavery*, ed. by M. McCurdy (NF)

4 Remember that magic moment in childhood when you looked at a book or a sign or even a cereal box and realized you could read it?

Tara Dawn Holland, 1997 Miss America, in the Jan. 5, 1997 *Parade* magazine (NF)

5 Until I feared I would lose it, I never loved to read. One does not love breathing.

Harper Lee, US author, said by Scout, *To Kill a Mockingbird* (F)

6 [T]hat's what reading is: using symbols to suggest a picture or an idea.

Robert C. O'Brien, US author, said by the rat Nicodemus, *Mrs. Frisby and the Rats of NIMH* (F)

7 Animal personalities have always intrigued me, and the desire to find out more about them made a reader out of me.

Bill Peet, US illustrator and author, *Bill Peet: An Autobiography* (NF)

8 [After Grayson realized he had read his first words,] his smile was so wide he'd have had to break it into sections to fit it through the doorway.

Jerry Spinelli, US author, *Maniac Magee* (F)

9 For the past year and a half [my cat Rosebud] has been reading *Gone with the Wind*. It sits open on a chair near the radiator so she can read whenever she's in the mood. Every few days I turn the page for her.

Thomas Wharton, US illustrator, from *Purr . . . Children's Book Illustrators Brag about Their Cats*, ed. by M. J. Rosen (NF)

Religion
(See also God*)*

1 Science without religion is lame, religion without science is blind.

Albert Einstein, German-American physicist, *Out of My Later Years* (NF)

2 [N]ever laugh at anyone's religion, because whether you take it seriously or not, they do. And more than that, people who think enough to even *have* a religion should be respected at least for the thinking.

Louise Fitzhugh, US author, said by Harriet's father, *The Long Secret* (F)

3 Everything [the Shoshoni Indians] do is connected to their religion. Every day they worship and praise the Great Spirit who, Jimmy knew, was God.

Kristiana Gregory, US author, *The Legend of Jimmy Spoon* (F)

4 It is in our lives, and not from our words, that our religion must be read.

Thomas Jefferson, 3rd US President, in an Aug. 6, 1816 letter to Mrs. M. Harrison Smith

5 I cannot imagine myself without religion. I could as easily fancy* a living body without a heart.

Helen Keller, US author and humanitarian, *My Religion* (NF)   *imagine

6 The basis for world peace is the teaching which runs through almost all the great religions of the world. "Love thy neighbor as thyself."

Eleanor Roosevelt, US diplomat, author, and wife of the 32nd President, found in *Eleanor and Franklin* by J. P. Lash (NF)

7 Our religion is the traditions of our ancestors—the dreams of our old men, given them in solemn hours of night by the Great Spirit . . . and written in the hearts of our people.

Chief Seattle, leader of six Indian tribes in the Pacific Northwest, in an 1854 speech to Gov. Isaac Stevens, found in *The American Reader*, ed. by D. Ravitch (NF)

8 [If religion] does not teach [people] to be good and kind to man and beast, it is all a sham.*

Anna Sewell, English-American author, said by John Manley, *Black Beauty* (F)   *fake

9 Doubt is part of all religion. All the religious thinkers were doubters.

Isaac Bashevis Singer, Polish-American author, in the Dec. 3, 1978 issue of *The New York Times* (NF)

Respect

1 The creature had mourned [on the mountain top] for a thousand years, in isolation so splendid, and with sorrows so infinitely greater than any of their own, that the people were struck with awe and respect.

Natalie Babbitt, US author, *Knee-Knock Rise* (F)

2 This Indian—*his* Indian—was behaving in every way like a real Indian brave, and despite the vast differences in their sizes and strengths, Omri respected him.

Lynne Reid Banks, US author, *The Indian in the Cupboard* (F)

3 There's still a lot of respect [in America] for the flag and duty and honor.

George Bush, 41st US President, in the Dec. 1, 1996 *Parade* magazine (NF)

4 One must always treat guests with respect . . . even when they are as brainless as gulls.

Michael Dorris, Native American author and anthropologist, said by Morning Girl, *Morning Girl* (F)

5 [T]o animals, might is right. I was biggest and I was oldest, and I was going to tell them so. I growled and snarled and hissed and snorted. It worked. [The raccoons and skunk] understood and moved away.

Jean Craighead George, US author, thought by Sam Gribley, *My Side of the Mountain* (F)

6 The Porcupine, whom one must
      Handle, gloved,
   May be respected, but is never Loved.

Arthur Guiterman, US poet, *A Poet's Proverbs*

7 If you once forfeit the confidence of your fellow citizens, you can never regain their respect and esteem. It is true that you may fool all the people some of the time; you can even fool some of the people all of the time; but you can't fool all of the people all of the time.

Abraham Lincoln, 16th US President, in a Sept. 8, 1858 speech in Clinton, IL, found in *Lincoln: A Photobiography* by R. Freedman (NF)

8 Respect others if you want to be respected.

Philippine proverb

9　I am eager to learn from others. My father believed you could learn from "*Un peon o un presidente*" —a farm worker or a president—and you should respect both equally.

Blandina Cardenas Ramirez, Mexican-American member of the US Commission on Civil Rights, found in *Famous Mexican Americans* by Morey and Dunn (NF)

10　I had never cared about acceptance as much as I cared about respect.

Jackie Robinson, US professional baseball player, found in *Jackie Robinson: Baseball Great* by R. Scott (NF)

11　When [Derek the mouse] went out briefly into the world, he noted that his friends treated him with more respect, perhaps because he was behaving in a more respect-commanding way.

William Steig, US author, *The Real Thief* (F)

12　From my father the storyteller I learned to respect the past, to respect my own heritage and myself.

Mildred D. Taylor, US author, the Author's Note in *Roll of Thunder, Hear My Cry* (F)

13　You have to demand respect in this world, ain't nobody gonna hand it to you. How you carry yourself, what you stand for—that's how you gain respect.

Mildred D. Taylor, US author, said by Papa, *Roll of Thunder, Hear My Cry* (F)

Responsibility

1　I *must* accept my responsibility so as to prove to [the crew of the ship] that it had been my head that was wrong, not my heart.

Avi, US author, thought by Charlotte, *The True Confessions of Charlotte Doyle* (F)

2　Unto whomsoever much is given, of him shall much be required.

Bible, Luke 12:48 (KJV)

3　I have an awesome responsibility and many opportunities as First Lady.

Rosalyn Carter, wife of the 39th US President, found in *The President: America's Leader* by M. O. Johnson (NF)

4　My duty to my country comes first [before my family].

James L. Collier and Christopher Collier, US authors, said by Sam, *My Brother Sam Is Dead* (F)

5　A man can stand up.

Esther Forbes, US author, *Johnny Tremain* (F)

6　[I]f you're the baddest dude on the block, you've got responsibilities. If you got the weight, you got to take the freight.

Walter Dean Myers, US author, said by Stuff, *Fast Sam, Cool Clyde, and Stuff* (F)

7　UNLESS someone like you
　　cares a whole awful lot,
　　　nothing is going to get better.
　It's not.

Dr. Seuss, US author, *The Lorax* (F)

8 Why should not we, who are the leaders, settle the matter between us alone, so that the blood of our fine young men need not be shed in the fight which presents itself?

Tecumseh, Shawnee leader, said to Army Com. William Harrison in 1813, found in *Tecumseh* by R. Cwiklik (NF)

9 The buck stops here.

Harry S Truman, 33rd US President, a sign he kept on his desk

Revolutionary War
(1775–1783)
(See also War)

1 Yesterday the greatest question was decided . . . and a greater [question] perhaps never was nor will be decided among men. A resolution was passed without one dissenting colony "that these United Colonies are, and of right ought to be, free and independent states."

John Adams, 2nd US President, in a July 3, 1776 letter to his wife Abigail

2 You will see, in a few days, a Declaration setting forth the causes which have impelled* us to this mighty revolution, and the reasons which will justify it in the sight of God and man.

Ibid.   *driven

3 I am apt to believe that [the second day of July, 1776] will be celebrated by succeeding generations . . . with pomp and parade, with shows, games, sports, guns, bells, bonfires, and illuminations,* from one end of this continent to the other, from this time forward forevermore.

Ibid.   *fireworks

4 What a glorious morning for America!

Samuel Adams, Revolutionary patriot and statesman, when he first heard shots fired at the Battle of Lexington on Apr. 19, 1775

5 The said states hereby severally enter into a firm league of friendship with each other, for their common defence, the security of their Liberties, and their mutual and general welfare.

Articles of Confederation, Nov. 15, 1777

6 Then join hand in hand,
    brave Americans all,
By uniting we stand, by
    dividing we fall.

John Dickinson, Revolutionary patriot and writer, words to the song "The Liberty Song," written in 1768, found in *The American Reader*, ed. by D. Ravitch (NF)

7 By the rude bridge that arched the flood,
    Their flag to April's breeze unfurled,
Here once the embattled farmers stood,
    And fired the shot heard 'round the world.

Ralph Waldo Emerson, US writer and poet, "Concord Hymn," found in *The Faber Book of America*, ed. by Ricks and Vance (NF)

8 It was dawn. . . . [I]n Lexington on the Village Green the first shot [of the Revolutionary War] was fired. One shot and then a volley.

Esther Forbes, US author, *Johnny Tremain* (F)

9 The die is now cast; the colonies must either submit or triumph. . . . We must not retreat.

George III, King of England, in a Sept. 11, 1774 letter to Lord North

10 We fight, get beat, rise, and fight again.

Nathanael Greene, Revolutionary general, in an Apr. 1781 letter, written after the Battle of Hobkirk's Hill, SC

13 The war is actually begun! The next gale that sweeps from the north will bring to our ears the clash of resounding arms!
Ibid.

14 Listen, my children, and you
    shall hear
Of the midnight ride of Paul Revere,
On the eighteenth of April, in
    Seventy-five;
Hardly a man is now alive
Who remembers that famous day
    and year.

Henry Wadsworth Longfellow, US poet, "Paul Revere's Ride," found in *From Sea to Shining Sea*, comp. by A. L. Cohn

11 I only regret that I have but one life to lose for my country.

Nathan Hale, Revolutionary patriot, said before the British hanged him as a spy on Sept. 22, 1776

12 The battle, sir, is not to the strong alone; it is to the vigilant,* the active, the brave.

Patrick Henry, Revolutionary leader, in a Mar. 23, 1775 speech to the second Virginia Convention   *alert*

15 Don't tread on me.

Motto on the first official American flag, raised on the ship *Alfred* at Philadelphia on Dec. 3, 1775

16 Stand your ground. Don't fire unless fired upon, but if they mean to have a war, let it begin here.

Capt. John Parker, Revolutionary patriot, addressing his men at the Lexington Green on Apr. 19, 1775

17 Yankee Doodle went to town,
A-ridin' on a pony,
Stuck a feather in his cap
And called it Macaroni.*

Attributed to Robert Shuckburg, British Army doctor, words to the song "Yankee Doodle," found in *The Anderson Book of American Folk Tales and Songs*, coll. by A. Durell
decorations on uniforms

18 The fate of unborn millions will now depend, under God, on the courage and conduct of this army. Our cruel and unrelenting enemy leaves us only the choice of brave resistance, or the most abject* submission. We have, therefore, to resolve to conquer or die.

George Washington, Revolutionary general and then 1st US President, addressing the Continental Army before the Battle of Long Island on Aug. 27, 1776   *humiliating*

19 Nothing short of independence, it appears to me, can possibly do. A peace on other terms would . . . be a peace of war.

George Washington, Revolutionary general and later 1st US President, in an Apr. 21, 1778 letter to John Banister

20 The injuries we have received from the British nation were so unprovoked, and have been so great and so many, that they can never be forgotten.

Ibid.

Right and Wrong

1 If you're for the right thing, then you do it without thinking.

Maya Angelou, US poet and author, *I Know Why the Caged Bird Sings* (NF)

2 I had been educated to the belief that when I was wrong . . . it was *my* responsibility—mine alone—to admit *my* fault and make amends.

Avi, US author, said by Charlotte, *The True Confessions of Charlotte Doyle* (F)

3 [N]ever tire of doing what is right.

Bible, 2 Thessalonians 3:13 (NIV)

4 I leave this rule for others when I'm dead: Be always sure you're right—then go ahead.

Davy Crockett, US frontiersman and politician, *Autobiography* (NF)

5 When things around me are right, I forget to notice: I don't remember days that aren't too hot or too wet.

Michael Dorris, Native American author and anthropologist, said by Morning Girl, *Morning Girl* (F)

6 Two wrongs will not make one right.

English proverb

7 I seize every opportunity to try to right a wrong, whether it's in schools, stores, or anywhere black people are being disrespected.

Jesse Jackson, US civil rights activist, found in *Jesse Jackson* by A. Kosof (NF)

8 Let us have faith that Right makes Might, and in that faith, let us, to the end, dare to do our duty as we understand it.

Abraham Lincoln, 16th US President, in a Feb. 27, 1860 speech, found in *Lincoln: A Photobiography* by R. Freedman (NF)

9 Why couldn't someone come along and make things right—Wonder Woman or Superman.

Norma Fox Mazer, US author, *Taking Terri Mueller* (F)

10 [W]e can't just take things into our own hands because we've decided they're wrong. We have to live by the rules, even when those rules don't always seem right.

Walt Morey, US author, said by Mark's father, *Gentle Ben* (F)

11 Crying is feeling . . . ain't nothing wrong with that.

Walter Dean Myers, US author, said by Sam, *Fast Sam, Cool Clyde, and Stuff* (F)

12 I'm thinking how nothing is as simple as you guess—not right or wrong.

Phyllis Reynolds Naylor, US author, said by Marty, *Shiloh* (F)

13 [Pa] didn't think it was right for him to go and kill other men over something that didn't matter one way or the other to him.

Carolyn Reeder, US author, said by Meg, *Shades of Gray* (F)

14 My doctrine* is this, that if we see cruelty or wrong that we have the power to stop, and do nothing, we make ourselves sharers in that guilt.

Anna Sewell, English-American author, said by an unnamed friend, *Black Beauty* (F)   *belief

15 [W]hoever has done a wrong deed and thinks that no one knows it, deceives himself.

Johanna Spyri, Swiss author, said by Mrs. Sesemann, *Heidi* (F)

16 It had been simple to have Daddy and Mama tell [Jade Snow] what was right and wrong; it was not simple to decide for herself.

Jade Snow Wong, Chinese-American author, *Fifth Chinese Daughter* (NF)

Rivers

(See Nature)

Sadness

1 I wish I had no heart, it aches so.

> Louisa May Alcott, US author, said by Meg, *Little Women* (F)

2 I think you are wrong to want a heart. It makes most people unhappy.

> L. Frank Baum, US author, said by the Wizard of Oz to the Tin Woodman, *The Wonderful Wizard of Oz* (F)

3 This morning's sermon reminded us that *great* though our grief and suffering be, others have suffered more.

> Joan W. Blos, US author, written by Catherine Cabot Hall, *A Gathering of Days* (F)

4 I have wept over my big feet and my skinny legs and my nose, I have even cried over my stupid shoes, and now when I have a true sadness there are no tears left.

> Betsy Byars, US author, said by Sara, *The Summer of the Swans* (F)

5 There's more sadness in [your mama's dying] than you and I have got tears to cry for it. But life's full of good things, too.

> Cynthia DeFelice, US author, said by Pa, *Weasel* (F)

6 After the death of my second husband, terrible grief came over me. But only then did I even begin to understand how young chimps can pine away* and die when they lose their mothers.

> Jane Goodall, English-American wildlife expert and author, found in *Jane Goodall: Naturalist* by J. A. Senn (NF)

> **slowly die from sadness*

7 The sadness [over my brother's death] was so vast and heavy, it filled up all the space in our house, suffocating everyone.

> Mary Downing Hahn, US author, thought by Margaret, *Stepping on the Cracks* (F)

8 [I]f you've been up all night and cried till you have no more tears left in you—you will know that there comes in the end a sort of quietness.

> C. S. Lewis, English author, *The Lion, the Witch, and the Wardrobe* (F)

9 Being sad means something bad is happening to you, like you're lonely, or something like that. Then you feel bad and that's kind of sad.

> Walter Dean Myers, US author, *Won't Know Till I Get There* (F)

10 If you've ever been sad, *really* sad, you know what I'm talking about. Sadness is with you all the time. Even when your friends are trying to make you laugh, sadness seems to be waiting right behind your smile.

Barbara Parks, US author, said by Howard, *The Kid in the Red Jacket* (F)

11 Whenever I feel like crying,
    I smile hard instead!
    I turn my sadness upside down
        and stand it on its head!

David Saltzman, US author and illustrator, said by the Jester, *The Jester Has Lost His Jingle* (F)

12 [Chester Cricket] began to chirp to ease his feelings. He found that it helped somehow if you sang your sadness.

George Selden, US author, *The Cricket in Times Square* (F)

13 When one had a sorrow that cannot be told to anybody on earth, it must be confided in God . . . for He can make our sorrows lighter, and teach us to bear them.

Johanna Spyri, Swiss author, said by Mrs. Sesemann, *Heidi* (F)

14 The bitterest tears shed over graves are for words left unsaid and deeds left undone.

Harriet Beecher Stowe, US author, *Little Foxes* (F)

15 I have born [thirteen] children, and seen em mos all sold off into slavery, and when I cried out with a mother's grief, none but Jesus heard.

Sojourner Truth, US civil rights activist, said in a speech at the 1851 Ohio Women's Rights Convention, found in *Great Lives: Human Rights* by W. J. Jacobs (NF)

16 One doesn't know another's sorrow.
Yiddish proverb

School

(See also Education, Learning, *and* Teachers*)*

1 No more pencils, no more books,
    No more teachers' dirty looks,
    No more things that bring us sorrow,
    For we won't be here come tomorrow.

Anonymous folk poetry, found in *And the Green Grass Grew All Around*, comp. by A. Schwartz

2 If a child comes to school hungry, the best school in the world won't help.

> Arthur Ashe, US professional tennis player, in the June 28, 1991 issue of the *USA Weekend* magazine (NF)

3 Maybe all the kids [at the next school] would hate me. Maybe I'd hate them. Maybe we'd hate each other.

> Judy Blume, US author, said by Peter Hatcher, *Superfudge* (F)

4 I remember I used never to be able to get along at school. I don't know what it was, but I was always at the foot of the class.

> Thomas Edison, US inventor, found in *The Thomas A. Edison Album* by L. F. Frost (NF)

5 It's now definite: there's no more school. The war has interrupted our lessons, closed down the schools, sent the children to cellars instead of classrooms.

> Zlata Filipovic, Sarajevian diarist, *Zlata's Diary*, May 17, 1992 entry (NF)

6 The first three years of school were wonderful. After that, it was the abyss* until I got into high school, where it became wonderful again.

> Madeleine L'Engle, US author, in the Jan. 1992 *Biography Today* (NF) *nothing

7 [W]hen you have a mother who's an angel and a father who is a cannibal king, and when you have sailed on the ocean all your whole life, then you don't know just how to behave in school.

> Astrid Lindgren, Swedish author, said by Pippi, *Pippi Longstocking* (F)

8 Close the barbecue.
Close the sun.
Close the home-run games we won.

Close the picnic.
Close the pool.

Close the summer.

Open school.

> Prince Redcloud, "Now," found in *The Sky Is Full of Song*, sel. by L. B. Hopkins

9 School just speeds things up. . . . Without school it might take another seventy years before you wake up and are able to count.

> Louis Sachar, US author, said by Mrs. Jewls, *Sideways Stories from Wayside School* (F)

10 At school I felt like a real nerd, the nerd of the block. The skinny acne-faced wimpy kind of kid who gets pushed around by big football jocks and picked on all the way home from school.

> Steven Spielberg, US movie director and producer, in the Jan. 1994 *Biography Today* (NF)

11 Monday morning found Tom Sawyer miserable. Monday morning always found him so—because it began another week's slow suffering in school.

> Mark Twain, US author, *The Adventures of Tom Sawyer* (F)

12 [When I was a slave,] I had the feeling that to get into a schoolhouse and study . . . would be about the same as getting into paradise.

> Booker T. Washington, US educator and author, *Up from Slavery* (NF)

Science

1 When a distinguished but elderly scientist states that something is possible, he is almost certainly right. When he states that something is impossible, he is very probably wrong.

Arthur C. Clark, English science-fiction author, *Profiles of the Future* (NF)

2 Matthew thinks about how science used to be so much easier to understand, how it was just one subject to study, and now it involves history, geography, math, and lots of other things.

Paula Danziger, US author, *Earth to Matthew* (F)

3 Better things for better living through chemistry.

Du Pont advertising slogan

4 When you are courting* a nice girl, an hour seems like a second. When you sit on a red-hot cinder, a second seems like an hour. That's relativity.

Albert Einstein, German-American physicist, in the Mar. 14, 1949 issue of the *New Chronicle* (NF)   *dating*

5 Science is a wonderful thing if one does not have to earn one's living at it.

Albert Einstein, German-American physicist, in a Mar. 24, 1951 letter to a California student

6 The whole of science is nothing more than a refinement of everyday thinking.

Albert Einstein, German-American physicist, *Out of My Later Years* (NF)

7 I liked it better when science didn't come so close to home. When it fit neatly inside a textbook, with five questions at the end of each chapter.

Karen Hesse, US author, thought by Nyle, *Phoenix Rising* (F)

8 We especially need imagination in science. It is not all mathematics, nor all logic, but it is somewhat beauty and poetry.

Maria Mitchell, US author, *Maria Mitchell: Life, Letters, and Journals* (NF)

9 Science is a joy. It is not just something for an isolated, remote elite. It is our birthright.

Carl Sagan, US astronomer and author, found in *Contemporary Heroes and Heroines*, ed. by R. B. Browne (NF)

10 What's interesting to me about [the movie *Jurassic Park*] is there is as much science as there is adventures and thrills.

Steven Spielberg, US movie director and producer, in the Jan. 1994 *Biography Today* (NF)

11 [Y]ou wouldn't expect a dumb subject like math or social studies to be interesting. But science could be fun. I mean, we could do experiments, like make bombs or something.

Todd Strasser, US author, said by Jake, *Help! I'm Trapped in My Teacher's Body* (F)

12 If you go into science, you must realize you are doing it for your own interest, not glory or fame. . . . You must think science is most important.

Samuel C. C. Ting, Chinese-American physicist, found in *Famous Asian Americans* by Morey and Dunn (NF)

13 [S]cientists must go beyond what is taught in the textbook, and they must think independently. Also, they cannot hesitate to ask questions, even when their view may be unpopular.

Ibid.

Sea Life

1 Six slippery seals slipping silently ashore.

Anonymous tongue twister, found in *A Twister of Twists, a Tangler of Tongues*, coll. by A. Schwartz

2 So God created the great creatures of the sea and every living and moving thing with which the water teems, according to their kinds.

Bible, Genesis 1:21 (NIV)

3 Why, if a fish came to *me*, and told me he was going on a journey, I would say "With what porpoise?"

Lewis Carroll, English author, said by the Mock Turtle, *Alice's Adventures in Wonderland* (F)

4 The fish that escaped is the big one.

Chinese proverb

5 [The whale] is bigger than a five-storied house, and . . . his mouth is so enormous and so deep that a railroad with its smoking engine would pass easily down his throat.

Carlo Collodi, Italian author, said by Dolphin, *The Adventures of Pinocchio* (F)

6 The dolphin can change color too— from deep blue to violet, red, yellow, and silvery white.

Erik Hesselberg, Norwegian associate of Thor Heyerdahl, *Kon-Tiki and I* (NF)

7 It's good luck to throw back the first fish of the season.

Mavis Jukes, US author, said by Austin, *Blackberries in the Dark* (F)

8 [The Whale] ate the starfish and the garfish, and the crab and the dab, and the plaice and the dace, and the skate and his mate, and the mackereel and the pickereel, and the really truly twirly-whirly eel.

Rudyard Kipling, English-American journalist and author, "How the Whale Got His Throat" from *Just So Stories* (F)

9 [Seals] are cool and slippery and they slide through the water like fish. They can cry and sing. And sometimes they bark, a little like dogs.

Patricia MacLachlan, US author, said by Sarah, *Sarah, Plain and Tall* (F)

10 I don't mind eels
Except as meals.
And the way they feels.

Ogden Nash, US poet, "The Eel" from *Custard and Company*, sel. by Q. Blake

11 Dolphins are animals of good omen. . . . I was very lonely before they appeared, but now I felt that I had friends with me.

Scott O'Dell, US author, said by Won-a-pa-lei (Karana), *Island of the Blue Dolphins* (F)

12 From the coasts of Scotland and northern New England come legends of seals who live among us, in human form. They are called *selkies*, these people of the sea.

Sylvia Peck, US author, said by Molly, *Seal Child* (F)

13 You have to be *out* of the sea really to know how good it is to be *in* it. . . . That is, if you're a whale.

William Steig, US author, said by a whale named Boris, *Amos and Boris* (F)

Seasons

1 Button to the chin,
Autumn's coming in.

Anonymous folk poetry, found in *And the Green Grass Grew All Around*, comp. by A. Schwartz

2 Even the seasons form a great circle in their changing, and always come back again to where they were.

Black Elk, member of the Oglala Sioux, found in *American Indian Voices*, ed. by K. Harvey (NF)

3 As my eyes
Search the prairie,
I feel the summer in the spring.

Chippewa, North American Indian tribe, found in *The Trees Stand Shining*, sel. by Hettie Jones

4 Spring is a wondrous necessity.

Vera and Bill Cleaver, US authors, said by Mary Call, *Where the Lilies Bloom* (F)

5 Spring is showery, flowery, bowery.
Summer: hoppy, choppy, poppy.
Autumn: wheezy, sneezy, freezy.
Winter: slippy, drippy, nippy.

"Four Seasons," anonymous poem, found in *The BFC Young Book of Poetry*, sel. by B. Mathias

6 I always like summer best
you can eat fresh corn . . .
and go barefooted
and be warm
all the time.

Nikki Giovanni, US poet, "Knoxville, Tennessee" from *Black Judgement*

7 No animal, according to the rules of animal-etiquette, is ever expected to do anything strenuous, or heroic, or even moderately active during the off-season of winter.

Kenneth Grahame, English author, *The Wind in the Willows* (F)

8 Autumn was blithely indifferent to the tumult in the land that year. Color splashed through the woods as if it had been thrown about by some madcap wastrel* who spilled out, during the weeks of one brief autumn, beauty enough to last for years.

Irene Hunt, US author, *Across Five Aprils* (F) *sprendthrift

9 Everything is good in its season.
Italian proverb

10 [Ariel] always watched for the geese; she almost believed that spring couldn't start until she'd heard them.

Natalie Kinsey-Warnock, US author, *The Canadian Geese Quilt* (F)

11 Is it robin o'clock?
Is it five after wing?
Is it quarter to leaf?
Is it nearly time for spring?

Eve Merriam, US poet, from *Blackberry Ink*

12 Sing a song of seasons!
Something bright in all!
Flowers in the summer,
Fires in the fall!

Robert Louis Stevenson, English poet, "Autumn Fires" from *A Child's Garden of Verses*

13 The days are short,
　The sun a spark
　Hung thin between
　The dark and the dark.

John Updike, US author, "January" from *A Child's Calendar*

14 [The Giant] did not hate the Winter now, for he knew that it was merely the Spring asleep, and that the flowers were resting.

Oscar Wilde, Irish poet and playwright, "The Selfish Giant," found in *The Book of Virtues*, ed. by W. J. Bennett (F)

15 We remember not the summer
　For it was long ago.
　We remember not the summer
　In this whirling blinding snow.
　I will leave this frozen region,
　I will travel farther south.
　If you say one word against it,
　I will hit you in the mouth.

Laura Ingalls Wilder, US author, written when she was 14 years old, found in *Laura Ingalls Wilder: A Biography* by W. Anderson (NF)

16 Don't you love it in the summer when it's so hot you can hardly move and you lie in the shade outside and you watch the clouds move and someone tells a slow story?

Vera Williams, US author, said by Elana Rosen, *Scooter* (F)

Secrets

1 Touch my heart,
　Touch my knee,
　This shall forever
　A secret be.

Anonymous American folk poem, found in *I Saw Esau*, ed. by I. and P. Opie

2 [The moon] rocks around us [were] unchanged throughout the history of man—whose three-billion-year-old secrets made them the treasures we sought.

Neil A. Armstrong, US astronaut, in a Sept. 16, 1969 speech to Congress

3 A gossip betrays a confidence, but a trustworthy man keeps a secret.

Bible, Proverbs 11:13 (NIV)

4 I had learned . . . that there are no secrets unless you keep them yourself, and this was the greatest secret I had ever had to keep in my life so far.

Roald Dahl, English author, *Roald Dahl, My Year* (NF)

5 If you would keep your Secret from an enemy, tell it not to a friend.

Benjamin Franklin, Revolutionary statesman, the 1741 *Poor Richard's Almanack* (NF)

6 Thomas admired the house for keeping [its secrets] so long.

Virginia Hamilton, US author, *The House of Dies Drear* (F)

7 [A]fter a time having a secret and nobody knowing you have a secret is not fun. And although you don't want others to know what the secret is, you want them to at least know you have one.

E. L. Konigsburg, US author and illustrator, *From the Mixed-up Files of Mrs. Basil E. Frankweiler* (F)

8 A secret of only one person after a while gets too hard to keep. To make it real, you have to tell someone else. . . . Otherwise, all you got left is just one small, dried-up secret that's not worth anything.

Joseph Krumgold, US author, thought by Miguel, . . . *And Now Miguel* (F)

9 The moment I picked up that box I could tell by the pricking in my fingers that I held some great secret in my hands.

C. S. Lewis, English author, said by Uncle Andrew, *Chronicles of Narnia: The Magician's Nephew* (F)

10 I had never wanted to know anybody's secrets—not Mother's, not Pop's. *Don't tell me*, that's what I used to say. I guess the secret I never wanted to find out was that life can be so hard.

Cynthia Rylant, US author, thought by Pete, *A Fine White Dust* (F)

11 [H]ere is my secret, a very simple secret: It is only with the heart that one can see rightly; what is essential is invisible to the eye.

Antoine de Saint-Exupéry, French author and illustrator, said by the fox, *The Little Prince* (F)

12 He who tells his own secret will hardly keep another's.

Spanish proverb

Senses
(See Smells and Sounds)

Sickness

1 I've scratched the measles, itched the pox,
The mumps, they made me drool.
They weren't no fun, not any one—
But they got me out of school!

Anonymous poem, found in *A Nonny Mouse Writes Again!,* sel. by J. Prelutsky

2 [Tinker Bell] was saying that she thought she could get well again if children believed in fairies.

J. M. Barrie, Scottish author, *Peter Pan* (F)

3 My stomach was doing dipsy-doodles and back flips.

Tom Birdseye, US author, said by Ryan, *Tarantula Shoes* (F)

4 [A heart attack is] bad enough to make a lion look like a turtle, I reckon.

Bruce Brooks, US author, said by Dooley, *Everywhere* (F)

5 You must know that wooden puppets have the privilege of being seldom ill and of being cured very quickly.

Carlo Collodi, Italian author, said by the Fairy, *The Adventures of Pinocchio* (F)

6 Health is not valued until sickness comes.

English proverb

7 [Harriet] managed to convince her mother that she was just about to come down with a terrible cold, the type of cold that could be nipped in the bud by only one little day home from school. There is, of course, no kind of a cold in the world like this.

Louise Fitzhugh, US author, *Harriet the Spy* (F)

8 [I]t is from despair that all your ailments have come. . . . And hope is always the best medicine.

Mollie Hunter, Scottish author, said by Howdy, *The Mermaid Summer* (F)

9 Sometimes I have hiccups and on Sunday I didn't feel very well after having eaten a dish of shoe polish and milk. . . . It must be the spink* which bothers me.

Astrid Lindgren, Swedish author, said by Pippi, *Pippi in the South Seas* (F)   * a word made up by Pippi

10 Teenagers are getting flabby, it's a national health problem.

Norma Fox Mazer, US author, said by Rachel, *After the Rain* (F)

11 I had a series of childhood illnesses. The first was scarlet fever. Then I had pneumonia. Polio followed. I walked with braces until I was at least nine years old. My life wasn't like the average person who grew up and decided to enter the world of sports.

Wilma Rudolph, US track star, in the Aug. 6, 1987 issue of *USA Today* (NF)

12 "I cannot go to school today,"
    Said little Peggy Ann McKay.
    "I have the measles and the mumps.
    A gash, a rash and purple bumps."

Shel Silverstein, US poet and illustrator, "Sick" from *Where the Sidewalk Ends*

13 Very sick people seem to . . . depart from themselves, from the people who love them. They make their way back very slowly. Some . . . just journey on and never do return.

Mary Stolz, US author, said by Mr. Emerson, *Quentin Corn* (F)

14 No one had a spare broomstick, so I had to fly home on a borrowed rake. . . . It's the only time in my life I've been airsick.

Patricia C. Wrede, US author, said by the witch Morwen, *Calling on Dragons* (F)

Singing

(See also Music)

1 An opera star named Maria
    Always tried to sing higher and higher,
        Till she hit a high note
        Which got stuck in her throat—
    Then she entered the Heavenly Choir.

Anonymous limerick, found in *Laughable Limericks*, comp. by S. and J. Brewton

2 Sing me a song of sneakers and
        snoopers:
    Snookers and sneapers and snappers
        and snacks,
    snorkels and snarkles, a seagull
        that gargles,
    and gargoyles and gryphons and other
        knickknacks.

N. M. Bodecker, "Sing Me a Song of Teapots and Trumpets," found in *The Random House Book of Poetry for Children*, sel. by J. Prelutsky

3 [Alyce's] song brightened the cold gray day so that a cowbird thought it was spring and began to sing in the old oak tree.

Karen Cushman, US author, *The Midwife's Apprentice* (F)

4 Slaves sing most when they are most unhappy. The songs of the slave represent the sorrows of his heart.

Frederick Douglass, US abolitionist and author, *Escape from Slavery*, ed. by M. McCurdy (NF)

5 Who cannot sing may whistle.

German proverb

6 I remember when I was about twelve . . . I'd close my eyes and sing all by myself, and imagine I was on stage singing to a packed house.

Whitney Houston, US singer and actress, in the Sept. 1994 *Biography Today* (NF)

7 Tonight is the night all the dragons
Awake in their lairs underground,
To sing in cacophonous* chorus
And fill the whole world with their
   sound. . . .
Some of their voices are treble,
And some of their voices are deep,
But all of their voices are thunderous,
And no one can get any sleep.

Jack Prelutsky, US poet, "The Dragons Are Singing Tonight" from *The Dragons Are Singing Tonight*
*having a harsh, unpleasant sound

Sisters

(*See* Brothers and Sisters)

Slavery

(*See also* Civil Rights *and* Equality)

1 Dogs and monkeys can ride first class [on trains] . . . but not Frederick Douglass.

Margaret Davidson, US author, said by a friend of Douglass's, found in *Frederick Douglass Fights* (NF)

2 No man can put a chain about the ankle of his fellow man without at last finding the other end fastened about his own neck.

Frederick Douglass, US abolitionist and author, in an Oct. 22, 1883 speech in Washington, D.C.

3 The more I read, the more I was led to abhor* and detest my enslavers. I could regard them in no other light than a band of successful robbers, who had . . . gone to Africa, and stolen us from our homes, and in a strange land reduced us to slavery.

Frederick Douglass, abolitionist and author, *Escape from Slavery*, ed. by M. McCurdy (NF)   *hate

4 A slave has no choice.

Egyptian proverb

5 You can be sure that [the British] wouldn't have passed laws against slaving if they hadn't found something else as profitable. That's the way of things.

Paula Fox, US author, said by Purvis, *The Slave Dancer* (F)

6 Harriet Tubman didn't take no stuff
Wasn't scared of nothing neither
Didn't come in this world to be no slave
And wasn't going to stay one either.

Eloise Greenfield, US author and poet, "Harriet Tubman," found in *From Sea to Shining Sea*, comp. by A. L. Cohn

7 [T]here ain't a white man, lean-bellied and hopeless as so many of them are, that would change lots with a slave belongin' to the kindest master in the South.

Irene Hunt, US author, said by John Creighton, *Across Five Aprils* (F)

8 Hate come over me strong today. I dont want to hear the preacher talk anymore bout hell, becaus I already been there.

Harriet A. Jacobs, US author, found in *Letters from a Slave Girl* by M. E. Lyons (F)

9 Whenever I hear anyone arguing for slavery, I feel a strong impulse to see it tried on him personally.

Abraham Lincoln, 16th US President, in a Mar. 17, 1865 speech to an IN regiment

10 Slavery was a kind of legal robbery. Slaveholders, instead of paying their workers, simply stole their labor.

Michele Stepto, US author and editor, *Our Song, Our Toil* (NF)

11 I was a conductor of the Underground Railroad for eight years, and I can say what most conductors can't say—I never ran my train off the track and I never lost a passenger.

Harriet Tubman, US abolitionist and liberator of about 300–400 slaves, found in *Women's Words: The Columbia Book of Quotations by Women* by M. Biggs (NF)

12 I vividly remember seeing a dozen black men and women chained to one another, once, and lying in a group on the pavement, awaiting shipment to the Southern slave market. Those were the saddest faces I have ever seen.

Mark Twain, US author, *Autobiography* (NF)

13 I could clearly foresee that nothing but rooting out of slavery can perpetuate* the existence of our union.

George Washington, 1st US President, said to a friend after the Revolutionary War, found in *George Washington* by R. Bruns (NF) *prolong

Sleep

1 Good night, sleep tight,
  Don't let the bedbugs bite.

Anonymous folk poetry, found in *And the Green Grass Grew All Around*, comp. by A. Schwartz

2 Now I lay me down to sleep,
  I pray the Lord my soul to keep.
  If I should die before I wake,
  I pray the Lord my soul to take.

Anonymous prayer, originally published in the 1781 *New England Primer*

3 "Good night, little girls!
  Thank the lord you are well!
  And now go to sleep!"
  said Miss Clavel.

Ludwig Bemelmans, Austrian-American illustrator and author, *Madeline* (F)

4 I will lie down and sleep in peace, for you alone, O Lord, make me dwell in safety.

Bible, Psalm 4:8 (NIV)

5 Early to Bed, and early to rise,
  Makes a Man healthy, wealthy,
    and wise.

Benjamin Franklin, Revolutionary statesman, the 1758 *Poor Richard's Almanack* (NF)

6 The worst of sleeping out of doors is that you wake up so dreadfully early.

C. S. Lewis, English author, *Prince Caspian* (F)

7 You lose such a lot of time just sleeping . . . when you might just be living! . . . It seems such a pity we can't live nights too.

Eleanor H. Porter, US author, said by Pollyanna, *Pollyanna* (F)

8 A yawn is quite catching, you see.
  Like a cough.
  It just takes one yawn to
    start other yawns off.

Dr. Seuss, US author, *Sleep Book* (F)

9 They're sleeping in bushes.
  They're sleeping in crannies.
  Some on their stomachs,
    and some on their fannies.

Ibid.

10 He that sleeps much,
learns little.

Spanish proverb

11 [Princess Miserella, Jane, and the fairy] slept through three and a half wars, one plague, six new kings, the invention of the sewing machine, and the discovery of a new continent.

Jane Yolen, US author, *Sleeping Ugly* (F)

Smells

1 At first I think [the empty inside of the box] smells like wood, and then I smell all the rest—a young farmer's stubbornness, a pioneer mother's sorrow, and a wondrous wild and lasting hope.

Pam Conrad, US author, said by the granddaughter of Spencer McClintic, "Hattie's Birthday Box," found in *Birthday Surprises*, ed. by J. Hurwitz (F)

2 [Brat] passed through the forest of bright booths with flags and pennants flying. . . . Her nostrils quivered at the smells of roasting meats and fresh hot bread and pies stuffed with pork and raisins, but . . . she was content just to smell.

Karen Cushman, US author, *The Midwife's Apprentice* (F)

3 All of the most wonderful smells in the world seemed mixed up in the air around them [in the chocolate factory]—the smell of roasting coffee and burnt sugar and melting chocolate and mint and violets and crushed hazelnuts and apple blossom and caramel and lemon peel.

Roald Dahl, English author, *Charlie and the Chocolate Factory* (F)

4 The smell of that buttered toast simply talked to Toad, and with no uncertain voice; talked of warm kitchens, of breakfasts on bright frosty mornings, of cozy parlour firesides on winter evenings.

Kenneth Grahame, English author, *The Wind in the Willows* (F)

5 Even a bad smell is found in sweet places.

Hawaiian proverb

6 The death smell flowed out—strong, and sweetly horrible, like a rotting animal under a summer rosebush.

Jan Hudson, Canadian author, said by Sweetgrass, *Sweetgrass* (F)

7 There is a certain odor in the room and not elsewhere in the house, the odor of my great-grandmother's old age. It is not unpleasant, but it is most particular and exclusive, as much hers as is her voice or her hair or the nails on her hands.

N. Scott Momaday, Native American poet and author, "Keahdinekeah" from *The Names* (NF)

8 Mama put her face right down close to mine, and I could smell her goodness.

Robert Newton Peck, US author, said by Rob, *A Day No Pigs Would Die* (F)

9 [W]hen you kill pigs for a living, you can't always smell like Sunday morning. You just smell like hard work.

Ibid.

10 I kept the sneakers outside in the garage. . . . [Mom] says the smell would make an elephant faint.

Donald J. Sobol, US author, said by Phoebe, "The Case of the Disgusting Sneakers" from *Encyclopedia Brown and The Case of the Disgusting Sneakers* (F)

11 Through all the frozen winter
My nose has grown most lonely
For lovely, lovely colored smells
That come in springtime only.

Kathryn Worth, US poet, "Smells," found in *The Random House Book of Poetry*, sel. by J. Prelutsky

12 All of the caves smelled of dragon, a somewhat musty, smoky, cinnamony smell.

Patricia C. Wrede, US author, *Dealing with Dragons* (F)

Sorrow

(See Sadness*)*

Sounds

1 What? Rescue a hundred princesses? Not likely! Just think of the chattering and giggling and gabbling—the very thought of it made [Dan's] head buzz.

Joan Aiken, English author, "Think of a Word" from *The Last Slice of Rainbow* (F)

2 Sounds often terrify more than realities.

American proverb

3 [The creature] moaned like a lonely demon, like a mad, despairing animal, like a huge and anguished something chained forever to its own great tragic disappointments.

Natalie Babbitt, US author, *Knee-Knock Rise* (F)

4 Honk shoe! Honk shoe! That's what Dad says when he sleeps.

Tom Birdseye, US author, said by Justin, *Tarantula Shoes* (F)

5 In that snowy wilderness [Lucy's] scream sounded thin, like a rabbit struck by a hawk.

    Carol Carrick, US author, *Stay Away from Simon!* (F)

6 The BFG [Big Friendly Giant] can hear the tread of a ladybug's footsteps as she walks across a leaf. He can hear the whisper of ants as they scurry around in the soil talking to one another. He can hear the sudden shrill cry of pain a tree gives out when a woodman cuts into it with an ax.

    Roald Dahl, English author, said by Danny's father, *Danny, The Champion of the World* (F)

7 [T]he clock would come to life, whirring and singing and striking the hour in a way that filled the whole household with joy.

    E. T. A. Hoffmann, German author, *Nutcracker* (F)

8 It was the noise [of the tiger's humming purr] that bewilders woodcutters and gipsies sleeping in the open, and makes them run sometimes into the very mouth of the tiger.

    Rudyard Kipling, English-American journalist and author, *The Jungle Book* (F)

9 A stubborn voice is loud. . . . A trusting voice can speak softly and still be heard.

    E. L. Konigsburg, US author and illustrator, said by Antonio, "In the Village of the Weavers" from *Throwing Shadows* (F)

10 New sounds to
walk on
today—

dry
leaves,
talking
in hoarse
whispers,
under bare trees.

    Lilian Moore, US poet, "New Sounds," found in *The Sky Is Full of Song*, sel. by L. B. Hopkins

11 The reason Mr. and Mrs. Neal did not know their pets could talk was that, when Marco and Polo conversed, it sounded like meowing. They could meow in hundreds of different ways that the Neals could not distinguish at all: soft and loud; short and long; wavy meows; sharp meows; meows that started out high and got low; meows that started out low and got high. Plus seventy-six different kinds of purrs.

    Phyllis Reynolds Naylor, US author, *The Great Escape* (F)

12 The moose bugled. . . . Bugling is a noise that no animal except a moose can really do right. . . . When the moose bugled, the whole house jumped and rattled, dishes clinked together in the cupboard, pots and pans clanged together, icicles fell off the house.

    Daniel Manus Pinkwater, US author and illustrator, *Blue Moose and Return of the Moose* (F)

13 [The mysterious sound] was like a quick stroke across the strings of a violin, or like a harp that had been plucked suddenly. If a leaf in a green forest far from New York had fallen at midnight through the darkness into a thicket, it might have sounded like that.

George Selden, US author, *The Cricket in Times Square* (F)

14 "Their mouths will hang open a
    minute or two
"Then the *Whos* down in *Who*-ville
    will all cry BOO-HOO!
"That's a noise," grinned the Grinch,
"That I simply MUST hear!"

Dr. Seuss, US author, *How the Grinch Stole Christmas* (F)

15 Oh
CRASH!
my
BASH!
it's
BANG!
the
ZANG!
Fourth
WHOOSH!
of
BAROOOM!
July
WHEW!

Shel Silverstein, US poet and illustrator, "The Fourth" from *Where the Sidewalk Ends*

16 [Matt] had grown used to the stillness. In fact he knew now that the forest is rarely quiet. As he tramped through it he was accompanied by the chirruping of birds, the chatter of squirrels, and the whine and twang of thousands of bothersome insects.

Elizabeth George Speare, US author, *The Sign of the Beaver* (F)

Space Exploration

1 Tranquility Base here. The Eagle has landed.

Neil A. Armstrong, US astronaut, the first words from the moon on July 20, 1969

2 That's one small step for a man, one giant leap for mankind.

Neil A. Armstrong, US astronaut, said as he took the first step onto the moon on July 20, 1969

3 Some people tell me that we've missed out on the golden age of spaceflight, but I disagree. I think that golden age is just beginning.

Mike Fincke, US astronaut who was chosen by NASA in 1996 to be one of the first 21st century astronauts, in the June 29, 1997 *Parade* magazine (NF)

4 I believe that this nation should commit itself to achieving a goal, before this decade is out, of landing a man on the moon and returning him safely to the earth.

John F. Kennedy, 35th US President, in a May 24, 1961 speech to Congress

5 Many years ago the great British explorer George Mallory . . . was asked why did he want to climb [Mt. Everest]. He said, "Because it is there." Well, space is there, and we're going to climb it, and the moon and the planets are there, and new hopes for knowledge and peace are there.

John F. Kennedy, 35th US President, in a Sept. 12, 1962 speech at Rice University

2 Spelling was never my strong point and I'm still not very good at it. But the school did its best. Every word that was spelled wrongly in an essay had to be written out correctly a hundred times after work.

Roald Dahl, English author, *Roald Dahl, My Year* (NF)

3 Take care that you never spell a word wrong . . . and if you do not remember it, turn to a dictionary.

Thomas Jefferson, 3rd US President, in a 1783 letter to his daughter Martha

4 When Milo looked up he saw an enormous bee, at least twice his size. . . . "I am the Spelling Bee. . . . Don't be alarmed— a-l-a-r-m-e-d."

Norton Juster, US author, *The Phantom Tollbooth* (F)

5 [M]y spelling is Wobbly. It's good spelling but it Wobbles, and the letters get in the wrong places.

A. A. Milne, English author, said by Winnie-the-Pooh, "Eeyore Has a Birthday" from *Winnie-the-Pooh* (F)

6 [Y]ou can't help respecting anybody who can spell TUESDAY, even if he doesn't spell it right.

A. A. Milne, English author, said by Rabbit, "Rabbit's Busy Day" from *The House at Pooh Corner* (F)

6 I want to be the first to walk on Mars.

Christopher "Gus" Loria, US astronaut who was chosen by NASA in 1996 to be one of the first 21st century astronauts, in the June 29, 1997 *Parade* magazine (NF)

7 Advanced civilizations—if they exist— aren't breaking their backs to save us before we destroy ourselves.

Carl Sagan, US astronomer and author, in the June 1978 *American Way* magazine (NF)

8 [T]he planet down below us was listed as *unexplored* on our charts.

Robert Silverberg, US author, said by Gus, "Collecting Team" from *Science Fiction Bestiary* (F)

Spelling

1 I'm greatly desirous of reading [your journal]. . . . But mind, I shall be on the lookout for spelling mistakes!

Avi, US author, said by Charlotte's father, *The True Confessions of Charlotte Doyle* (F)

7 I consider it a very fine thing to spell words correctly and I strongly urge every one of you [students] to buy a *Webster's Collegiate Dictionary* and consult it whenever you are in the slightest doubt. So much for spelling.

E. B. White, US author, said by the mouse Stuart, *Stuart Little* (F)

Sports

(See also Baseball, Basketball, Football, *and* Winning and Losing*)*

1 I started boxing because I thought this was the fastest way for a black person to make it in this country.

Muhammad Ali, US professional boxer, found in *Words to Make My Dream Children Live*, ed. by D. Mullane (NF)

2 Sports is a major part of American life.

Avi, US author, said by Mr. Lester, *S.O.R. Losers* (F)

3 As for our guys [on the soccer team] . . . they were doing one of four things: standing around, running the wrong way, backing up furiously, or falling down.

Ibid.

4 I like when people are watching. What's the reason for figure skating without spectators?

Oksana Baiul, Ukrainian figure skater, found in *Women in Sports* by J. Layden (NF)

5 I'm really into violence. . . . I think hockey's a great game. It's a lot bloodier than football, and there are more team fights.

Judy Blume, US author, said by Jimmy Fargo, *Superfudge* (F)

6 As they say in sports, "If you win the world championship by one point, you're still the world champion."

Bill Bradley, US professional basketball player and senator, in the Jan. 7, 1996 *Parade* magazine (NF)

7 There has never been a great athlete who died not knowing what pain is.

Bill Bradley, US professional basketball player and senator, found in *A Sense of Where You Are* by J. McPhee (NF)

8 Sports do not build character, they reveal it.

Heywood Hale Broun, US sportswriter, found in *Sports in America* by J. Michener (NF)

9 I know that if I can stay on the [tennis] court long enough, I can figure out what I have to do to beat most players.

Michael Chang, Chinese-American professional tennis player, found in *Famous Asian Americans* by Morey and Dunn (NF)

10 The only good reason for swimming, so far as I can see, is to escape drowning.

Helen Cresswell, English author, said by Uncle Parker, *Ordinary Jack* (F)

11 I learned how to visualize. If I have a match the next day, I visualize serving the ball and playing the game—and winning. So, when I actually play the match, I've already done it in my mind, fifty times, and I don't feel panic.

> Beatriz "Gigi" Fernandez, Puerto Rican-American professional tennis player, found in *Famous Hispanic Americans* by Morey and Dunn (NF)

12 I was the last one picked on every team when I was a kid. I was a klutz. If you had ever told me that I would make being an athlete my profession, I would have laughed at you.

> Diana Golden, US one-legged World Champion skier, found in *Champions* by B. Littlefield (NF)

13 At age six, there were no six-year-old [hockey] leagues, so I played on a ten-year-old team. By my third, fourth, and fifth seasons, I knew I was gifted and fortunate.

> Wayne Gretzky, Canadian professional hockey player, in the Jan. 12, 1997 *Parade* magazine (NF)

14 Talent wins games, but teamwork and intelligence win championships.

> Michael Jordan, US professional basketball player, *I Can't Accept Not Trying* (NF)

15 I want to be remembered as a person who felt there was no limitation to what the human body and human mind can do.

> Carl Lewis, US track star and winner of 17 gold medals in four Olympics, in the Feb. 18, 1996 *Parade* magazine (NF)

16 Sports ideally teach discipline and commitment. They challenge you and build character for everything you do in life.

> Howie Long, US professional football player and sports commentator, in the Nov. 3, 1996 *Parade* magazine (NF)

17 You can't teach fearlessness. It has to be inborn. And you can't be a gymnast without it.

> Bud Marquette, US coach of Cathy Rigby, found in *Women in Sports* by J. Layden (NF)

18 For it is [the] enlarging of the human adventure that sports are all about.

> James Michener, US author, *Sports in America* (NF)

19 It's becoming increasingly difficult to be a great athlete and not be smart.

> Edwin Moses, US track star, in the Oct. 1988 *Life* magazine (NF)

20 The most important thing in the Olympic Games is not to win but to take part, just as the most important thing in life is not the triumph but the struggle. The essential thing is not to have conquered but to have fought well.

> The Olympic Creed, found in *100 Greatest Moments in Olympic History* by B. Greenspan (NF)

21 Tiger [Woods] has an opportunity to become one of the greatest golfers, or maybe even the greatest golfer, of all time.

Arnold Palmer, US professional golfer, in the Mar. 31, 1997 *Time* magazine (NF)

22 Climbing is unadulterated* hard labor. The only pleasure is the satisfaction of going where no man has been before and where few can follow.

Annie Smith Peck, US mountain climber, in the Dec. 1977 *WomenSports* magazine (NF)

*pure

23 I knew how to play soccer on the street, without shoes, without a professional ball, without a uniform. When I moved on to a very comfortable field . . . why wouldn't I win?

Pelé, Brazilian soccer player, found in *Champions* by B. Littlefield (NF)

24 Kids need to know that there is no such thing as a superstar. Many think that if they make it big as an athlete, their worries are over. I'm here to tell you that [the worries are] just beginning.

Wilma Rudolph, US track star, found in *Wilma Rudolph: Champion Athlete* by T. Biracree (NF)

25 One day [Dad] asked me why I wanted to travel with [a local track club] and add to an already busy school schedule. Didn't I want to have fun? he wondered. I told him running is fun.

Joan Benoit Samuelson, US Olympic runner, found in *Champions* by B. Littlefield (NF)

26 And the bullfighter was some kind of an athlete. He was graceful, too, like a ballet dancer, and had the steadiest nerves I'd ever seen.

Allen Say, Japanese author, *El Chino* (F)

27 [T]rack is kind of like football. Sure, there's no ball and no shoulder pads, and nothing in your way except the string across the finish line. But you can demolish a kid just as much by beating him in a race as by plowing him under on a football field.

Jerry Spinelli, US author, thought by Crash, *Crash* (F)

28 The curious thing about fishing is you never want to go home. If you catch something, you can't stop. If you don't catch anything, you hate to leave in case something might bite.

Gladys Taber, US author, in a 1941 *Ladies Home Journal* (NF)

Stars
(See Moon and Stars)

Success and Failure

1 It takes time to win success.

Aesop, Greek writer, the moral in the fable "The Goose with the Golden Eggs," found in *The Children's Treasury*, ed. by P. S. Goepfert (F)

2 Any definition of a successful life must include service to others.

George Bush, 41st US President, in the Dec. 1, 1996 *Parade* magazine (NF)

3 Success [to American Indians] isn't what you have, it's what you've given away. The most revered* member of the tribe may be the poorest, because . . . we place greater value on what we contribute to society rather than on what we accumulate.

Ben Nighthorse Campbell, Native American US senator, in the June 2, 1996 *Parade* magazine (NF)   *honored

4 We can only do the best we can with what we have. That, after all, is the measure of success.

Marguerite de Angeli, English author and illustrator, said by Brother Luke, *The Door in the Wall* (F)

5 Success is counted sweetest
By those who ne'er succeed.

Emily Dickinson, US poet, "Success," found in *The American Reader*, ed. by D. Ravitch (NF)

6 To want in one's head to do a thing, for its own sake; to enjoy doing it; to concentrate all of one's energies upon it—that is not only the surest guarantee of its success. It is also being true to oneself.

Amelia Earhart, US aviation pioneer, found in *Sky Pioneer* by C. Szabo (NF)

7 Women must try to do things as men have tried. When they fail, their failure must be but a challenge to others.

Amelia Earhart, US aviation pioneer, *Last Flight* (NF)

8 [Thomas Edison] never hesitated out of fear of failure.

Charles Edison, US son of Thomas Edison, "It's Plain Hard Work That Does It," found in *The Book of Virtues*, ed. by W. J. Bennett (NF)

9 Edison was a giant. He had gigantic successes and gigantic failures.

Keith Ellis, US author, *Thomas Edison: Genius of Electricity* (NF)

10 A first failure may prepare the way for later success.

Arnold Lobel, US author and illustrator, the moral in "The Young Rooster" from *Fables* (F)

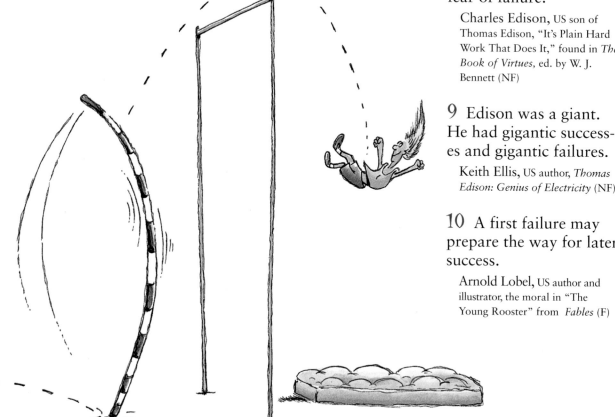

11 Some people say that success equals money, but frankly, I don't think success is money at all. . . . Success is being the best at whatever you want to do well at.

> Ann M. Martin, US author, found in *Ann M. Martin: The Story of the Author of the Baby-sitters Club* by M. Becker R. (NF)

12 Rather than leaning back and criticizing how things are, [successful people] work to make things the way they should be.

> Ellison S. Onizuka, Hawaiian astronaut, found in *Famous Asian Americans* by Morey and Dunn (NF)

13 **Our own success, to be real, must contribute to the successes of others.**

> Eleanor Roosevelt, US diplomat, author, and wife of the 32nd President, found in *Contemporary Heroes and Heroines*, ed. by R. B. Browne (NF)

14 It is common sense to take a method and try it; if it fails, admit it frankly, and try another. But above all, try something.

> Franklin D. Roosevelt, 32nd US President, in a May 22, 1932 speech in Atlanta, GA

15 Failure teaches you more than success.

> Russian proverb

16 Real success is knowing that you helped others to change their lives for the better.

> Dan Sosa, Jr., Mexican-American Justice on the New Mexico State Supreme Court, found in *Famous Mexican Americans* by Morey and Dunn (NF)

17 My recipe for success is hard work, patience, honesty, and total commitment.

> Dave Thomas, US founder of Wendy's, in the Apr. 1996 *Biography Today* (NF)

18 All my life people have said I wasn't going to make it.

> Ted Turner, US creator of CNN, in a 1984 TV interview

19 The man with a new idea is a Crank until the idea succeeds.

> Mark Twain, US author, *Following the Equator* (NF)

20 I have learned that success is to be measured not so much by the position that one has reached in life as by the obstacles* which he has overcome while trying to succeed.

> Booker T. Washington, US educator and author, *Up from Slavery* (NF)   *problems

21 [W]e considered our experiments a failure. At this time [in 1901] I made the prediction that man would sometime fly, but that it wouldn't be in our lifetime.

> Wilbur Wright, US inventor, found in *The Wright Brothers* by R. Freedman (NF)

22 Our new machine is a very great improvement over anything we had built before. . . . Everything is so much more satisfactory that we now believe [in 1902] that the flying problem is really nearing its solution.

> Wilbur Wright, US inventor, writing to his father, found in *The Wright Bothers* by R. Freedman (NF)

Talent

1 [T]alent is like electricity. We don't understand electricity. We use it.

Maya Angelou, US poet and author, found in *Black Women Writers at Work* by C. Tate (NF)

2 A winner is someone who recognizes his Godgiven talents, works his tail off to develop them into skills, and uses these skills to accomplish his goals.

Larry Bird, US professional basketball player and coach, *Bird on Basketball* (NF)

3 I started [writing] with two talents: 1) An ease with words (which came from a lifelong habit of reading), 2) An ease with dialogue* (which came from being born into a family of talkers). Everything else I acquired the hard way—I learned it.

Betsy Byars, US author, *The Moon and I: A Memoir* (NF)
talk or conversation

4 Great talent takes time to ripen.

Greek proverb

5 All of us do not have equal talent, but all of us should have an opportunity to develop our talents.

John F. Kennedy, 35th US President, in a June 18, 1962 speech at San Diego State College

6 God has given each normal person a capacity to achieve some end. True, some are endowed* with more talent than others, but God has left none of us talentless.

Martin Luther King, Jr., US civil rights leader, in a Dec. 19, 1956 speech in Montgomery, AL   *supplied*

7 We can't take any credit for our talents. It's how we use them that counts.

Madeleine L'Engle, US author, *A Wrinkle in Time* (F)

8 [T]alent is something rare and beautiful and precious, and it must not be allowed to go to waste.

George Selden, US author, said by Tucker Mouse, *The Cricket in Times Square* (F)

Talking

(See also Conversation and Language)

1 Sometimes you have to do that with adults — just say what they need you to say — so they'll get out of your face.

Tom Birdseye, US author, said by Ryan, *Tarantula Shoes* (F)

2 It's too late to correct it . . . when you've once said a thing, that fixes it, and you must take the consequences.

Lewis Carroll, English author, said by the Red Queen, *Through the Looking Glass* (F)

3 Tecumseh's voice resounded over the multitude* — now sinking in low and musical whispers, now rising to the highest key, hurling out his words like a succession of thunderbolts.

Robert Cwiklik, US author, said by Capt. Sam Dale, US soldier, describing the great Shawnee leader, *Tecumseh* (NF)

*huge crowd

4 We don't talk much.
My father never was a talker.
Ma's dying hasn't changed that.
I guess he gets the sound out of him
  with the songs he sings.

Karen Hesse, US author, written by Billie Jo, *Out of Dust* (F)

5 King Miraz had been talking in the tiresome way that some grown-ups have, which makes it quite clear that they are not really interested in what you are saying.

C. S. Lewis, English author, *Prince Caspian* (F)

6 Wouldn't it be nice if roses could talk? I'm sure they could tell us such lovely things.

L. M. Montgomery, Canadian author, said by Anne, *Anne of Green Gables* (F)

7 Dave is very shy. . . . He would appreciate it if you didn't say anything to him until he knows you better, maybe in ten or fifteen years.

Daniel Manus Pinkwater, US author and illustrator, said by the moose to Mr. Breton, *Blue Moose and Return of the Moose* (F)

8 But it is in the old story that all the beasts can talk, in the night between Christmas Eve and Christmas Day in the morning (though there are very few folk that can hear them, or know what it is that they say).

Beatrix Potter, English author, "The Tailor of Gloucester" from *The Complete Tales of Beatrix Potter* (F)

9 Cats have a lot to say and not very much of it is complimentary.

Michael J. Rosen, US author, the Introduction to *Purr . . . Children's Book Illustrators Brag about Their Cats* (NF)

10 Cletus had some gifts . . . and knowing when to talk and when not to was turning out to be one of them.

Cynthia Rylant, US author, said by Summer, *Missing May* (F)

11 Cats purr.
Lions roar.
Owls hoot.
Bears snore.
Crickets creak.
Mice squeak.
Sheep baa.
But I SPEAK!

Arnold L. Shapiro, "I speak, I say, I talk" found in *The BFC Young Book of Poetry*, sel. by B. Mathias

12 The horse talked with his ears. You could tell exactly how he felt about every-thing by the way his ears pointed. . . . They went back when he was angry or fearful, and forward when he was anxious and curious and pleased.

John Steinbeck, US author, *The Red Pony* (F)

13 Perhaps if people talked less, animals would talk more.

E. B. White, US author, said by Dr. Dorian, *Charlotte's Web* (F)

14 Nine times out of ten, talking is a way of avoiding doing things.

Patricia C. Wrede, US author, said by a frog, *Dealing with Dragons* (F)

15 Animals have long tongues but can't speak; men have short tongues and shouldn't speak.

Yiddish proverb

Tall Tale Heroes

1 Raised in the woods so's he knew
ev'ry tree.
Kilt him a b'ar when he was only three.
Davy, Davy Crockett, King of the wild
Frontier!

Tom Blackburn, US lyricist, words to the song "The Ballad of Davy Crockett" from Walt Disney's TV production *Davy Crockett*

2 Davy's wife, Sally Ann Thunder Ann Whirlwind Crockett . . . could laugh the bark off a pine tree, blow out the moonlight, and sing a wolf to sleep.

Walter Blair, US author, a retelling of "The Amazing Crockett Family" from *Tall Tale America* (F)

3 If you happened to land on the tip of one horn [of Paul Bunyan's ox Babe], it's doubtful if you could have seen the tip of the other, even on a clear day.

Harold Courlander, US author, a retelling of "Paul Bunyan's Cornstalk" from *Ride with the Sun* (F)

4 Paul Bunyan was the fellow who invented the ax with two edges so a man could stand between two trees and chop them both down at the same time.

Ibid.

5 I personally have always been on the best of terms with God's wild creatures, and my name, it seems, is widely known among them.

Andrew Glass, US author and illustrator, said by Johnny Appleseed, a retelling of *Folks Call Me Appleseed John* (F)

6 [This mush pot] is more useful than any hat. It keeps my head dry. I can cook in it, and once I used it to discourage an unreasonable copperhead. Ain't much a man need fear when he's got a mush pot on his head.

Ibid.

7 [Pecos Bill] was the doggonedest, goldingest, dad-blamest son of the prairie sod who ever rode across these here United States.

Brian Gleeson, US author, a retelling of "Ride 'em, Rope 'em: The Story of Pecos Bill," found in *From Sea to Shining Sea*, comp. by A. L. Cohn (F)

8 The cyclone spun faster and faster to try to get [Pecos] Bill to loosen his grip. Fat chance, *amigo*!

Ibid.

9 [Pecos] Bill chased [the wild stallion named] Lightning north to the Arctic Circle . . . and south to the bottom of the Grand Canyon. Finally he cornered the stallion and jumped onto his back. Lightning exploded from the canyon, leaping and bucking across three states.

Steven Kellogg, US author and illustrator, a retelling of *Pecos Bill* (F)

10 Just as the bull whirled around to trample him, [Pecos] Bill snagged him with the rattlesnake and yanked with all his might. "Cattle roping has just been invented!"

Ibid.

11 [The giant rattlesnake] slapped its coils around him. The snake squeezed hard, but [Pecos] Bill squeezed harder and he didn't let up until every drop of poison was out of that reptile, leaving it skinny as a rope and mild as a goldfish.

Ibid.

12 [Johnny] liked to sleep outdoors, even in the coldest weather. . . . He could walk through snow in his bare feet and feel no cold. He could go through the deepest forest and never lose his way. For all of these reasons the Indians had great respect for Johnny, and treated him as a friend.

Patrick McGrath, US author, a retelling of *Johnny Appleseed* (F)

13 As [John Henry's] hammer glowed white-hot, he tunneled deeper into the darkness, driving steel so hard that the mighty ribs on his body began to crack, and his insides broke in two, and his great heart burst.

Mary Pope Osborne, US author, a retelling of "John Henry" from *American Tall Tales* (F)

17 When next heard of, Paul [Bunyan] was headed to Arizona. He dragged his pickaxe behind him on that trip, not realizing he was leaving a big ditch in his tracks. Today that ditch is called the Grand Canyon.

Ibid.

18 I can wade the Mississippi without getting wet, outholler a mountain lion, and dance down any fellow in Arkansas or Texas. And my granddaughter [Slue-Foot Sue] is just like me.

Robert D. San Souci, US author, said by Sue's grandmother to Pecos Bill, a retelling of "Slue-Foot Sue and Pecos Bill" from *Larger Than Life* (F)

14 Soon [Stormalong] became the best farmer around. He planted over five million potatoes and watered his whole crop with the sweat of his brow.

Mary Pope Osborne, US author, a retelling of "Stormalong" from *American Tall Tales* (F)

15 The towering masts of [Stormalong's ship] had to be hinged to let the sun and moon go by. The tips of the masts were padded so they wouldn't punch holes in the sky. The trip to the crow's nest took so long, the sailors who climbed to the top returned with gray beards.

Ibid.

16 [Paul Bunyan's] strangest feature [when he was a baby] was his big, curly black beard. It was so big and bushy that every morning his poor mother had to comb it with a pine tree.

Mary Pope Osborne, US author, a retelling of "Paul Bunyan, the Mightiest Logger of Them All," found in *From Sea to Shining Sea*, comp. by A. L. Cohn (F)

19 [T]he worst [part of the storm] was the barn blew down, and I had to keep the cows and horses under my slicker until the rain let up.

Robert D. San Souci, US author, said by Sue, a retelling of "Slue-Foot Sue and Pecos Bill" from *Larger Than Life* (F)

20 Paul Bunyan tackled the tough logging problems before him with characteristic courage. He was sure that his inventiveness and resourcefulness would, as always, triumph over every obstacle.

James Stevens, US author, a retelling of *Paul Bunyan* (F)

21 There wasn't another steel-driving man in the world who could touch John Henry for speed and power. He could hammer every which way, up or down or sidewise. He could drive for ten hours at a stretch and never miss a stroke.

Adrien Stoutenburg, US author, a retelling of "Hammerman" from *American Tall Tales* (F)

Teachers

(See also School)

1 Nobody seemed scared of [Mr. Benedict, the sixth grade teacher] at all and you should always be a little scared of your teacher.

Judy Blume, US author, said by Margaret, *Are You There, God? It's Me, Margaret* (F)

2 A loving caring teacher took a liking to me. She noticed the potential* [in me] and wanted to help shape it.

Tom Bradley, US mayor of Los Angeles, CA, found in *My Soul Looks Back, 'Less I Forget*, ed. by D. W. Riley (NF)

*possibilities

3 [Mr. Birkway] was one of those energetic teachers who loved his subject half to death and leaped about the room dramatically, waving his arms and clutching his chest and whomping people on the back.

Sharon Creech, US author, said by Salamanca, *Walk Two Moons* (F)

4 Better than a thousand days of diligent* study is one day with a great teacher.

Japanese proverb   *steady

5 I think [my teacher] Mrs. Westvessel is probably over 100 years old. . . . Probably about 120.

Lois Lowry, US author, said by Anastasia, *Anastasia Krupnik* (F)

6 [As your teacher,] I work for *you*, for the tilling of your minds and the fruit of your ever-growing souls.

George Ella Lyons, US author, said by Amanda's teacher, *Borrowed Children* (F)

7 It was rather comfortable . . . to know that your [school] work was judged on its merits and was not affected by the teacher's personal opinion of the person doing the work.

Katherine Paterson, US author, thought by Gilly, *The Great Gilly Hopkins* (F)

8 [I]t's never wise to disagree with a teacher.

Richard Peck, US author, said by Blossom Culp, "The Special Powers of Blossom Culp," found in *Birthday Surprises*, ed. by J. Hurwitz (F)

9 For everyone of us that succeeds, it's because there's somebody there to show you the way out. The light doesn't always necessarily have to be in your family; for me it was teachers and school.

Oprah Winfrey, US actress and TV personality, in the Apr. 5, 1995 issue of *The Star* (NF)

Technology

1 The fabulous wizard of Oz
Retired from business becoz
  What with up-to-date science
  To most of his clients
He wasn't the wiz that he woz.

Anonymous limerick, found in *A Nonny Mouse Writes Again!*, sel. by J. Prelutsky

2 The computer's sucked out your brain.

Susan Cooper, US author, said by Emily to Jessup, *The Boggart* (F)

3 [Television] rots the senses in the head!
It kills imagination dead!
It clogs and clutters up the mind!
It makes a child so dull and blind
He can no longer understand
A fantasy, a fairyland!
His brain becomes as soft as cheese!
His powers of thinking rust and freeze!
He cannot think—he only sees!

Roald Dahl, English author, words to an Oompa-Loompas song, *Charlie and the Chocolate Factory* (F)

4 I suspect that this motorcar has thought out, all by herself, certain improvements, certain very extraordinary mechanical devices, just as if she had a mind of her own.

Ian Fleming, English writer, said by Com. Pott, *Chitty Chitty Bang Bang: The Magical Car* (F)

5 Man is still the most extraordinary computer of all.

John F. Kennedy, 35th US President, in a May 21, 1963 speech

6 The daily ration [of television] was one hour. More than that, [Peter's mother and father] believed, would rot the brain. They offered no medical evidence for this theory.

Ian McEwan, English author, *The Daydreamer* (F)

7 When television is good, nothing—not the theater, not the magazines or news-papers—nothing is better. But when television is bad, nothing is worse. [It can be] a vast wasteland.

Newton Minow, US public official, in a May 9, 1961 speech to the National Association of Broadcasters

8 I didn't plan . . . for a computer to become my new best friend.

Justine Rendal, US author, said by Pollard Gunning, *A Very Personal Computer* (F)

9 But I *do* know this clock does one very slick trick.
It doesn't tick tock. How it goes is tock tick.
So, with ticks in its tocker, and tocks in its ticker
It saves lots of time and the sleepers sleep quicker.

Dr. Seuss, US author, *Sleep Book* (F)

10 The day may soon come when the concept of student and teacher will be obsolete. All knowledge will be acquired electronically.

Todd Strasser, US author, said by Mr. Dirksen, *Help! I'm Trapped in My Teacher's Body* (F)

11 Technology feeds on itself. Technology makes more technology possible.

Alvin Toffler, US author, *Future Shock* (NF)

12 There are days when any electrical appliance in the house, including the vacuum cleaner, seems to offer more entertainment possibilities than the TV set.

Attributed to Harriet Van Horne, US journalist

13 Television had a chance to become the greatest social force for good in this country . . . [b]ut it failed.

Vladimir Zworykin, Russian-American inventor, the one person most responsible for bringing TV into the world, found in *American Profiles: 20th Century Inventors* by N. Aaseng (NF)

Thinking

1 [To fly] you just think lovely wonderful thoughts, and they lift you in to the air.

J. M. Barrie, Scottish author, said by Peter Pan, *Peter Pan* (F)

2 [I]f anything is excellent or praiseworthy—think about such things.

Bible, Philippians 4:8 (NIV)

3 [T]houghts . . . are as powerful as electric batteries — as good for one as sunlight is, or as bad for one as poison.

Frances Hodgson Burnett, English-American author, *The Secret Garden* (F)

4 To let a sad thought or a bad one get into your mind is as dangerous as letting a scarlet-fever germ get into your body. If you let it stay there after it has got in, you may never get over it as long as you live.

Ibid.

5 Minds, like diapers, need occasional changing.

Karen Cushman, US author, said by Lucy's mother, *The Ballad of Lucy Whipple* (F)

6 Think before you speak, and look before you leap.

Irish proverb

7 Ordinance 175389-J: It shall be unlawful, illegal, and unethical to think, think of thinking, surmise, presume, reason, meditate, or speculate while in the Doldrums.

Norton Juster, US author, said by a Lethargarian, *The Phantom Tollbooth* (F)

8 [L]ying in bed just before going to sleep is the worst time for organized thinking; it is the best time for free thinking. Ideas drift like clouds in an undecided breeze, taking first this direction and then that.

E. L. Konigsburg, US author and illustrator, *From the Mixed Up Files of Mrs. Basil E. Frankweiler* (F)

9 Owl . . . you and I have brains. The others have fluff. If there is any thinking to be done in this Forest — and when I say thinking I mean *thinking* — you and I must do it.

A. A. Milne, English author, said by Rabbit, "Rabbit's Busy Day" from *The House at Pooh Corner* (F)

10 [W]hen you are a Bear of Very Little Brain, and you Think of Things, you find sometimes that a Thing which seemed Thingish inside you is quite different when it gets out into the open and has other people looking at it.

A. A. Milne, English author, said by Winnie-the-Pooh, "Eeyore Joins a Game" from *The House at Pooh Corner* (F)

11 Think! Think and wonder.
Wonder and think.
How much water can fifty-five
elephants drink?

Dr. Seuss, US author, *Oh, The Thinks You Can Think!* (F)

12 We know what a person thinks not
when he tells us what he thinks, but by
his actions.

Isaac Bashevis Singer, Polish-American author, in the
Nov. 26, 1978 issue of *The New York Times Magazine* (NF)

13 I really believe the most handicapped
[person] in the whole world is a negative
thinker.

Heather Whitestone, 1995 Miss America, in the
Apr. 1995 *Biography Today* (NF)

Time

1 There is a time for everything, a season
for every activity under heaven.

Bible, Ecclesiastes 3:1 (NIV)

2 Little drops of water, little grains
of sand,
Make the mighty oceans, and the
pleasant land.
So the little minutes, humble though
they be,
Make the mighty ages of eternity.

Julia Carney, US poet, "Little Things" found in
American Quotations by Carruth and Ehrlich (NF)

3 The past is a ghost, the future a
dream, and all we ever *have* is now.

Bill Cosby, US comedian and author, *Time Flies* (NF)

4 Time waits for no one.
Danish proverb

5 The bed was his own, the room was his
own. Best and happiest of all, the Time
before [Scrooge] was his own, to make
amends in!

Charles Dickens, English author, *A Christmas Carol* (F)

6 [T]he seconds trudged by so slowly they
seemed to be wearing boots made of
concrete.

Fred D'Ignazio, US author, "The Case of the Computer
Bully" from *Chip Mitchell* (F)

7 [I]f the day starts before you do, you
never catch up. You spend all your time
running after what you should have
already done, and no matter how much
you hurry, you never finish the race in a tie.
The day wins.

Michael Dorris, Native American author and anthropologist, said by Morning Girl, *Morning Girl* (F)

8 No time like the present.

English proverb

9 Time softened my memory as though it was kneading wax.

Paula Fox, US author, thought by Jessie Bollier, *The Slave Dancer* (F)

10 Lost Time is never found again.

Benjamin Franklin, Revolutionary statesman, the 1738 *Poor Richard's Almanack* (NF)

11 Remember that time is money.

Benjamin Franklin, Revolutionary statesman, the 1748 *Poor Richard's Almanack* (NF)

12 You may delay, but Time will not.

Benjamin Franklin, Revolutionary statesman, the 1758 *Poor Richard's Almanack* (NF)

13 For the most part, time seems to proceed at a reasonable pace, but once you have gone through quite a bit of it and look back, it seems no more than a snap of the fingers.

Jean Fritz, US author, *China Homecoming* (NF)

14 [The forest animals] didn't bother themselves about the past—they never do; they're too busy. . . . And they don't bother about the future, either.

Kenneth Grahame, English author, *The Wind in the Willows* (F)

15 Time works wonders.

Hebrew proverb

16 [T]he present was an egg laid by the past that had the future inside its shell.

Zora Neal Hurston, US anthropologist and author, *Moses, Man of the Mountain* (NF)

17 God invented time to keep everything from happening at once.

Bill Keane, US cartoonist, "The Family Circus" cartoon

18 [T]ime is neutral. It can be used either destructively or constructively.

Martin Luther King, Jr., US civil rights leader, *Letter from a Birmingham City Jail*, found in *The American Reader*, ed. by D. Ravitch (NF)

19 Time, you agree, is everybody's gift,
   But the packages aren't the same.
   The lid of each is there to lift,
   Yet only one package bears your name.

David McCord, US poet, "No Present Like the Time" from *One at a Time*

20 Never before have we had so little time in which to do so much.

Franklin D. Roosevelt, 32nd US President, in a Feb. 23, 1942 radio speech

21 [T]ime soothes all sorrows.

Antoine de Saint-Exupéry, French author and illustrator, *The Little Prince* (F)

22 Martha had never paid much attention to time, because there was always more of it than she knew what to do with.

Zilpha Keatley Snyder, US author, *The Changeling* (F)

23 The Great TV Turn-Off had begun. . . . Brenda had already done the arithmetic. She would have to go without TV for 168 hours. Or 1,080 minutes. Or 640,800 seconds.

Jerry Spinelli, US author, "Brenda" from *The Library Card* (F)

24 Time lies frozen [in the castle.] It's always Then. It's never Now.

James Thurber, US author, *The 13 Clocks* (F)

Trees

1 Once, long ago, when you could get four ounces of fruit drops for a penny . . . there was a tree that loved a girl.

Joan Aiken, English author, "The Tree That Loved a Girl" from *The Last Slice of Rainbow* (F)

2 A tree draws its strength from the roots of the earth. That's beyond the power of any enchanter.

Lloyd Alexander, US author, said by the wizard Arbican, *The Wizard in the Tree* (F)

3 And the Lord God made all kinds of trees grow out of the ground—trees that were pleasing to the eye and good for food.

Bible, Genesis 2:9 (NIV)

4 A single tree does not make a forest.

Chinese proverb

5 I prayed to trees. This was easier than praying directly to God. There was nearly always a tree nearby.

Sharon Creech, US author, said by Salamanca, *Walk Two Moons* (F)

6 [A]ll the people rushed to the faerie's little garden and laid their troubles under the third apple tree which was a thousand miles tall and had red and green apples on it as big as balloons.

e. e. cummings, US poet, "The Old Man Who Said 'Why'" from *Fairy Tales* (F)

7 I think that I shall never see,
A poem lovely as a tree.

Joyce Kilmer, US poet, "Trees," found in *The American Reader*, ed. by D. Ravitch (NF)

8 Poems are made by fools like me.
But only God can make a tree.
Ibid.

9 [The Leopard and the Ethiopian] saw a great, high, tall forest full of tree trunks all 'sclusively speckled and sprottled and spottled, dotted and splashed and slashed and hatched and cross-hatched with shadows.

Rudyard Kipling, English-American journalist and author, "How the Leopard Got His Spots" from *Just So Stories* (F)

10 The whole wood is full of [the White Witch's] spies. Even some of the trees are on her side.

C. S. Lewis, English author, said by Mr. Tumnus, *The Lion, the Witch, and the Wardrobe* (F)

11 Woodman, spare that tree!
Touch not a single bough!
In youth it sheltered me,
And I'll protect it now.

George Perkins Morris, US poet and journalist, "Woodman, Spare That Tree," found in *The American Reader*, ed. by D. Ravitch (NF)

12 I think that I shall never see
A billboard lovely as a tree.
Perhaps unless the billboards fall,
I'll never see a tree at all.

Ogden Nash, US poet, "Song of the Open Road," found in *The Anthology of American Poetry*, ed. by G. Gesner

13 "Mister!" he said with a sawdusty
sneeze,
"I am the Lorax. I speak for the trees.
I speak for the trees, for the trees have
no tongues."

Dr. Seuss, US author, *The Lorax* (F)

14 As far as man could go to the north in a day, or a week, or a whole month . . . [t]here were only trees and the wild animals who had their homes among them.

Laura Ingalls Wilder, US author, *Little House in the Big Woods* (F)

Trouble
(See also Problems and Solutions*)*

1 When Noah sailed the waters blue,
He had his troubles, same as you.
For forty days he drove his ark
Before he found a place to park.

Anonymous poem, found in A *Nonny Mouse Writes Again!*, sel. by J. Prelutsky

2 Nobody knows the trouble I've
seen,
Nobody knows but Jesus.

Anonymous words from a spiritual, *c.* 1845

3 The trouble was that although grown-ups usually knew what to do, *what* they did was very seldom what children wanted to be done.

Lynne Reid Banks, US author, *The Indian in the Cupboard* (F)

4 There is nothing written in the Bible, Old or New Testament, that says: "If you believe in Me, you ain't going to have no troubles."

Ray Charles, US singer and composer, in the Oct. 10, 1988 *Parade* magazine (NF)

5 [The faerie] would examine all the troubles no matter how big or how little they were, or whether they were just plain troubles or troubles in fancy boxes (tied up with pink and green ribbons) and he'd give advice to all the people who brought him these troubles.

e. e. cummings, US poet, "The Old Man Who Said 'Why'" from *Fairy Tales* (F)

6 I always tumble into trouble when I lose my temper.

Jane Louise Curry, US author, said by Robin Hood, a retelling of *Robin Hood and His Merry Men* (F)

7 [O]nce you start taking credit for your luck, you're in for trouble.

Peter Dickinson, English author, *Time and the Clock Mice, Etcetera* (F)

8 The way I see it, hard times aren't only
about money,
or drought,
or dust.
Hard times are about loosing spirit,
and hope,
and what happens when dreams dry up.

Karen Hesse, US author, written by Billie Jo, *Out of Dust* (F)

9 My mama says that what comes most naturally to me is getting into trouble.

Athena V. Lord, US author, said by Zach, *Today's Special: Z.A.P. and Zoe* (F)

10 When there's trouble waitin' for you, you jest as good go to meet it.

Marjorie Kinnan Rawlings, US author, said by Jody's father, *The Yearling* (F)

11 One of the basic causes for all the trouble in the world today is that people talk too much and think too little.

Margaret Chase Smith, US politician, in a June 7, 1953 speech in Portland, ME

12 [S]omething [to make you happy] will come out of the trouble, but one must keep perfectly quiet, and not run away.

Johanna Spyri, Swiss author, said by Heidi, *Heidi* (F)

13 There was peace and harmony in the kingdom once again, except for the little troubles that come up every so often even in the best of circumstances, since nothing is perfect.

William Steig, US author, *The Real Thief* (F)

14 The fat is in the fire, the die is cast, the jig is up, the goose is cooked, and the cat is out of the bag.

James Thurber, US author, said by the Goluz, *The 13 Clocks* (F)

15 Trouble trouble and it will trouble you!

P. L. Travers, Australian-English author, said by Mary Poppins, *Mary Poppins* (F)

16 He who bears trouble patiently receives his reward.

Turkish proverb

17 "Thomas Sawyer!" Tom knew that when his name was pronounced in full, it meant trouble.

Mark Twain, US author, *The Adventures of Tom Sawyer* (F)

18 'Tis easy enough to be pleasant,
When life flows along like a song;
But the man worthwhile is the one
who will smile
When everything goes dead wrong.

Ella Wheeler Wilcox, US poet, "Worthwhile" from *Collected Poems*

Truth

1 Then you will know the truth, and the truth will set you free.

Bible, John 8:32 (NIV)

2 Always speak the truth—think before you speak—and write it down afterwards.

Lewis Carroll, English author, said by the Red Queen, *Through the Looking Glass* (F)

3 Some of this story is true. Some of it's lies. No brontosaurus has ever been found in Nebraska.

Pam Conrad, US author, the Foreword to *My Daniel* (F)

4 Sooner or later, the truth comes to light.
Dutch proverb

5 The truth came slowly like a story told by people interrupting each other.

Paula Fox, US author, thought by Jessie Bollier, *The Slave Dancer* (F)

6 I have nothing new to teach the world. Truth and nonviolence are as old as the hills.

Mohandas Gandhi, Indian civil rights leader, found in *Contemporary Heroes and Heroines*, ed. by R. B. Browne (NF)

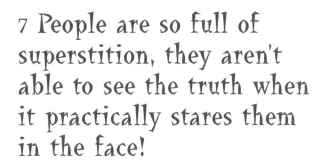

7 People are so full of superstition, they aren't able to see the truth when it practically stares them in the face!

Virginia Hamilton, US author, said by Mr. Small, *The House of Dies Drear* (F)

8 Sometimes the truth is the hardest to understand.

Michael Morpurgo, English author, said by Uncle Sung, *King of the Cloud Forests* (F)

9 I'm so far gone that I'm telling the truth. It sounds like a foreign language.

Richard Peck, US author, thought by Jim Atwater, *Father Figure* (F)

10 [Tory] couldn't define truth with an unabridged dictionary.

Mary Francis Shura, US author, said by Jason, *The Josie Gambit* (F)

11 When in doubt, tell the truth.

Mark Twain, US author, *Following the Equator* (NF)

12 There is nothing so powerful as truth; and often nothing so strange.

Daniel Webster, US lawyer, in his argument in a murder trial on Apr. 6, 1830

Understanding

1 Understand, rubber band?

Anonymous folk poetry, found in *And the Green Grass Grew All Around*, comp. by A. Schwartz

2 Man must understand his universe in order to understand his destiny.*

Neil A. Armstrong, US astronaut, in a Sept. 16, 1969 speech to Congress   *future*

3 [Sarah and the Indian children] did not speak in the same words but somehow they understood each other. When they couldn't understand, it did not seem to matter.

Alice Dalgliesh, US author, *The Courage of Sarah Noble* (F)

4 Even though the Nutcracker was made of wood, he felt and understood all of Marie's goodness and love.

E. T. A. Hoffmann, German author, *Nutcracker* (F)

5 I want the white people to understand my people. Some of you think an Indian is like a wild animal. This is a great mistake. I will tell you about our people, and then you can judge whether an Indian is a man or not.

Chief Joseph, leader of the Nez Perce, in an 1879 speech to President Rutherford B. Hayes, found in *Indian Chiefs* by R. Freedman (NF)

6 You never really understand a person until you consider things from his point of view . . . until you climb into his skin and walk around in it.

Harper Lee, US author, said by Atticus, *To Kill a Mockingbird* (F)

7 Making lists of reasons was sometimes a good way to figure things out.

Lois Lowry, US author, *Anastasia Krupnik* (F)

8 What people don't understand, they laugh at.

Geraldine McCaughrean, English author, the retelling of *Coppelia* from *The Random House Book of Stories from the Ballet* (F)

9 I sort of got the feeling that [Mark and the brown bear Ben] were in . . . some sort of world all their own. And I couldn't get in. . . . It doesn't make sense, but they actually seemed to understand each other.

Walt Morey, US author, said by Mark's father, *Gentle Ben* (F)

10 Sometimes I think you have to live through something yourself before you can really understand it.

Walter Dean Myers, US author, said by Stuff, *Fast Sam, Cool Clyde, and Stuff* (F)

11 It's funny how dogs and cats know the insides of folks better than other folks do.

Eleanor H. Porter, US author, said by Pollyanna, *Pollyanna* (F)

12 [May] understood people and she let them be whatever way they needed to be. . . . Seems people knew she saw the very best of them, and they'd turn that side to her to give her a better look.

Cynthia Rylant, US author, said by Summer, *Missing May* (F)

13 Grown-ups never understand anything by themselves, and it is tiresome for children to be always and for-ever explaining things to them.

Antoine de Saint-Exupéry, French author and illustrator, *The Little Prince* (F)

14 Things you don't understand are mysterious.

Mary Francis Shura, US author, said by Greg, *The Josie Gambit* (F)

15 [I]t is very clever of humans to understand a [dog's] wagging tail . . . as they have no tails of their own.

Dodie Smith, English author, *The 101 Dalmatians* (F)

16 [M]any dogs can understand almost every word humans say, while humans seldom learn to recognize more than half a dozen barks, if that.

Ibid.

United States
(See America and Americans)

Universe
(See World)

Voting

1 [E]ven if the right to vote brought to women no better work, no better pay, no better conditions in any way, she should have it for her own self-respect and to compel man's respect for her.

> Susan B. Anthony, US suffragist and reformer, found in *The Life and Work of Susan B. Anthony* by I. H. Harper (NF)

2 Sensible and responsible women do not want to vote.

> Grover Cleveland, 22nd US President, in an Apr. 1905 *Ladies Home Journal* (NF)

3 Slavery is not abolished until the black man has the ballot.

> Frederick Douglass, US abolitionist and author, in a Feb. 1, 1865 speech to the Anti-Slavery Society

4 People who do not vote have no line of credit with people who are elected.

> Marian Wright Edelman, US lawyer and public official, in a Sept. 26, 1987 speech

5 There's a freedom train a coming. . . . But you got to be registered to ride. Get on board . . . [and] we can move from the slaveship to the championship, from the guttermost to the uppermost . . . from the state house to the White House.

> Jesse Jackson, US civil rights activist, found in *Jesse Jackson* by A. Kosof (NF)

6 The vote is the most powerful instrument ever devised by man for breaking down . . . the terrible walls which imprison men because they are different from other men.

> Lyndon B. Johnson, 36th US President, in an Aug. 6, 1965 speech at the signing of the Voting Rights Bill

7 The ballot is stronger than the bullet.

> Abraham Lincoln, 16th US President, in a May 19, 1856 speech

8 I want to stand by my country, but I cannot vote for war. I vote *no*.

> Jeannette Rankin, US politician, said before voting against declaration of war against Germany in 1917, found in *Women of the U.S. Congress* by I. V. Morin (NF)

9 During the post-baseball years, I became increasingly persuaded that there were two keys to the advancement of blacks in America — the ballot and the buck.

Jackie Robinson, US professional baseball player, found in *Jackie Robinson: Baseball Great* by R. Scott (NF)

10 The ultimate rulers of our democracy are not a President and senators and congressmen and government officials, but the voters of this country.

Franklin D. Roosevelt, 32nd US President, in a July 8, 1938 speech in Marietta, OH

11 An election is a very serious thing; at least it ought to be, and every man ought to vote according to his conscience, and let his neighbor do the same.

Anna Sewell, English-American author, said by the cab driver, *Black Beauty* (F)

12 Voters don't decide issues, they decide who will decide the issues.

George F. Will, US news commentator and writer, in the Mar. 8, 1976 *Newsweek* magazine (NF)

13 When you vote for the president, you also vote for his wife.

Oprah Winfrey, US actress and TV personality, in the Oct. 4, 1988 *Woman's Day* magazine (NF)

War

(See also Civil War,
Peace, *and* Revolutionary War)

1 I've too often longed to see war, and now I have my wish . . . but as I can't fight, I will content myself with working for those who can.

> Louisa May Alcott, US author, found in *Louisa May* by N. Johnston (NF)

2 It is wise statesmanship which suggests that in time of peace we must prepare for war.

> Clara Barton, US founder of the American Red Cross, found in *Herstory,* ed. by Ashby and Ohrn (NF)

3 These [young] lads . . . don't know what I know, and I can't tell them: men actually die in war.

> Ray Bradbury, US author, said by the general, "The Drummer Boy of Shiloh" from *The Machineries of Joy* (F)

4 We know more about war than we know about peace, more about killing than we know about living.

> Omar Bradley, US military general, in a Nov. 10, 1948 speech in Boston, MA

5 War is hard. . . . Sometimes we do a lot of things we don't want to do. A lot of very good men have been killed in this [American Revolutionary] war, and all we can do is hope that it's been worth it.

> James L. Collier and Christopher Collier, US authors, said by Col. Parsons, *My Brother Sam Is Dead* (F)

6 War is never fair. Who chooses which men get killed and which ones don't?

> James L. Collier and Christopher Collier, US authors, said by Col. Read, *My Brother Sam Is Dead* (F)

7 No nation ever had an army large enough to guarantee it against attack in time of peace or insure it victory in time of war.

> Calvin Coolidge, 30th US President, in an Oct. 6, 1925 speech

8 War begins where reason ends.

> Frederick Douglass, US abolitionist and author, found in *My Soul Looks Back, 'Less I Forget*, ed. by D. W. Riley (NF)

9 What, oh, what is the use of the war? Why can't people live peacefully together? Why all this destruction?

> Anne Frank, Dutch diarist, *Anne Frank: The Diary of a Young Girl,* May 3, 1944 entry (NF)

10 [T]here never was a good war or a bad peace.

> Benjamin Franklin, Revolutionary statesman, in a Sept. 11, 1783 letter to Josiah Quincy

11 In history books war seemed to be a simple matter of two sides fighting, the right side against the wrong.

> Jean Fritz, US author, *My Own Story* (NF)

12 The art of war is simple enough. Find out where your enemy is. Get at him as soon as you can. Strike at him as hard as you can and as often as you can, and keep moving on.

> Ulysses S. Grant, Union general and later the 18th US President, found in *Our American Presidents* by Bumann and Patterson (NF)

13 Mankind must put an end to war or war will put an end to mankind.

John F. Kennedy, 35th US President, in a Sept. 25, 1961 speech to the United Nations

14 What a cruel thing is war . . . to fill our hearts with hatred instead of love for our neighbors, and to devastate the fair face of this beautiful world.

Robert E. Lee, Confederate general, in a Dec. 15, 1862 letter to his wife

15 I know war as few other men now living know it, and nothing to me is more revolting.

Douglas MacArthur, US military general, in an Apr. 19, 1951 speech to Congress

16 Last night I had the strangest dream,
I'd never dreamed before,
I dreamed the world had all agreed
To put an end to war.

Ed McCurdy, US singer and composer, words to the song "Last Night I Had the Strangest Dream," found in *The American Reader*, ed. by D. Ravitch (NF)

17 My philosophy of war is that what you need to win a war is money.

Jean F. Merrill, US author, said by Maxie, *The Pushcart War* (F)

18 The quickest way of ending a war is to lose it.

George Orwell, English author, "Shooting an Elephant" from *Shooting an Elephant and Other Essays* (NF)

19 More than an end to war, we want an end to the beginnings of all wars.

Franklin D. Roosevelt, 32nd US President, in an Apr. 13, 1945 radio broadcast that was aired the day after his death

20 Sometime they'll give a war and nobody will come.

Carl Sandburg, US poet and biographer, a line from *The People, Yes*, found in *Rainbows Are Made*, sel. by L. B. Hopkins

21 In war all suffer defeat; even the victors.
Swedish proverb

22 War is fear cloaked* in courage.

William Westmoreland, US military general, in the Dec. 1966 *McCall's* magazine (NF)
*disguised

Water

1 So [the Tucks] decided at last that the source of their changelessness was the [water from the] spring.

Natalie Babbitt, US author, *Tuck Everlasting* (F)

2 Water, water, every where,
   And all the boards did shrink;
   Water, water, every where,
   Nor any drop to drink.

Samuel Taylor Coleridge, English poet, *The Rime of the Ancient Mariner*

3 [Beetle] could not swim. No one could. Water was for horses to drink and an occasional quick bath before weddings and such.

Karen Cushman, US author, *The Midwife's Apprentice* (F)

4 Each year there are more and more people living on the Earth, yet the amount of water we have to use remains the same. . . . If you imagine a day without water, you realize how precious it is.

Marydele Donnelly, US member of the Center for Marine Conservation, found in *50 Simple Things Kids Can Do To Save the Earth* by the EarthWorks Group (NF)

5 Still waters run deep.

English proverb

6 And at the end of the day, the sun could stain the water yellow as cane stalks, green as limes, pink and orange as shrimps.

Paula Fox, US author, thought by Jessie Bollier, *The Slave Dancer* (F)

7 The sound of the water is . . . very calming.

Maya Lin, Chinese-American creator of the Vietnam Memorial in Washington, D.C., found in *Maya Lin, Architect and Artist* by M. Malone (NF)

Wealth And Poverty

1 God made the bees,
   And the bees make honey.
   The miller's man does all the work,
   But the miller makes the money.

Anonymous poem, found in the *Oxford Book of Poetry for Children*, comp. by E. Blishen

2 An honest crew makes a fair voyage. A fair voyage brings a profit, and profit, my good gentlemen, doth turn the world.

Avi, US author, said by Capt. Jaggery, *The True Confessions of Charlotte Doyle* (F)

3 Do not store up for yourselves treasures on earth, where moth and rust destroy, and where thieves break in and steal. But store up for yourselves treasures in heaven. . . . For where your treasure is, there your heart will be also.

Bible, Matthew 6:19-21 (NIV)

4 We will win in the end. We learned many years ago that the rich may have the money, but the poor have the time.

César Chávez, Mexican-American labor activist and organizer of farm workers, in the Sept. 22, 1975 *Newsweek* magazine (NF)

5 [The sheriff of Nottingham] robs the poor to make himself rich. Robin Hood's men rob the rich and greedy to feed the poor and needy.

Jane Louise Curry, US author, said by Little John, a retelling of *Robin Hood and His Merry Men* (F)

6 The greatest wealth is contentment with a little.

English proverb

7 Money is like an arm or a leg—use it or lose it.

Henry Ford, US car manufacturer, in an interview in the Nov. 8, 1931 issue of *The New York Times* (NF)

8 The old Eskimo hunters . . . thought the riches of life were intelligence, fearlessness, and love.

Jean Craighead George, US author, *Julie of the Wolves* (F)

9 We are poor folk . . . but poverty isn't so bad when you're willing to own up to it, and a contented spirit is a great help, too.

Edith Hamilton, German-American author, said by Baucis, a retelling of "Baucis and Philemon" (F)

10 Some people's money is merited And other people's money is inherited.

Ogden Nash, US poet, "The Terrible People," from *Happy Days*

11 When you are poor enough, everything has some value.

Barbara Ann Porte, US author, "What the Princess Discarded," found in *Birthday Surprises*, ed. by J. Hurwitz (F)

12 Money buys food, clothes, houses, land, guns, jewels, men, women, time to be lazy and listen to music.
Money buys everything except love, personality, freedom, immortality,* silence, peace.

Carl Sandburg, US poet and biographer, an excerpt from *The People, Yes*, found in *Rainbows Are Made*, sel. by L. B. Hopkins   *no death*

13 From borrowing one gets poorer and from work one gets richer.

Isaac Bashevis Singer, Polish-American author, "Utzel & His Daughter, Poverty" from *Stories for Children* (F)

14 If more of us valued food and cheer and song above hoarded gold, it would be a merrier world.

J. R. R. Tolkien, English author, said by the dwarf Thorin, *The Hobbit* (F)

Weather

(See also Nature*)*

1 It's raining, it's pouring,
  The old man is snoring,
  He got into bed and bumped his head
  And didn't get up until morning.

  Anonymous folk poetry, found in *And the Green Grass Grew All Around*, comp. by A. Schwartz

2 [In Chewandswallow] . . . it never rained rain. It never snowed snow. And it never blew just wind. It rained things like soup and juice. It snowed mashed potatoes and green peas. And sometimes the wind blew in storms of hamburgers.

  Judi Barrett, US author, *Cloudy with a Chance of Meatballs* (F)

3 It had been raining for seven years; thousands upon thousands of days compounded and filled from one end to the other with rain. . . . And this was the way life was forever on the planet Venus.

  Ray Bradbury, US author, "All Summer in a Day" (F)

4 The summer fog was so low the whole world seemed to drip.

  Beverly Cleary, US author, written by Leigh, *Strider* (F)

5 The rain, when it came, didn't fall in the proper way but rushed to the west, fast as a flock of sparrows chasing a hungry gull from their nests.

  Michael Dorris, Native American author and anthropologist, said by Star Boy, *Morning Girl* (F)

6 Every cloud has a silver lining.
  English proverb

7 Rained all night the day I left, the
    weather it was dry;
  The sun so hot I froze to death, Susanna
    don't you cry.

  Stephen Foster, US songwriter, words to the song "Oh, Susanna!," found in *Gonna Sing My Head Off!*, coll. and arr. by K. Krull

8 The wind came in at hurricane strength. The tips of trees bent over and aimed toward the ground, like fishing rods hooked on a big one.

  Eddy Harris, US author, *Mississippi Solo* (NF)

9 Snow is snowy when it's snowing,
  I'm sorry it's slushy when it's going.

  Ogden Nash, US poet, "Winter Morning" found in *Custard and Company*, sel. by Q. Blake

10 The Black Snake Wind came to me,
   The Black Snake Wind came to me,
   Came and wrapped itself about
   Came here running with its song.

   Pima, North American Indian tribe, found in *The Trees Stand Shining*, sel. by Hettie Jones

11 I am Boom the thunder dragon.
   Taller than the tallest trees,
   I stir whirlwinds when I whisper.
   Mighty cyclones when I sneeze.

   Jack Prelutsky, US poet, "I AM **BOOM!**" from *The Dragons Are Singing Tonight*

12 Who has seen the wind?
   Neither you nor I:
   But when the trees bow down
   their heads,
   The wind is passing by.

   Christina Rossetti, English poet, "Who Has Seen the Wind?" found in the *Oxford Book of Poetry for Children*, comp. by E. Blishen

13 The fog comes
    on little cat feet.
It sits looking
    over the harbor and city
    on silent haunches
    and then moves away.

Carl Sandburg, US poet and biographer, "Fog," found in *Rainbows Are Made*, sel. by L. B. Hopkins

14 I know it is wet
And the sun is not sunny.
But we can have
Lots of good fun that is funny.

Dr. Seuss, US author, said by Cat, *The Cat in the Hat* (F)

15 The storm raged as if it had lost its mind completely. . . . The storm was turning into a full-fledged, screaming hurricane.

William Steig, US author and illustrator, *Abel's Island* (F)

16 [T]he wind was a separate thing, not part of the winter, but a lost, unloved soul, screaming and moaning and rushing about looking for a place to rest and reckon up its woes.

Ibid.

17 I saw you
    toss the
    kites on high
And blow the
    birds around the sky;
And all around I heard
    you pass,
Like ladies' skirts across the grass—
    O Wind, a-blowing all day long,
    O Wind, that sings so loud a song!

Robert Louis Stevenson, English poet, "The Wind" from *A Child's Garden of Verses*

18 Thunder is good, thunder is impressive; but it is lightning that does the work.

Mark Twain, US author, in a 1908 letter

19 Everybody talks about the weather, but nobody does anything about it.

Attributed to Charles Dudley Warner, US journalist

20 Whether the weather be fine,
Or whether the weather be not,
Whether the weather be cold,
Or whether the weather be hot,
We'll weather the weather
Whatever the weather,
Whether we like it or not.

"Weather," anonymous poem, found in *The BFC Young Book of Poetry*, sel. by B. Mathias

21 The wind shrieked and howled like nothing under heaven but a blizzard wind.

Laura Ingalls Wilder, US author, found in *Laura Ingalls Wilder: A Biography* by W. Anderson (NF)

Whales

(See Sea Life)

Winning and Losing

1 I try to do the right thing at the right time. They may just be little things, but usually they make the difference between winning and losing.

Kareem Abdul-Jabbar, US professional basketball player, in the May 1986 *Star* (NF)

2 The moral is clear: The wisest folks know
That it's so nice to win, but it's foolish to crow.

Aesop, Greek writer, the moral in the retelling of "The King of the Barnyard" from *Androcles and the Lion and Other Aesop's Fables* by T. Paxton (F)

3 I never thought about losing, but now that it's happened, the only thing is to do it right. . . . We all have to take defeats in life.

Muhammad Ali, US professional boxer, in a Mar. 31, 1973 speech after losing his first fight

4 Some of us are timid. We think we have something to lose so we don't try for that next hill.

Maya Angelou, US poet and author, in the Mar. 5, 1988 issue of *USA Today* (NF)

5 Everybody plays, everybody wins. That's the motto of our [soccer] program.

Avi, US author, said by Mr. Lester, *S.O.R. Losers* (F)

6 People have the right to be losers.

Avi, US author, said by Radosh, *S.O.R. Losers* (F)

7 You never conquer a mountain. You stand on the summit a few moments; then the wind blows your footprints away.

Arlene Blum, US mountain climber, *Annapurna* (NF)

8 Yes, it is a victory for me to win the Iditarod.* But it isn't amazing that I, a woman, did it. I did it because I am capable, and women are capable.

Susan Butcher, first US woman to win the Alaskan Iditarod, found in *Champions*, by B. Littlefield (NF)

1,100-mile Alaskan sled dog race

9 If you win non-violently, then you have a double victory, you have not only won your fight, but you remain free.

César Chávez, Mexican-American labor activist and organizer of farm workers, found in *The Fire in Our Souls* by R. Gonzalez (NF)

10 Winning [a title] once can be a fluke;* winning it twice proves you are the best.

Althea Gibson, US professional tennis player and golfer, *I Always Wanted To Be Somebody* (NF)   *accident*

11 Failure always makes me try harder the next time.

Michael Jordan, US professional basketball player, *I Can't Accept Not Trying* (NF)

12 Obstacles are challenges for winners, and excuses for losers.

M. E. Kerr, US author, said by Buddy's grandfather, *Gentlehands* (F)

13 Losing's just a number on a scoreboard.

Joseph Krumgold, US author, said by Andy's father, *Onion John* (F)

14 Winning is great, sure, but if you are really going to do something in life, the secret is learning how to lose.

Wilma Rudolph, US track star, found in *Wilma Rudolph* by T. Biracree (NF)

15 Without losing, you cannot win.

Russian proverb

16 Winning is neither everything nor the only thing. It is one of many things.

Joan Benoit Samuelson, US Olympic runner, found in *Champions* by B. Littlefield (NF)

17 I think that all of [Charlie Brown's] readers can sympathize with him since everybody has had experiences in losing. Only one person can win, but the rest have to lose. Besides, what's so funny about winning?

Charles Schultz, US cartoonist and creator of "Peanuts," *Charles Brown, Snoopy, and Me* (NF)

18 Let others cheer the winning man,
There's one I hold worthwhile;
'Tis he who does the best he can,
Then loses with a smile.

"A Smile," anonymous poem, found in *The Book of Virtues*, ed. by W. J. Bennett

19 I've never been number two in my life. I can't stand to lose. More than that, I won't. Like one of my T-shirts says:
REFOOZE TO LOOZE.

Jerry Spinelli, US author, thought by Crash, *Crash* (F)

Wishes

1 Do you seriously believe anything worthwhile can be had merely for the wishing?

Lloyd Alexander, US author, said by the wizard Arbican, *The Wizard in the Tree* (F)

2 [P]eople always said to put things under your pillow when you go to bed, and if you make a wish, it will come true.

William H. Armstrong, US author, *Sounder* (F)

3 If I had my way, I'd remove January from the calendar altogether and have an extra July instead.

Roald Dahl, English author, *Roald Dahl, My Year* (NF)

4 I wish I were like you. . . . You're not afraid of anything.

Sid Fleischman, US author, said by the prince to Jemmy, *The Whipping Boy* (F)

5 The things are mighty few on earth
That wishes can attain.
Whate'er we want of any worth
We've got to work to gain.

Edgar A. Guest, English-American journalist and poet, "Results and Roses," found in *The Book of Virtues*, ed. by W. J. Bennett

6 Wishes on their way to coming true will not be rushed.

Arnold Lobel, US author and illustrator, the moral in "The Poor Old Dog" from *Fables* (F)

7 Wishes are free.

George Ella Lyons, US author, said by Amanda's father, *Borrowed Children* (F)

8 Even the wishes of an ant reach heaven.

Japanese proverb

9 Wishes are funny, aren't they? . . . Sometimes they come true differently than you think they will.

Patricia Polacco, US author, *My Rotten Redheaded Older Brother* (F)

10 Because you . . . wished too much, you received nothing.

Isaac Bashevis Singer, Polish-American author, said by an old man, "A Tale of Three Wishes" from *Stories for Children* (F)

11 I wish *we* had tails to wag.

Dodie Smith, English author, said by Mr. Dearly, *The 101 Dalmatians* (F)

12 Peace with all the world is my sincere wish.

George Washington, 1st US President, in an Aug. 15, 1798 letter to the Rev. Jonathan Boucher

13 When you wish upon a star, makes no difference who you are,
Anything your heart desires will come to you.

Ned Washington, US lyricist, words to the song "When You Wish Upon a Star" from Walt Disney's *Pinocchio*

Witches and Wizards

1 Which is the witch that wished the wicked wish?

Anonymous tongue twister, found in *A Twister of Twists, A Tangler of Tongues*, col. by A. Schwartz

2 In the civilized countries I believe there are no witches left; nor wizards, nor sorceresses, nor magicians. But, you see, the Land of Oz has never been civilized, for we are cut off from the rest of the world. Therefore we still have witches and wizards among us.

L. Frank Baum, US author, said by the Witch of the North, *The Wonderful Wizard of Oz* (F)

3 The Witch did not bleed where she was bitten [by Toto], for she was so wicked that the blood in her had dried up many years before.

L. Frank Baum, US author, *The Wonderful Wizard of Oz* (F)

4 I'm not much good as a witch. I don't like mixing the brews or making spells to hurt people.

Elizabeth Coatsworth, US author and poet, said by Pretty, "Witch Girl," found in *A Newbery Halloween*, Introduction by L. Alexander (F)

5 [The woman's] furious oaths made Beetle truly fear she was a witch, for only someone who had truck* with the devil could know such words.

Karen Cushman, US author, thought by Beetle, *The Midwife's Apprentice* (F)   *dealings

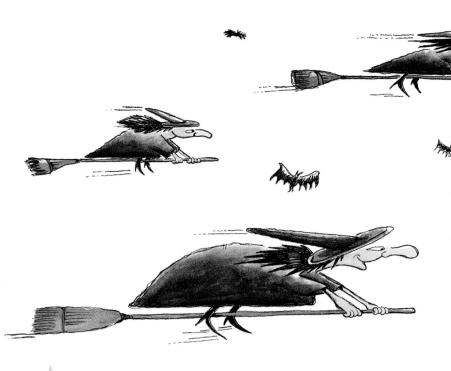

Women's Rights

1 If particular care and attention is not paid to the Ladies, we are determined to foment* a Rebellion, and will not hold ourselves bound by any Laws in which we have no voice, or Representation.

> Abigail Adams, wife of the 2nd US President, in a Mar. 31, 1776 letter to her husband, John   *stir up

6 On Halloween, what bothers some
About these witches is, how come
In sailing through the air like bats
They never seem to lose their hats?

> David McCord, US poet, "Witch's Broom Notes" from *One at a Time*

7 Day and night these witches boiled up wicked thoughts in a cauldron . . . lying in wait for people they could tempt, lives they could ruin. They could not tempt good people, only people whose thoughts were already evil.

> Bernard Miles, English actor and author, the retelling of *Macbeth* from *Favorite Tales from Shakespeare* (F)

8 The wizard, watchful, waits alone
within his tower of cold gray stone
and ponders in his wicked way
what evil deeds he'll do this day.

> Jack Prelutsky, US poet, "The Wizard" from *Nightmares: Poems to Trouble Your Sleep*

9 Wizards don't need magic to do nasty things.

> Patricia C. Wrede, US author, said by Trouble the cat, *Calling on Dragons* (F)

2 In the new code of laws which I suppose it will be necessary for you to make, I desire you would remember the Ladies and be more generous and favorable to them than your ancestors.

> *Ibid.*

3 I believe that it is as much a right and duty for women to do something with their lives as for men.

> Louisa May Alcott, US author, *Rose in Bloom* (NF)

4 Let the professions be open to [women]; let fifty years of college education be hers, and then we shall see what we shall see. Then, and not until then, shall we be able to say what woman can and what she cannot do.

> Louisa May Alcott, US author, in an 1874 letter to Maria S. Porter, found in *Great Americans in Their Own Words* (NF)

5 Join the union, girls, and together say *Equal Pay for Equal Work*.

> Susan B. Anthony, US suffragist and reformer, in the Mar. 18, 1869 issue of her newspaper *The Revolution* (NF)

6 You, you blind men, have become slave-holders of your own mothers and wives.

Susan B. Anthony, US suffragist and reformer, "Susan B. Anthony," by Strong and Leonard, found in *The Book of Virtues*, ed. by W. J. Bennett (NF)

7 Within the stable economy, it's necessary to eliminate all forms of sexual discrimination, and to provide women for the first time in our history with economic opportunities equal to those of men.

Jimmy Carter, 39th US President, in an Oct. 2, 1976 speech in Washington, D.C.

8 The law cannot do it for us. *We must do it for ourselves.* Women in this country must become revolutionaries.

Shirley Chisholm, US politician, found in *Words to Make My Dream Children Live*, ed. by D. Mullane (NF)

11 [Women] are half the people; [women] should be half the Congress.

Jeannette Rankin, US politician, in the Feb. 14, 1966 *Newsweek* magazine (NF)

12 I am Woman, hear me roar
In numbers too big to ignore.

Helen Reddy, Australian-American singer and composer, words to the song "I Am Woman"

13 *Resolved*, that woman is man's equal, was intended to be so by the Creator, and the highest good of the race demands that she should be recognized as such.

Seneca Falls Declaration of Women's Rights, July 19, 1848

9 I think it's important to credit the women's movement with creating the climate that made [it possible for me to be the first woman to compete in the Indianapolis 500].

Janet Guthrie, US professional car racer, found in *Women in Sports* by J. Layden (NF)

10 I had no idea when I was appointed [the first woman on the U.S. Supreme Court] how *much* it would mean to many people around the country. . . . [P]eople saw the appointment as a signal that there are virtually unlimited opportunities for women.

Sandra Day O'Connor, US Supreme Court Associate Justice, in the July 1992 *Biography Today* (NF)

14 We hold these truths to be self—evident, that all men and women are created equal.

Elizabeth Stanton, US women's rights leader, in a speech at the first Women's Rights Convention on July 19–20, 1848

15 Farm women have always been wage earners and partners in their husband's businesses, but no one ever noticed.

Laura Ingalls Wilder, US author, found in *Laura Ingalls Wilder: A Biography* by W. Anderson (NF)

Words

(See also Language)

1 We have too many high sounding words, and too few actions that correspond to them.

Abigail Adams, wife of the 2nd US President, in a 1774 letter to her husband, John

2 Trees are swayed by winds, men by words.

Joan Aiken, English author, said by Dan, "Think of a Word" from *The Last Slice of Rainbow* (F)

3 Words are like spices. Too many is worse than too few.

Ibid.

4 I like good strong words that mean something.

Louisa May Alcott, US author, said by Jo, *Little Women* (F)

5 Words mean more than what is set down on paper. It takes the human voice to infuse* them with shades of deeper meaning.

Maya Angelou, US poet and author, *I Know Why the Caged Bird Sings* (NF)   *fill

6 [Because of Gordon's southern accent] his words sounded like they were covered with maple syrup, kind of gooey with sliding sounds all over them.

Tom Birdseye, US author, said by Ryan, *Tarantula Shoes* (F)

7 Words do wonderful things. They sound purr. They can urge, they can wheedle, whip, whine. They can sing, sass, singe. They can churn, check, channelize. They can be a hup 2, 3, 4.

Gwendolyn Brooks, US poet, the Afterword to *Contending Forces* (NF)

8 Words are wonderful. By writing them and putting them together, I could make them say whatever I wanted to say. It was a kind of magic.

Clyde Robert Bulla, US author, *A Grain of Wheat: A Writer Begins* (NF)

9 *[L]ook* was Pa's favorite word; it meant admire, wonder, goggle at the beauty and excitement all around us.

Karen Cushman, US author, said by Lucy, *The Ballad of Lucy Whipple* (F)

10 Bah! Humbug!

Charles Dickens, English author, said by Scrooge, *A Christmas Carol* (F)

11 A word is dead
   When it is said.
      Some say.
   I say it just
   Begins to live
      That day.

Emily Dickinson, US poet, "A Word" from *The Collected Poems of Emily Dickinson*

12 You can't take [words] back. . . . They sit there like big damp frogs.

Paula Fox, US author, said by Aaron, *Western Wind* (F)

13 *Tough* and *tuff* are two different words. *Tough* is the same as rough; *tuff* means cool, sharp—like a tuff looking [car]. . . . In our neighborhood both are compliments.

S. E. Hinton, US author, said by Ponyboy, *The Outsiders* (F)

14 Good words do not last long unless they amount to something. Words do not pay for my dead people. They do not pay for my country, now overrun by white men. . . . I am tired of talk that comes to nothing. It makes my heart sick when I remember all the good words and broken promises [of the white men].

Chief Joseph, leader of the Nez Perce, found in *Bury My Heart at Wounded Knee* by D. Brown (NF)

15 You see . . . Dictionopolis is the place where all the words in the world come from. They're grown right here in our orchards.

Norton Juster, US author, said by one of the king's ministers, *The Phantom Tollbooth* (F)

16 "Steady! . . . Down! . . . Stay!" Shepherding suited Farmer Hogget—there was no waste of words in it.

Dick King-Smith, English author, *Babe the Gallant Pig* (F)

17 Words are, of course, the most powerful drug used by mankind.

Rudyard Kipling, English-American journalist and author, in a Feb. 14, 1923 speech

18 Words can destroy. What we call each other ultimately becomes what we think of each other, and it matters.

Jeane Kirkpatrick, US Ambassador to the United Nations, in a Feb. 11, 1982 speech

19 The ballpoint pen has been the biggest single factor in the decline of Western Civilization. It makes the written word cheap, fast, and totally without character.

E. L. Konigsburg, US author and illustrator, said by Noah Gershom, *The View from Saturday* (F)

20 Just think of the words they make up— "tub" and "stopper" and "string" and words like that. Where they get them from, nobody knows. But a wonderful word like "spink," they don't bother to invent.

Astrid Lindgren, Swedish author, said by Pippi, *Pippi in the South Seas* (F)

21 [Anastasia] was listening . . . to the words that were appearing in her own head, floating there and arranging themselves into groups, into lines, into poems.

Lois Lowry, US author, *Anastasia Krupnik* (F)

22 Inside this pencil
couch words that have
never been written
never been spoken
never been thought
they're hiding.

W. S. Merwin, US poet, "The Unwritten" from *Writings to an Unfinished Accompaniment*

23 For Owl, wise though he was in many ways . . . somehow went all to pieces over delicate words like MEASLES and BUTTERED TOAST.

A. A. Milne, English author, "Eeyore Loses a Tail" from *Winnie-the-Pooh* (F)

24 A trite word is an overused word which has lost its identity like an old coat in a second-hand shop. The familiar grows dull and we no longer see, hear, or taste it.

Anaïs Nin, French-American author, *The Diary of Anaïs Nin* (NF)

25 I found things I could say with color and shapes that I couldn't say in any other way . . . things I had no words for.

Georgia O'Keeffe, US painter, found in *Painting: Great Lives* by S. Glubok (NF)

26 Some words clink
As ice in a drink.
Some move with grace
A dance, a lace.
Some sound thin:
Wail, scream and pin.
Some words are squat:
A mug, a pot.

Mary O'Neill, US poet, "Feelings About Words" found in *The Random House Book of Poetry for Children*, sel. by J. Prelutsky

27 *Need* is a weak word. Has nothing to do with what people get.

Robert Newton Peck, US author, said by Rob's father, *A Day No Pigs Would Die* (F)

28 Look out how you use proud words,
When you let proud words go, it is not easy to call them back.

Carl Sandburg, US poet and biographer, "Primer Lesson," found in *Rainbows Are Made*, sel. by L. B. Hopkins

29 Polite words open iron gates.

Serbo-Croatian proverb

30 The rest of the Abbotts fought quietly and politely by using words that said one thing and meant another.

Zilpha Keatley Snyder, US author, *The Changeling* (F)

31 Supercalifragilisticexpialidocious

Song title from Walt Disney's *Mary Poppins*

32 That night . . . [Bobby and Jamie] had flung words into the darkness and, like fireworks, the words had burst and showered their future with light.

Jerry Spinelli, US author, "Mongoose" from *The Library Card* (F)

Work

1 By the seventh day God had finished the work He had been doing; so on the seventh day He rested from all his work.

Bible, Genesis 2:2-3 (NIV)

2 Tell our children they're not going to jive their way up the career ladder. They have to work their way up hard. There's no fast elevator to the top.

Marian Wright Edelman, US lawyer and public official, in the Aug. 1988 *Ebony* magazine (NF)

3 All work and no play makes Jack a dull boy.

English proverb

4 Laziness may *appear* attractive, but work *gives* satisfaction.

Anne Frank, Dutch diarist, *Anne Frank: The Diary of a Young Girl*, July 6, 1944 entry (NF)

5 I've always believed that if you put in the work, the results will come.

Michael Jordan, US professional basketball player, *I Can't Accept Not Trying* (NF)

6 Whatever your life's work is, do it well.

Martin Luther King, Jr., US civil rights leader, found in *I Have a Dream: The Life and Words of Martin Luther King, Jr.* by J. Haskins (NF)

7 I grumbled as a child with all the housework and practicing I had to do. . . . Now, when I look back, I am grateful because hard work made me stronger and a more responsible person.

June Kuramoto, Japanese-American musician and composer, found in *Famous Asian Americans* by Morey and Dunn (NF)

8 It seemed the ordained order of things that dogs should work. . . . They hauled cabin logs and firewood, freighted up to the mines, and did all manner of work that horses did in the Santa Clara Valley.

Jack London, US author, *The Call of the Wild* (F)

9 Just whistle while you
    work.
  Put on that grin and
    start right in,
  To whistle loud and long.

Larry Morey, US lyricist, words to the song "Whistle While You Work" from Walt Disney's *Snow White*

10 Far and away the best prize that life offers is the chance to work hard at work worth doing.

Theodore Roosevelt, 26th US President, in a Sept. 7, 1903 Labor Day speech

11 I'm tired and I'm bored
And I've kinks in my leg
From sitting, just sitting here day
   after day.
It's *work*! How I hate it!
I'd *much* rather play.

Dr. Seuss, US author, said by Horton, *Horton Hatches the Egg* (F)

12 I don't claim anything of the work. It is [God's] work. I am like a little pencil in His hand. . . . The pencil has only to be allowed to be used.

Mother Teresa, Yugoslavian missionary in India, in a 1986 speech at the Awakening Conference in CO

13 Work consists of whatever a body is *obliged** to do, and Play consists of whatever a body is not obliged to do.

Mark Twain, US author, *The Adventures of Tom Sawyer* (F)   *forced

14 No race can prosper till it learns that there is as much dignity in tilling a field as in writing a poem.

Booker T. Washington, US educator and author, *Up from Slavery* (NF)

15 Nothing ever comes to one, that is worth having, except as a result of hard work.
Ibid.

16 Luck had nothing to do with [the hatching of seven goslings]. It was good management and hard work.

E. B. White, US author, said by a goose, *Charlotte's Web* (F)

17 We should all do what, in the long run, gives us joy, even if it is only picking grapes or sorting the laundry.

E. B. White, US author, in a Nov. 10, 1963 letter to Judith Preusser

18 I worked sixteen hours a day and had never been happier in my life.

Laurence Yep, Chinese-American author, said by Moon Shadow, *Dragonwings* (F)

World

1 In the beginning God created the heavens and the earth.

Bible, Genesis 1:1 (NIV)

2 [C]ontact the space probe. I want to invade that primitive ball of mud called Earth before lunch.

Claire Boiko, US playwright, said by Think-Tank in the play *The Book That Saved the Earth* (F)

3 If everyone minded their own business . . . the world would go round a deal faster than it does.

Lewis Carroll, English author, said by the Duchess, *Alice's Adventures in Wonderland* (F)

4 Each of us has his place in the world. If we cannot serve in one way, there is always another. If we do what we are able, a door always opens to something else.

Marguerite de Angeli, English author and illustrator, said by Sir Peter, *The Door in the Wall* (F)

5 I began to wonder if the Branton Town Hall Clock wasn't a bit like this old earth of ours, . . . the way it's all got to balance to keep going, and bits of it we'll never understand, and us messing around with it not knowing what we're doing, and us sharing it with things like mice, and it needing them as much as it needs us, and all that.

Peter Dickinson, English author, *Time and the Clock Mice, Etcetera* (F)

6 Oh, I'm all for rockets
And worlds cold or hot,
But I'm wild in love
With the planet we've got!

Frances Frost, US poet, "Valentine for Earth" from *The Little Naturalist*

7 Take the world as it is, not as it ought to be.

German proverb

8 No one on this entire planet was separate from anyone else. We were all connected, by the water we drank, the air we breathed. The release of radiation from Cookshire had risen into the atmosphere. . . . Halfway around the world it had tainted rice crops, poisoned grazing fields, turned the air toxic where babies slept in the open.

Karen Hesse, US author, thought by Nyle, *Phoenix Rising* (F)

9 We must use our lives to make the world a better place, not just to acquire things. That is what we are put on earth for.

Dolores Huerta, Mexican-American Vice President of the United Farm Workers, found in *Famous Mexican Americans* by Morey and Dunn (NF)

10 What happens to the country, to the world, depends on what we do with what others have left us.

Robert F. Kennedy, US Attorney General and brother of the 35th US President, the Foreword to *Profiles in Courage* by J. F. Kennedy (NF)

11 It is going to take an act of Congress to deal with poverty and hunger, not only in this country, but throughout the world. We have the resources, but we don't have the will.

Coretta Scott King, US civil rights activist and wife of Martin Luther King, Jr., found in *In Search of Our Mothers' Gardens* by A. Walker (NF)

12 But do you really mean . . . there could be other worlds — all over the place, just around the corner — like that?

C. S. Lewis, English author, said by Peter, *The Lion, the Witch, and the Wardrobe* (F)

13 What's the matter with the world? There ain't nothing but one word wrong with every one of us, and that's selfishness.

Will Rogers, US humorist and author, found in *Will Rogers: Quotable Cowboy* by C. L. Bennett (NF)

14 We don't have two planets — one to live on and one to squander. We have to keep this world from deteriorating.*

George Schaller, US naturalist and field biologist, in the Feb. 2, 1997 *Parade* magazine (NF)   *worsening

15 A person who is able to contribute something to the world is a fortunate person, and each of us should be able at least to "brighten the corner" where we are.

Charles Schultz, US cartoonist and creator of "Peanuts," *Charles Brown, Snoopy, and Me* (NF)

Writers and Writing

(See also Books *and* Reading*)*

1 I have written mostly animal stories. . . . They must take off from something funny. . . . Kids like to be happy and my books give them the opportunity.

Jose Aruego, Philippine-American author and illustrator, found in *Famous Asian Americans* by Morey and Dunn (NF)

2 I think I write the kinds of books I would have liked to read when young.

Judy Blume, US author, in the Jan. 1992 *Biography Today* (NF)

3 I am a writer perhaps *because* I am not a talker.

Gwendolyn Brooks, US poet, found in *My Soul Looks Back, 'Less I Forget*, ed. by D. W. Riley (NF)

4 Writing is like anything — baseball, playing, piano playing, sewing, hammering nails. The more you work at it, the better you get. But it seems to take a longer time to get better at writing than hammering nails.

Betsy Byars, US author, *The Moon and I: A Memoir* (NF)

5 A real live author had called *me* an author. A real live author had told me to keep it up. Mom was proud of me when I told her.

Beverly Cleary, US author, said by Leigh Botts, *Dear Mr. Henshaw* (F)

6 It was a lot easier to write what I thought or felt than to say it out loud. I could write things I'd never say to someone's face.

Karen Cushman, US author, thought by Lucy, *The Ballad of Lucy Whipple* (F)

7 Writers "get started" the day they are born. The minds they bring into the world with them are the amazing machines their stories will come out of, and the more they feed into it, the richer those stories will be.

Lois Duncan, US author, *Chapters: My Growth as a Writer* (NF)

8 A writer needs three things: experience, observation, and imagination.

William Faulkner, US author, found in *The International Thesaurus of Quotations*, ed. by Ehrlich and DeBruhl (NF)

9 The Indian needs no writing. Words that are true sink deep into his heart where they remain. He never forgets them. On the other hand, if the white man loses his paper, he is helpless.

Four Guns, member of the Oglala Sioux, found in *American Indian Voices*, ed. by K. Harvey (NF)

10 I can shake off everything if I write; my sorrows disappear, my courage is reborn.

Anne Frank, Dutch diarist, *Anne Frank: The Diary of a Young Girl*, Apr. 4, 1944 entry (NF)

11 [Playing the tuba] is exactly the same with writing. You sit down and you do it, and you do it, and you do it, until you have learned how to do it. Of course, there are differences. Writing makes no noise, except groans, and it can be done any-where, and it is done alone.

Ursula K. Le Guin, US author, "Talking about Writing" from *The Language of the Night: Essays on Fantasy and Science Fiction* (NF)

12 I wrote my first story when I was five, and have been writing ever since.

Madeleine L'Engle, US author, in the Jan. 1992 *Biography Today* (NF)

13 I am a believer in regular work, and [I] never wait for inspiration.

Jack London, US author, found in *Jack London: A Biography* by D. Dyer (NF)

14 One interesting thing about writing is that when you're making up a story, you're in charge. You can solve problems the way you wish they could be solved in real life.

Ann M. Martin, US author, in *Ann M. Martin: The Story of the Author of the Baby-sitters Club* by M. Becker R. (NF)

15 This writing business. Pencils and what-not. Over-rated, if you ask me. Silly stuff. Nothing in it.

A. A. Milne, English author, said by Eeyore, "We Say Good-Bye," found in *The House at Pooh Corner* (F)

16 I don't do any of the so-called fun things in life. Writing is what I do, for me that is where it is — where the vacation is, the fun is, the danger, the excitement — all of that is in my work.

Toni Morrison, US author, in the Jan. 1994 *Biography Today* (NF)

17 When people ask me what qualifies me to be a writer for children, I say I was once a child.

Katherine Paterson, US author, *Gates of Excellence* (NF)

18 The challenge [in writing] is to find cheap thrills . . . like the cat is boiled in the spaghetti, a girl pours honey over a boy and sets ants on him. [Children] like the gross stuff.

R. L. Stine, US author of the Goosebumps books, in the Apr. 1994 *Biography Today* (NF)

19 Vigorous* writing is concise. A sentence should contain no unnecessary words, a paragraph no unnecessary sentences, for the same reason that a drawing should have no unnecessary lines and a machine no unnecessary parts.

William Strunk, Jr., US author, *The Elements of Style* (1918) (NF)   *strong, effective

20 There ain't nothing more to write about, and I am rotten glad of it, because if I'd knowed what a trouble it was to make a book I wouldn't a tackled it, and ain't agoing to no more.

Mark Twain, US author, the last paragraph of *The Adventures of Huckleberry Finn* (F)

Youth

(See Children*)*

Zoos

1 Roses are red,
   Violets are blue,
   A face like yours
   Belongs in the zoo.

Anonymous folk poetry, found in *And the Green Grass Grew All Around*, comp. by A. Schwartz

2 Come to the Central Park Zoo Cafeteria. Let the animals watch you eat for a change.

Central Park Zoo advertising slogan

3 Once upon a time, not so long ago, zoos were little more than jails. Animals were kidnapped from the wild and imprisoned in bleak cells.

Charles Hirshberg, US journalist, "Miracle Babies," in the Mar. 1997 *Life* magazine (NF)

4 Conservationists warn that within a generation, one out of five species living on earth today may be gone forever. For all too many animals, zoos may be the last best hope.

Ibid.

5 I've been to the zoo
      where the thing that you do
      is watching the things
      that the animals do —

   and watching
      the animals
      all watching
            you!

Myra Cohn Livingston, US poet and teacher, "At the Zoo," found in *To the Zoo: Animal Poems,* sel. by L. B. Hopkins

6 Now we've been collected, too. This whole damned place is just a zoo—a zoo for aliens so far ahead of us we don't dare dream what they're like.

Robert Silverberg, US author, said by Gus, "Collecting Team" from *Science Fiction Bestiary* (F)

7 I dreamed we were at the Zoo . . . and instead of animals in the cages there were human beings, and all the animals were outside.

P. L. Travers, Australian-English author, said by Jane, *Mary Poppins* (F)

Bibliography of Secondary Sources

Aaseng, Nathan. *American Profiles: 20th Century Inventors.* New York: Facts on File, 1997.

Alexander, Lloyd, Introduction to *A Newbery Halloween.* New York: Delacorte Press, 1993.

Allen, Paula Gunn and Patricia Clark Smith. *As Long as the Rivers Flow: The Stories of Nine Native Americans.* New York: Scholastic Inc., 1996.

Anderson, William. *Laura Ingalls Wilder: A Biography.* New York: HarperCollins, 1992.

Anthony, Carl S. *America's Most Influential First Ladies.* Minneapolis: Oliver Press, Inc., 1992.

Aparicio, Francis R., ed. *Latino Voices.* Brookfield, CT: The Millbrook Press, 1994.

Ashby, Ruth and Deborah Gore Ohrn, eds. *Herstory: Women Who Changed the World.* New York: Viking, 1995.

Bauer, Caroline Feller, ed. *Valentine's Day: Stories and Poems.* New York: HarperCollins, 1993.

Becker R., Margot, with Ann M. Martin. *Ann M. Martin: The Story of the Author of the Baby-sitters Club.* New York: Scholastic Inc., 1993.

Bennett, Cathereen L. *Will Rogers: Quotable Cowboy.* Minneapolis: Runestone Press, 1995.

Bennett, William J., ed. *The Book of Virtues: A Treasury of Great Moral Stories.* New York: Simon & Schuster, 1993.

_____, ed. *The Book of Virtues for Young People: A Treasury of Great Moral Stories.* New Jersey: Silver Burdett Press, Inc., 1996.

Biggs, Mary. *Women's Words: The Columbia Book of Quotations by Women.* New York: Columbia University Press, 1966.

Biracree, Tom. *Wilma Rudolph: Champion Athlete.* New York: Chelsea House, 1988.

Blake, Quintin, poems selected and illustrated by. *Custard and Company: Poems by Ogden Nash.* Boston: Little, Brown and Co., 1980.

Blishen, Edward, compiled by. *Oxford Book of Poetry for Children.* New York: Franklin Watts, 1963.

Bober, Natalie S. *A Restless Spirit: The Story of Robert Frost.* New York: Henry Holt, 1991.

Brewton, Sara and John E., compiled by. *Laughable Limericks.* New York: Thomas Y. Crowell Co., 1965.

Brown, Dee. *Bury My Heart at Wounded Knee.* New York: Henry Holt & Company, 1970.

Browne, Ray B., ed. *Contemporary Heroes and Heroines.* Detroit: Gale Research Inc., 1990.

Bruns, Roger. *George Washington.* New York: Chelsea House, 1987.

Bumann, Joan and John Peterson. *Our American Presidents: From Washington through Clinton.* St. Petersburg, FL: Willowwisp Press, 1993.

Carey, John, ed. *Eyewitness to History.* New York: Avon Books, 1987.

Carruth, Gorton and Eugene Ehrlich. *American Quotations.* New York: Wings Books, 1988.

Cohn, Amy L., compiled by. *From Sea to Shining Sea: A Treasury of American Folklore and Folk Songs.* New York: Scholastic Inc., 1993.

Cox, Clinton. *Mark Twain: America's Humorist, Dreamer, Prophet.* New York: Scholastic Inc., 1955.

Cwiklik, Robert. *Tecumseh: Shawnee Rebel.* New York: Chelsea House, 1993.

Davidson, Margaret. *Frederick Douglass Fights for Freedom.* New York: Four Winds Press, 1968.

Donadio, Stephen and others, ed. *The New York Public Library Book of Twentieth-Century American Quotations*. New York: Warner Books, Inc., 1993.

Douglass, Frederick. *Escape from Slavery*, edited by Michael McCurdy. New York: Alfred A. Knopf, 1994.

Durell, Ann, collected by. *The Anderson Book of American Folk Tales*. London: Anderson Press, 1989.

Dyer, Daniel. *Jack London: A Biography*. New York: Scholastic Inc., 1997.

The EarthWorks Group. *50 Simple Things Kids Can Do to Save the Earth*. Kansas City, MO: Andrews and McNeil Books, 1990.

Ehrlich, Eugene and Marshall De Bruhl, eds. *The International Thesaurus of Quotations*. New York: Harper Perennial, 1996.

Freedman, Russell. *Eleanor Roosevelt: A Life of Discovery*. New York: Clarion Books, 1993.

_____. *Indian Chiefs*. New York: Holiday House, 1987.

_____. *Lincoln: A Photobiography*. New York: Clarion Books, 1987.

_____. *The Wright Brothers: How They Invented the Airplane*. New York: Holiday House, 1991.

Frost, Lawrence F. *The Thomas A. Edison Album*. Seattle: Superior Publishers, 1969.

Gallo, Donald, ed. *Within Reach: Ten Stories*. New York: HarperCollins, 1993.

Gesner, George, ed. *The Anthology of American Poetry*. Roanoke, VA: Avenel Books, 1983.

Glubok, Shirley. *Painting: Great Lives*. New York: Charles Scribner's Sons, 1994.

Goepfert, Paula S., ed. *The Children's Treasury: Best-Loved Stories and Poems from Around the World*. Ontario: Discovery Books, 1987.

Gonzalez, Rosie. *The Fire in Our Souls: Quotations of Wisdom and Inspiration by Latino Americans*. New York: A Plume Book, 1996.

Great Americans in Their Own Words: Extracts by 20 Heroic Men and Women. New York: Mallard Press, 1990.

Greene, Richard and Katherine Barrett. *The Man Behind the Magic: The Story of Walt Disney*. New York: Viking Children's Books, 1991.

Greenspan, Bud. *100 Greatest Moments in Olympic History*. Los Angeles: General Publishing Group, Inc., 1995.

Halifax, Joan. *Shamanic Voices*. New York: Viking Penguin, 1991.

Harper, Ida Husted. *The Life and Work of Susan B. Anthony*. New York: Arno, 1969.

Harvey, Karen, ed. *American Indian Voices*. Brookfield, CT: The Millbrook Press, 1995.

Haskins, Jim. *I Have a Dream: The Life and Words of Martin Luther King, Jr.* Brookfield, CT: The Millbrook Press, 1992.

_____. *The Story of Stevie Wonder*. New York: Lothrop, Lee & Shepard Co., 1976.

Hopkins, Lee Bennett, selected by. *Rainbows Are Made: Poems by Carl Sandburg*. New York: Harcourt Brace Jovanovich, 1982.

_____, selected by. *The Sky Is Full of Song*. New York: Harper & Row, 1983.

_____, selected by. *To the Zoo: Animal Poems*. Boston: Little, Brown and Co., 1992.

Hurwitz, Johanna, ed. *Birthday Surprises: Ten Great Stories to Unwrap*. New York: Morrow Junior Books, 1995.

Igus, Toyomi and others. *Book of Black Heroes, Vol. Two: Great Women in the Struggle*. East Orange, NJ: Just Us Books, 1991.

Jacobs, William Jay. *Great Lives: Human Rights*. New York: Atheneum Books for Young Readers, 1990.

Jezer, Marty. *Rachel Carson: Biologist and Author*. New York: Chelsea House, 1988.

Johnson, Mary Oates. *The President: America's Leader*. Austin, TX: Raintree, Steck Vaughan, 1993.

Johnston, Norma. *Louisa May: The World and Works of Louisa May Alcott.* New York: Four Winds Press, 1991.

Jones, Hettie, selected by. *The Trees Stand Shining: Poetry of the North American Indians.* New York: Dial Press, 1971.

Josephy, Alvin M. Jr. *500 Nations: An Illustrated History of North American Indians.* New York: Alfred A. Knopf, 1994.

Kent, Deborah and Kathryn A. Quinlin. *Extraordinary People with Disabilities.* New York: Children's Press, 1996.

Kosof, Anna. *Jesse Jackson.* New York: Franklin Watts, 1987.

Krull, Kathleen, songs collected and arranged by. *Gonna Sing My Head Off! American Folk Songs for Children.* New York: Alfred A. Knopf, 1992.

Lash, Joseph P. *Eleanor and Franklin.* New York: Norton, 1971.

Layden, Joe. *Women in Sports: The Complete Book of the World's Greatest Female Athletes.* Santa Monica, CA: General Publishing Group, 1997.

Lazo, Caroline. *Jimmy Carter: On the Road to Peace.* New Jersey: Silver Burdett Press, 1996.

Littlefield, Bill. *Champions: Stories of Ten Remarkable Athletes.* Boston: Little, Brown and Company, 1993.

Livingston, Myra Cohn, selected by. *Cat Poems.* New York: Holiday House, 1987.

_____, selected by. *Poems for Grandmothers.* New York: Holiday House, 1990.

Lyons, Mary E. *Letters from a Slave Girl: The Story of Harriet Jacobs.* New York: Charles Scribner's Sons, 1992.

Maggio, Rosalie, compiled by. *The Beacon Book of Quotations by Women.* Boston: Beacon Press, 1992.

Malone, Mary. *Maya Lin: Architect and Artist.* Springfield, NJ: Enslow Publishing, Inc., 1995.

Mathias, Beverly. *The BFC Young Book of Poetry.* St. Albans, VT: David Bennett Books, 1992.

McCaughrean, Geraldine, retold by. *The Random House Book of Stories from the Ballet.* New York: Random House, 1994.

McKissack, Patricia C. *Jesse Jackson: A Biography.* New York: Scholastic Inc., 1989.

McPhee, John. *A Sense of Where You Are: A Profile of William Warren Bradley.* New York: Farrar, Straus, Giroux, 1978.

Michener, James. *Sports in America.* New York: Random House, 1976.

Mieder, Wolfgang. *The Prentice-Hall Encyclopedia of World Proverbs: A Treasury of Wit and Wisdom Through the Ages.* Paramus, NJ: Prentice-Hall, Inc., 1986.

Miles, Bernard. *Favorite Tales from Shakespeare.* London: Hamlyn Publishing Group, 1976.

Miller, Merle. *Plain Speaking: An Oral Biography of Harry S Truman.* New York: Berkley Publishing, 1986.

Morey, Janet Nomura and Wendy Dunn. *Famous Asian Americans.* New York: Cobblehill Books, 1992.

_____. *Famous Hispanic Americans.* New York: Cobblehill Books, 1996.

_____. *Famous Mexican Americans.* New York: Puffin Books, 1989.

Morin, Isobel V. *Women of the U.S. Congress.* Minneapolis: The Oliver Press, Inc., 1994.

Mullane, Deirdre, ed. *Words to Make My Dream Children Live: A Book of African American Quotations.* New York: Anchor Books, 1995.

The New Illustrated Disney Songbook. New York: Harry N. Abrams, Inc., Publishers, 1986.

Opie, Iona and Peter, eds. *I Saw Esau: The Schoolchild's Pocket Book.* Cambridge: Candlewick Press, 1992.

Otfinoski, Steve. *Marian Wright Edelman: Defender of Children's Rights.* Woodbridge, CT: Blackbirch Press Inc., 1993.

_____. *Oprah Winfrey: Television Star.* Woodbridge, CT: Blackbirch Press Inc., 1993.

Paine, Albert B. *Mark Twain: A Biography*. New York: Chelsea House, 1980.

Potter, Robert R. *Benjamin Franklin*. Morristown, NJ: Silver Burdett Press, Inc., 1992.

Prelutsky, Jack, selected by. *A Nonny Mouse Writes Again!* New York: Dragonfly Books, 1993.

_____, selected by. *For Laughing Out Loud*. New York: Alfred A. Knopf, 1991.

_____, selected by. *For Laughing Out Louder*. New York: Alfred A. Knopf, 1995.

_____, selected by. *The Random House Book of Poetry for Children*. New York: Random House, 1983.

Ravitch, Diane, ed. *The American Reader: Words That Moved a Nation*. New York: HarperCollins, 1990.

Resnick, Jane P., ed. *The Classic Treasury of Silly Poetry*. Philadelphia: Courage Books, 1995.

Richardson, Polly, compiled by. *Animal Poems*. Hauppauge, NY: Barron's Educational Series, Inc., 1992.

Ricks, Christopher and William L. Vance, eds. *The Faber Book of America*. Boston: Faber and Faber, 1992.

Riley, Dorothy Winbush, ed. *My Soul Looks Back, 'Less I Forget: A Collection of Quotations by People of Color*. New York: HarperCollins, 1993.

Ross, Ishbel. *Angel of the Battlefield*. New York: Harper, 1956.

Schwartz, Alvin, compiled by. *And the Green Grass Grew All Around: Folk Poetry from Everyone*. New York: HarperCollins, 1992.

_____, collected by. *A Twister of Twists, A Tangler of Tongues*. New York: Harper & Row, 1972.

Scott, Richard. *Jackie Robinson: Baseball Great*. New York: Chelsea House, 1987.

Senn, J. A. *Jane Goodall: Naturalist*. Woodbridge, CT: Blackbirch Press, Inc., 1993.

Smith, John David. *Black Voices from Reconstruction: 1865-1877*. Brookfield, CT: The Millbrook Press, 1996.

Stepto, Michele, ed. *Our Song, Our Toil: The Story of American Slavery as Told by Slaves*. Brookfield, CT: The Millbrook Press, 1994.

Sterling, Philip. *Sea and Earth: The Life of Rachael Carson*. New York: Crown Publishing Co., 1970.

Sternburg, Janet, ed. *The Writer on Her Work*. New York: Norton, 1980.

Szabo, Corinne. *Sky Pioneer: A Photobiography of Amelia Earhart*. Washington, DC: National Geographic Society, 1997.

Tate, Claudia, ed. *Black Women Writers at Work*. New York: Continuum, 1983.

Untermeyer, Louis, ed. *The Golden Treasury of Animal Stories and Poems*. New York: Golden Press, 1971.

Vare, Ethlie A. and Greg Ptacek. *Women Inventors & Their Discoveries*. Minneapolis: Oliver Press, 1993.

Walker, Alice. *In Search of Our Mothers' Gardens*. New York: Harcourt Brace, 1984.

Ward, Geoffrey C. and Ken Burns. *Baseball, the American Epic: Who Invented the Game*. New York: Alfred A. Knopf, 1994.

Wepman, Dennis. *Helen Keller: Humanitarian*. New York: Chelsea House, 1987.

Whipple, Laura, compiled by. *Celebrating America: A Collection of Poems and Images of the American Spirit*. New York: Philomel Books, 1994.

People Index

*A listing of all the real people who
said or wrote the quotations in this book.*

Aaron, Hank (baseball player) Baseball 1;
ABOUT Aaron: Baseball 12

Aaseng, Nathan (author) Inventions and
Inventors 1

Abbott, Jim (baseball pitcher) Disabilities 1

Abdul-Jabbar, Kareem (basketball player)
Confidence 1; Education 1; Goals 1; Heroes
1; Winning and Losing 1

Adams, Abigail (wife of the 2nd President)
Women's Rights 1, 2; Words 1

Adams, John (2nd President) Government 1, 2;
The Presidency 1, 2, 3; Revolutionary War 1,
2, 3; ABOUT Adams: Peace 1

Adams, Samuel (Revolutionary patriot)
Revolutionary War 4

Adamson, Joy (wildlife conservationist)
Animals 1; Intelligence 1

Aesop (ancient Greek writer) Appearances 1;
Birds 1; Clothes 1; Courage 1; Friendship 1;
Kindness 1; Lies and Lying 1; Possible and
Impossible 1; Success and Failure 1;
Winning and Losing 2

Aiken, Joan (author) Birds 2; Dreams and
Nightmares 2; Monsters and Dragons 1;
Sounds 1; Trees 1; Words 2, 3

Alcott, Louisa May (author) Adventure 1;
Advice 1; Brothers and Sisters 1, 2; Death 1;
Equality 1; Fame 1, 2; Libraries 2; Reading
1; Sadness 1; War 1; Women's Rights 3, 4;
Words 4

Alexander, Cecil Frances (poet) Animals 2

*****Alexander, Lloyd** (author) Action 1; Advice 2;
Age 1; Appearances 2; Change 1; Good and
Bad 1; Hope 1; Magic 1; Trees 2; Wishes 1

Ali, Muhammad, *Cassius Clay* (boxer)
Disabilities 2; Fame 3; Occupations 1; Pride
1; Sports 1; Winning and Losing 3

Allen, Fred (radio comedian) Fame 4

Allen, Paula Gunn (author) Native Americans 1

Alou, Felipe (baseball manager) Brothers and
Sisters 3

Anderson, Marian (opera singer) Racism 1, 2

Anderson, William (author) Books 2

Angell, Judie (author) Change 2; Parents 1

Angell, Roger (sports writer) Excellence 1

Angelou, Maya (author and poet) Appearances
3; Change 3; Education 2; Fear 1; Home 2;
Language 1; Love 1; Mothers 1; Music 1;
Right and Wrong 1; Talent 1; Winning and
Losing 4; Words 5

Annixter, Paul (author) Animals 3

Anthony, Edward (poet) Advice 3

Anthony, Susan B. (suffragist) Education 3;
Equality 2; Voting 1; Women's Rights 5, 6

Arbus, Diane (photographer) Occupations 2

Armstrong, Neil A. (astronaut) Democracy 1;
Moon and Stars 1; Problems and Solutions 1;
Secrets 2; Space Exploration 1, 2; Under-
standing 2

*****Armstrong, William H.** (author) Change 4;
Death 3; Music 3; Peace 2; Wishes 2

Aruego, Jose (author and illustrator) Writers
and Writing 1

Ash, Mary Kay (Mary Kay Cosmetics founder)
Confidence 3

Ashe, Arthur (tennis player) Racism 3, 4, 5;
School 2

Asimov, Isaac (author) Monsters and Dragons
2

Avi, *Avi Wortis,* (author) Advice 4; Democracy
2; Responsibility 1; Right and Wrong 2;
Spelling 1; Sports 2, 3; Wealth and Poverty 2;
Winning and Losing 5, 6

B

Babbitt, Natalie (author) Change 5; Choices 1;
Conversation 2; Death 4; Dreams and
Nightmares 3; Future 1; Life 2; Names 2;
Nature 1; Respect 1; Sounds 3; Water 1

Bagert, Brod (poet) Birds 3

Bailey, Pearl (singer) God 1

Baiul, Oksana (skater) Sports 4

C

Cameron, Ann (author) Cats 2

Cameron, Eleanor (author) Differences 1; Dreams and Nightmares 4

Campbell, Ben Nighthorse (senator) Native Americans 3; Success and Failure 3

Carey, Mariah (singer) Determination 2

Carlson, Natalie Savage (author) Family 3

Carmichael, Stokely (civil rights activist) Racism 8

Carney, Julia (poet) Time 2

Carrick, Carol (author) Sounds 5

Carroll, Lewis (author) Age 5, 6; Beauty 2; Books 5; Cats 3; Conversation 3; Courage 3; Names 4; Possible and Impossible 4, 5; Sea Life 3; Talking 2; Truth 2; World 3; ABOUT Carroll: Likes and Dislikes 5

Carson, Benjamin (surgeon) Anger 5; Books 6

Carson, Rachel (environmentalist) Birds 6; Nature 3; Occupations 8; Pollution 2

Carter, Jimmy (39th President) Government 4; Peace 4; The Presidency 4, 5; Women's Rights 7

Carter, Rosalyn (wife of the 39th President) Responsibility 3

Castro, Raùl H. (ambassador) ABOUT Castro: Pride 8

Chang, Michael (tennis player) Life 7; Sports 9

Charles, Ray (singer) Disabilities 3; Music 5; Trouble 4

Chávez, César (labor organizer) Wealth and Poverty 4; Winning and Losing 9

Child, Lydia Maria (suffragist) Nature 4

Chippewa (Native American tribe) Seasons 3

Chisholm, Shirley (politician) Racism 9; Women's Rights 8

Christopher, John (author) Friendship 5; Goals 3

Clark, Arthur C. (author) Possible and Impossible 6; Science 1

Clay, Henry (politician) Constitution 1

*Cleary, Beverly (author) Anger 7; Animals 10; Basketball 3; Books 7; Clothes 4; Dogs 3; Heroes 4; Libraries 4; Life 8; Likes and Dislikes 5; Parents 5; Weather 4; Writers and Writing 5

Cleaver, Vera and Bill (authors) Action 5; Food 7; Seasons 4

Clemente, Roberto (baseball player) Baseball 2; ABOUT Clemente: Excellence 1

Cleveland, Grover (22nd President) Voting 2

Clifford, Eth (author) Grandparents 3

Clinton, Bill (42nd President) Grandparents 4; Mothers 5

Clinton, Hillary Rodham (lawyer and wife of the 42nd President) Differences 2; Justice and Injustice 1

Coatsworth, Elizabeth (author) Witches and Wizards 4

Cobb, Jewel Plummer (biologist) Anger 8

Cofer, Judith Ortiz (author) Grandparents 5

Cohen, Daniel (author) Dreams and Nightmares 5

Cole, Johnnetta B. (educator) History 1

Coleridge, Samuel Taylor (poet) Water 2

Collier, James L. and Christopher (authors) Eating 5; Freedom 3; Responsibility 4; War 5, 6

Collodi, Carlo (author) Advice 6; Clothes 5; Eating 6; Lies and Lying 6; Manners 1; Sea Life 5; Sickness 5

Colón, Willie (composer) Music 6

Commoner, Barry (biologist) Pollution 3

Conly, Jane Leslie (author) Courage 4; Education 4; Heroes 5; Learning 1

Conrad, Pam (author) Animals 11; Good and Bad 4; Grandparents 6; Monsters and Dragons 4; Smells 1; Truth 3

Cooke, Alistair (author) The Presidency 6

Coolidge, Calvin (30th President) War 7

Cooper, Ilene (author) Choices 4

*Cooper, Susan (author) Fairies and Ghosts 3; Good and Bad 5; Hope 4; Technology 2

Cosby, Bill (comedian) Education 5; Parents 6; Time 3

Coulander, Harold (author) Tall Tale Heroes 3, 4

Coutant, Helen (teacher) Death 9

*Creech, Sharon (author) Courage 5; Death 10; Fear 2; Good and Bad 6; Grandparents 7; Life 9; Problems and Solutions 4; Teachers 3; Trees 5

Einstein, Albert (physicist) Future 3; Religion 1; Science 4, 5, 6; ABOUT Einstein: Fame 9

Eisenhower, Dwight D. (34th President) Democracy 3; History 2; Occupations 9; Peace 7; The Presidency 7

Eliot, T. S. (poet and playwright) Cats 4

Ellis, Keith (author) Success and Failure 9

Emerson, Ralph Waldo (poet) Friendship 8; Revolutionary War 7

Enright, Elizabeth (author) Mice and Rats 4

Erickson, John R. (author) Beauty 4; Dogs 5; Food 8; Heroes 6

Erving, Julius (basketball player) Basketball 4

Escalante, Jaime (teacher) Learning 3

Esterl, Arnica (author) Hope 5

Euwer, Anthony Beauty 5

Evers, Medgar (civil rights activist) Change 8

Ewing, Patrick (basketball player) Education 9

F

Faulkner, William (author) Writers and Writing 8

Faulkner, William J. (author) Equality 5

Fenwick, Millicent (politician) Government 5

Fernandez, Beatriz "Gigi" (tennis player) Sports 11

Ferris, Jeri (author) Advice 8; Racism 10, 11

Field, Rachel (author) Change 9

Filipovic, Zlata (diarist) Children 3; School 5

Fillmore, Parker Nature 5

Fincke, Mike (astronaut) Space Exploration 3

Fitzgerald, John D. (author) Brothers and Sisters 6; Differences 6

Fitzhugh, Louise (author) Action 8; Advice 9; Anger 9; Arithmetic 3; Dreams and Nightmares 8; Friendship 9; God 7; Learning 4; Lies and Lying 7; Likes and Dislikes 8; Manners 3; Mothers 7; Religion 2; Sickness 7

*Fleischman, Paul (author) Civil War 4, 5; Horses 1

*Fleischman, Sid (author) Clothes 6; History 3; Intelligence 7; Mice and Rats 5; Wishes 4

Fleming, Ian (author) Adventure 4; Change 10; Inventions and Inventors 4; Technology 4

Fletcher, Susan (author) Animals 17

*Forbes, Esther (author) Differences 7; Responsibility 5; Revolutionary War 8

Ford, Betty (Betty Ford Clinic founder and wife of the 38th President) Accomplishment 3

Ford, Gerald (38th President) The Presidency 8

Ford, Henry (car manufacturer) America and Americans 3; Colors 2; Wealth and Poverty 7

Foster, Stephen (songwriter) Weather 7

Four Guns (Oglala Sioux tribe) Writers and Writing 9

*Fox, Paula (author) Colors 3; Family 5, 6; Fear 4; Happiness 4; Life 14; Slavery 5; Time 9; Truth 5; Water 6; Words 12

Frank, Anne (diarist) Good and Bad 9; Happiness 5; Justice and Injustice 3; War 9; Work 4; Writers and Writing 10

Frank, Otto (father of Anne Frank) Children 4

Franklin, Benjamin (statesman) Action 9; Age 8; Anger 10, 11; Arithmetic 4; Birds 9; Constitution 4; Declaration of Independence 5; Eating 7; Love 7; Secrets 5; Sleep 5; Time 10, 11, 12; War 10; ABOUT Franklin: Inventions and Inventors 9

*Freedman, Russell (author) Death 13; Future 4; Parents 7

Fritz, Jean (author) America and Americans 4; Time 13; War 11

Frost, Frances (poet) World 6

Frost, Robert (poet) Baseball 3

G

Gandhi, Mohandas (civil rights leader) Truth 6

Garagiola, Joe (baseball player) Baseball 4

Gardner, John (author) Fear 5; Monsters and Dragons 6

Gates, Bill (CEO of Microsoft) Democracy 4; Libraries 6

George III (king of England) Revolutionary War 9; ABOUT George: Declaration of Independence 6

*George, Jean Craighead (author) Animals 19, 20; Birds 10; Differences 8; Home 8; Moon and Stars 6; Respect 5; Wealth and Poverty 8

Geronimo (Apache leader) Nature 6

Gibbon, Col. John (military officer) Native Americans 5

Holland, Tara (1997 Miss America) Reading 4

Holman, Felice (author) Life 16

Hoover, Herbert (31st President) Pride 4

Horvath, Polly (author) Food 11

Hosier, John Magic 8

Houston, Whitney (singer) Singing 6

Howe, Deborah and James (authors) Birds 12; Cats 7; Dogs 6; Intelligence 9; Occupations 10; Rabbits 3

Hudson, Jan (author) Death 15; Future 7; Smells 6

Huerta, Dolores (Vice President of the United Farm Workers) Racism 12, World 9

Hughes, Langston (poet) Death 16; Democracy 5; Dreams and Nightmares 10; Friendship 13

Hughes, Ted (poet) Pets 3

Humphrey, Hubert H. (politician) Civil Rights 1

*Hunt, Irene (author) Civil War 9; Confidence 7; Music 12; Seasons 8; Slavery 7

Hunter, Mollie (author) Magic 9; Sickness 8

Hunter-Gault, Charlayne (journalist) Racism 13

Hurston, Zora Neale (anthropologist) Goals 9; Time 16

Hurwitz, Johanna (author) Eating 9; Food 12

Hyman, Trina Schart (illustrator) Friendship 14

Iacocca, Lee A. (business executive) Advice 11; Family 8

Irving, Washington (author) Change 12

Jackson, Andrew (7th President) The Presidency 9

Jackson, Jesse (civil rights activist) America and Americans 7; Change 13; Children 5; Confidence 8; Differences 11; Education 10; Hope 8; Right and Wrong 7; Voting 5

Jackson, Michael (singer) Children 6

Jacobs, Harriet A. (diarist) Children 7; Family 9; Freedom 7; Slavery 8

Jacques, Brian (author) Food 13; Nature 8

Jefferson, Thomas (3rd President) Constitution 5; Declaration of Independence 7; Future 9; Government 6; History 4; Religion 4; Spelling 3

Jehl, Francis (Thomas Edison employee) Problems and Solutions 9

Jennings, Peter (news anchor) Fathers 3

Johnson, Clifton Appearances 8

Johnson, Earvin "Magic" (basketball player) Children 9

Johnson, Lyndon B. (36th President) Civil Rights 2; The Presidency 10, 11; Voting 6

Johnson, Marilyn (journalist) Books 8

Jones, James Earl (actor) Disabilities 9

Jordan, Barbara (politician) Action 10; America and Americans 8; Disabilities 10; Equality 6; Intelligence 10; Occupations 12

Jordan, I. King (college president) Disabilities 11

Jordan, Michael (basketball player) Basketball 5, 6; Parents 8; Problems and Solutions 10; Sports 14; Winning and Losing 11; Work 5

Joseph (Nez Perce Chief) Change 14; Differences 13; Equality 7; Freedom 8; Native Americans 6; Understanding 5; Words 14; ABOUT Joseph: Death 13

Josephy, Alvin M., Jr. (author) Native Americans 7

Joyce, William (illustrator) Dogs 7

Joyner-Kersee, Jackie (track star) Goals 10

Jukes, Marvis (author) Sea Life 7

Juster, Norton (author) Advice 12; Food 14; Happiness 7; Spelling 4; Thinking 7; Words 15

Keane, Bill (cartoonist) Time 17

Keehn, Sally M. (author) Change 15; Family 10

Keller, Helen (humanitarian) Adventure 6; Disabilities 12; Happiness 8; Imagination 2; Religion 5

Keller, Mollie (author) Fathers 4

Kellogg, Steven (author and illustrator) Tall Tale Heroes 9, 10, 11

Kennedy, John F. (35th President) America and Americans 9; Civil Rights 3, 4; Courage 8, 9; Peace 8, 9; Space Exploration 4, 5; Talent 5; Technology 5; War 13

Kennedy, Robert F. (public official and brother of the 35th President) World 10

Kerr, M. E. (author) Birds 13; Fathers 5; Names 7; Winning and Losing 12

Moore, Clement Clarke (professor) Laughter 11

Moore, Lilian (poet) Sounds 10

Moore, Rosalie (poet) Cats 12

Morey, Larry (lyricist) Work 2

Morey, Walt (author) Love 17; Right and Wrong 10; Understanding 9

Morison, Samuel Eliot, (historian) America and Americans 13; Declaration of Independence 8; History 5

Morpurgo, Michael (author) Truth 8

Morris, George Perkins (poet) Trees 11

Morrison, Lillian (poet) Baseball 6; Basketball 8; Football 3

Morrison, Toni (author) Writers and Writing 16

Moses, Edwin (track star) Fathers 7; Sports 19

Moses, Grandma, *Anna Mary Robertson* (painter) Occupations 14

Mother Teresa *(See: Teresa, Mother)*

Myers, Walter Dean, (author) Death 19; Fairies and Ghosts 7; Friendship 20; Happiness 14; Imagination 7; Problems and Solutions 11; Responsibility 6; Right and Wrong 11; Sadness 9; Understanding 10

N

Nader, Ralph (consumer advocate) Democracy 9

Nash, Ogden (poet) Cats 13; Parents 13; Sea Life 10; Trees 12; Wealth and Poverty 10; Weather 9

*Naylor, Phyllis Reynolds (author) Cats 14; Children 13; Clothes 10; Conversation 5; Food 17; Home 11; Language 4; Names 11; Occupations 15; Right and Wrong 12; Sounds 11

Nhuong, Huynh Quang (author) Grandparents 14

Nin, Anaïs (author) Animals 25; Words 24

Nixon, Joan Lowery (author) Rabbits 5

Nixon, Richard (37th President) Equality 11; The Presidency 12

Nootka Tribe Colors 7

Norton, Mary (author) Fear 11; Names 12

Norworth, Jack (actor) Baseball 7

Nyad, Diana (swimmer) Determination 6

O

*O'Brien, Robert C. (author) Libraries 8; Reading 6

Ochoa, Ellen (astronaut) Occupations 16

O'Connor, Sandra Day (Supreme Court Justice) Women's Rights 10

*O'Dell, Scott (author) Conversation 6; Courage 13; Names 13; Sea Life 11

O'Donnell, Rosie (actress) Imagination 8

O'Keeffe, Georgia (painter) Nature 11; Words 25

Olsen, Mary-Kate and Ashley (actresses) Brothers and Sisters 10

O'Neill, Mary (poet) Words 26

Onizuka, Ellison S. (astronaut) Education 13; Success and Failure 12

Orwell, George (author) War 18

Osborne, Mary Pope (author) Tall Tale Heroes 13, 14, 15, 16, 17

P

Paige, Leroy "Satchel" (baseball player) Advice 14; Age 11; Baseball 8

Palmer, Arnold (golfer) Sports 21

Park, Ruth (author) Clothes 11

Parker, Capt. John (patriot) Revolutionary War 16

Parks, Barbara (author) Parents 14; Sadness 10

Parks, Rosa (civil rights activist) Action 11; Imagination 9

*Paterson, Katherine (author) Death 20; Fear 12, 13; Life 19; Parents 15; Teachers 7; Writers and Writing 17

Paulsen, Gary (author) Advice 15; Confidence 10; Death 21; Dogs 11, 12; Fear 14; Intelligence 13; Learning 8

Payne, John Howard (actor) Home 12

Peck, Anne Smith (mountain climber) Sports 22

Peck, Richard (author) Children 14; Death 22, 23; Fairies and Ghosts 8; Fathers 8; Intelligence 14; Mothers 9; Teachers 8; Truth 9

Peck, Robert Newton (author) Action 12; Animals 26; Music 18; Occupations 17; Smells 8, 9; Words 27

Peck, Sylvia (author) Beauty 10; Happiness 15; Love 18; Music 19; Sea Life 12

Peet, Bill (illustrator) Laughter 12; Reading 7

Pelé *Edson Arantes do Nascimento*, (soccer player) Sports 23

Pepper, Claude (politician) Democracy 10

Pima Tribe Weather 10

Pinkwater, Daniel Manus (author and illustrator) Clothes 12; Occupations 18; Pets 8, 9; Sounds 12; Talking 7

Polacco, Patricia (author) Wishes 9

Polk, James K. (11th President) The Presidency 13

Porte, Barbara Ann (author) Happiness 16; Inventions and Inventors 8; Wealth and Poverty 11

Porter, Eleanor H. (author) Appearances 12; Fathers 9; Good and Bad 15; Home 13; Sleep 7; Understanding 11

Potter, Beatrix (author) Advice 16; Food 19; Occupations 19; Talking 8

Potter, Robert R. (author) Inventions and Inventors 9

Powell, Colin (general) America and Americans 17

Prelutsky, Jack (poet) Brothers and Sisters 11; Bugs 6; Fathers 10; Monsters and Dragons 9; Singing 7; Weather 11; Witches and Wizards 8

Price, Leontyne (opera singer) Accomplishment 8

Quirot, Ana (track star) Fame 7

Ramirez, Blandina C. (civil rights activist) Respect 9

Rankin, Jeannette (politician) Voting 8; Women's Rights 11

*__**Raskin, Ellen** (author) Dreams and Nightmares 15

Rawlings, Marjorie Kinnan (author) Trouble 10

Rawls, Betsy (golfer) Children 15

Rawls, Wilson (author) Conversation 7

Redcloud, Prince School 8

Red Cloud (Oglala Sioux Chief) Native Americans 10

Reddy, Helen (singer) Women's Rights 12

Reeder, Carolyn (author) Civil War 14, 15; Good and Bad 16; Right and Wrong 13

Rendal, Justine (author) Imagination 10; Life 20; Problems and Solutions 12; Technology 8

Revere, Paul (patriot) ABOUT Revere: Revolutionary War 14

Richie, Lionel (singer and composer) Children 6

Ritter, Lawrence S. (author) Baseball 9

Robinson, Jackie (baseball player) Baseball 10; Life 21; Mothers 10; Respect 10; Voting 9; ABOUT Robinson: Baseball 9; Heroes 1

Rockwell, Thomas (author) Eating 14; Lies and Lying 13

Rodda, Emily (author) Imagination 11

Rogers, Will (humorist) Heroes 8; Home 14; Likes and Dislikes 10; Native Americans 11; Occupations 20; World 13

Roosevelt, Eleanor (diplomat and wife of the 32nd President) Disabilities 13; Fear 15; Good and Bad 17; Happiness 17; History 6; Peace 13; Possible and Impossible 12; Racism 15; Religion 6; Success and Failure 13

Roosevelt, Franklin D. (32nd President) Democracy 11; Fear 16; Future 11; Lies and Lying 14; Success and Failure 14; Time 20; Voting 10; War 19; ABOUT Roosevelt: Disabilities 13

Roosevelt, Theodore (26th President) Government 8; Nature 12; Work 10

Rosen, Michael J. (author) Dogs 13; Home 15; Talking 9

Rossetti, Christina (poet) Bugs 7; Weather 12

Rudolph, Wilma (track star) Accomplishment 9; Determination 7; Mothers 11; Sickness 11; Sports 24; Winning and Losing 14

Ruskin, John (author) Beauty 12

Russell, Bill (basketball player) Libraries 9; Racism 16

Ruth, Babe (baseball player) Baseball 11
ABOUT Ruth: Baseball 1

*__Rylant, Cynthia__ (author) Death 24; Differences 14, 15; God 11; Love 19; Secrets 10; Talking 10; Understanding 12

S

Sachar, Louis (author) Arithmetic 5; School 9

Sagan, Carl (astronomer) Death 25; Future 12; Science 9; Space Exploration 7

Saint-Exupéry, Antoine de (author and illustrator) Friendship 22; Moon and Stars 8; Secrets 11; Time 21; Understanding 13

Saltzman, David (author and illustrator) Laughter 13, 14; Sadness 11

Samuelson, Joan Benoit (runner) Sports 25; Winning and Losing 16

Sandburg, Carl (poet) Animals 27; Arithmetic 6, 7, 8; Language 5; Native Americans 12; War 20; Wealth and Poverty 12; Weather 13; Words 28

San Souci, Robert D. (author) Horses 3; Tall Tale Heroes 18, 19

Sargent, Sarah (author) Monsters and Dragons 10

Say, Allen (author) Names 14; Sports 26

Schaller, George (naturalist) Animals 28; Future 13; World 14

Schultz, Charles (cartoonist) Names 15; Occupations 21; Winning and Losing 17; World 15

Seattle (Chief of six Pacific NW tribes) Death 26; Differences 16; God 13; Hope 12; Native Americans 13; Religion 7

Selden, George (author) Bugs 8; Dogs 14; Fame 8; Fathers 11; Magic 14; Music 20; Names 16; Sadness 12; Sounds 13; Talent 8

Selena, *Quintanilla Perez* (singer) Music 21

Seuss, Dr., *Theodor Seuss Geisel* (author) Animals 29; Books 12; Eating 15; Equality 12; Food 20; Freedom 14; Inventions and Inventors 10; Lies and Lying 15; Pollution 10; Pride 7; Rabbits 6; Responsibility 7; Sleep 8, 9; Sounds 14; Technology 9; Thinking 11; Trees 13; Weather 14; Work 11

Seward, William H. (statesman) Constitution 8

Sewell, Anna (author) Advice 17; Excellence 7; Horses 4, 5; Religion 8; Right and Wrong 14; Voting 11

Shapiro, Arnold L. Talking 11

Shuckburg, Robert (doctor) Revolutionary War 17

Shura, Mary Francis (author) Children 16; Food 21; Truth 10; Understanding 14

Silverberg, Robert (author) Space Exploration 8; Zoos 6

Silverstein, Shel (poet and illustrator) Brothers and Sisters 12; Friendship 23; Inventions and Inventors 11; Magic 15; Sickness 12; Sounds 15

Simmons, Curt (journalist) Baseball 12

Simonton, Dean Keith (professor) Excellence 8; Fame 9; History 7

Simpson, Don (movie producer) Disabilities 14

Singer, Isaac Bashevis (author) Action 13; Death 27; Intelligence 15; Religion 9; Thinking 12; Wealth and Poverty 13; Wishes 10

Sitting Bull (Sioux Chief) Native Americans 14, 15

Smith, Charlotte (basketball player) Brothers and Sisters 13

Smith, Dodie (author) Clothes 13; Dogs 15; Intelligence 16; Language 6; Pets 10; Understanding 15, 16; Wishes 11

Smith, Margaret Chase (politician) Trouble 11

Smith, Robert Kimmel (author) Arithmetic 9; Baseball 13, 14

Smith, Samuel F. (clergyman) Freedom 15

Smith, Will (actor and rapper) Occupations 22

Snyder, Zilpha Keatley (author) Age 12; Horses 6; Time 22; Words 30

Sobol, Donald J. (author) Books 13; Smells 10

Sosa, Dan, Jr. (judge) Success and Failure 16

Soto, Gary (author) Clothes 14; Happiness 18

*__Speare, Elizabeth George__ (author) Clothes 15; Manners 8; Nature 13; Sounds 16

Spielberg, Steven (movie director) Arithmetic 10; School 10; Science 10

*__Spinelli, Jerry__ (author) Books 14, 15; Colors 9; Differences 17; Fear 17; Football 4, 5; Grandparents 15; Home 16; Imagination

V

Van Horne, Harriet (journalist) Technology 12

Viorst, Judith (poet) Pets 12

*Voigt, Cynthia (author) Books 19

Vonnegut, Kurt, Jr. (author) Equality 16

W

Walesa, Lech (Polish President) Government 11

Walker, Alice (author) Grandparents 17; Mothers 13

Warner, Charles Dudley (journalist) Weather 19

Washington, Booker T. (educator) Civil Rights 7; Determination 10; Freedom 18; Learning 10, 11; School 12; Success and Failure 20; Work 14, 15

Washington, Denzel (actor) Fathers 13

Washington, George (1st President) Freedom 19; Goals 12; Government 12; Peace 15; The Presidency 17; Revolutionary War 18, 19, 20; Slavery 13; Wishes 12; ABOUT Washington: Fathers 4

Washington, Ned (lyricist) Wishes 13

Webster, Daniel (lawyer) Truth 12

Weller, Frances Ward (author) Friendship 26

Westmoreland, William (general) War 22

Wharton, Thomas (illustrator) Dogs 17; Reading 9

Wheelock, Warren H. (author) Pride 8

White, E. B. (author) Advice 19; Bugs 10; Cats 17; Children 17, 18; Death 30; Friendship 27; Mice and Rats 10; Spelling 7; Talking 13; Work 16, 17

Whitestone, Heather (1995 Miss America) Disabilities 15; Mothers 14; Thinking 13

Whitman, Walt (poet) Nature 15

Wiggin, Kate Douglas (author) Choices 8

Wilcox, Ella Wheeler (poet) Trouble 18

Wilde, Oscar (poet) Seasons 14

Wilder, Laura Ingalls (author) America and Americans 18; Determination 11; Excellence 10; Manners 10; Seasons 15; Trees 14; Weather 21; Women's Rights 15; ABOUT Wilder: Books 2

Wilkins, Roy (civil rights activist) Racism 17

Will, George F. (news commentator) Voting 12

Williams, Jody (Nobel Prize winner) Goals 13

Williams, Margery (author) Beauty 13; Happiness 20; Rabbits 7

Williams, Vera (author) Colors 10; Seasons 16

Wilson, Woodrow (28th President) Democracy 12; Government 13

Winfrey, Oprah (actress) Excellence 11; Goals 14; God 17; Teachers 9; Voting 13; ABOUT Winfrey: Books 8

Winnemucca, Sarah (daughter of an Indian chief) Justice and Injustice 9

*Wojciechowska, Maia (author) Animals 32; Courage 14; Fear 18; Occupations 23

Wonder, Stevie (singer) Disabilities 16

Wong, Jade Snow (author) Eating 16; Right and Wrong 16

Woods, Tiger (golfer) ABOUT Woods: Sports 21

Worth, Kathryn (poet) Smells 11

Wrede, Patricia C. (author) Advice 20; Colors 11; Fairies and Ghosts 10; Horses 9; Manners 11; Sickness 14; Smells 12; Talking 14; Witches and Wizards 9

Wright, Milton (Wright brothers' father) Inventions and Inventors 12

Wright, Orville (inventor) Birds 18; Imagination 13; ABOUT Wright: Birds 4; Brothers and Sisters 16; Inventions and Inventors 12; Parents 7

Wright, Wilbur (inventor) Brothers and Sisters 16; Success and Failure 21, 22; ABOUT Wright: Birds 4, 18; Parents 7; Inventions and Inventors 12

Y

Yellen, Jack (songwriter) Happiness 21

Yep, Laurence (author) Family 15; Kindness 8; Monsters and Dragons 12; Names 20; Work 18

Yolen, Jane (author) Anger 19; Bugs 11; Choices 10; Fairies and Ghosts 11,12; Justice and Injustice 10; Life 22; Magic 18; Manners 12; Monsters and Dragons 13; Sleep 11

Z

Zworykin, Vladimir (inventor) Technology 13; ABOUT Zworykin: Inventions and Inventors 1

Subject Index

*A listing of all subjects, topics, and
fictional characters included in this book.*

Best
> *See:* Age 12; Beauty 6; Excellence 7; Goals 14; Good and Bad 10; Government 3, 6; Laughter 16; Life 7; Racism 4

Bible Verses
> *See:* **New Testament** Accomplishment 2; Anger 2; Children 1; Clothes 2; Food 6; Friendship 4; Life 3; Love 5; Parents 2; Peace 3; Possible and Impossible 2; Racism 7; Responsibility 2; Right and Wrong 3; Thinking 2; Truth 1; Wealth and Poverty 3; **Old Testament** Age 4: Animals 8: Change 6; Choices 3; Death 5; God 2; Happiness 1; Heroes 2; Hope 2; Pride 2; Sea Life 2; Secrets 3; Sleep 4; Time 1; Trees 3; Work 1; World 1

Bill of Rights
> *See:* Books 10

Birds 1-18
> *See also:* Advice 2; Animals 30; Beauty 12; Clothes 1, 12; Dreams and Nightmares 10; Freedom 4; Grandparents 3; Magic 7; Mice and Rats 2, 3; Pets 6; Respect 4; Seasons 10; Singing 3; Sounds 5, 16; Talking 11; Weather 5, 17; Words 23

Boasting and Bragging
> *See:* Accomplishment 1; Action 7; Birds 5, 11; Clothes 4; Love 5; Winning and Losing 2

Books 1-19
> *See also:* Cats 2; History 7, 9; Intelligence 9; Libraries 2, 5; Likes and Dislikes 3; Magic 17; Reading 1, 2; School 1; Science 7, 13; War 11; Writers and Writing 2, 20

Boys
> *See:* Grandparents 2; Writers and Writing 18

Boy Scout Oath
> *See:* Excellence 2

Bravery
> *See:* Courage 1-14

Brotherhood
> *See:* America and Americans 1; Dreams and Nightmares 11; Equality 8; Peace 10; Racism 6

Brothers and Sisters 1-16
> *See also:* Friendship 7, 14; Good and Bad 4; Names 14; Pets 3; Sadness 7

Brown, Charlie
> *See:* Winning and Losing 17

Buffalo
> *See:* Home 10; Monsters and Dragons 4; Native Americans 12; Pets 7

Bugs 1-11
> *See also:* Animals 30; Appearances 7; Dogs 4; Fame 5; God 8; Magic 18; Mothers 8; Music 7, 20; Pets 11; Sadness 12; Sleep 1; Sounds 6, 16; Spelling 4; Talking 11; Wealth and Poverty 1; Wishes 8; Writers and Writing 18

Bunyan, Paul
> *See:* Animals 27; Tall Tale Heroes 3, 4, 16, 17, 20

Butterflies
> *See:* Bugs 5, 7; Change 9; God 8

Careers
> *See in this Index:* Occupations

Cats 1-17
> *See also:* Advice 2; Animals 26, 30; Change 1; Colors 8, 11; Conversation 3; Language 4; Learning 5; Mice and Rats 3; Occupations 19; Pets 4; Reading 9; Sounds 11; Talking 9, 11; Understanding 11; Writers and Writing 18

Challenge
> *See:* Democracy 1; Sports 16; Success and Failure 7; Winning and Losing 12; Writers and Writing 18

Chance
> *See in this Index:* Opportunities

Change 1-19
> *See also:* Action 11; Death 9, 23, 26; Democracy 11; Education 1; History 10; Lies and Lying 14; Life 5; Magic 11; Names 20; Occupations 4; Peace 9; Pollution 7; The Presidency 5; Seasons 2; Secrets 2; Slavery 7; Success and Failure 16; Thinking 5; Water 1; Zoos 2

Chickens
> *See:* Eating 10; Learning 5; Occupations 14; Pets 9

Children 1-18
> *See also:* Action 10; Advice 11; America and Americans 18; Change 7; Civil Rights 4; Democracy 12; Differences 17; Dogs 7; Future 13; Goals 9; Horses 8; Imagination 8; Libraries 4, 6; Manners 9, 10; Moon and Stars 7; Native Americans 5, 6; Parents 2, 4, 11, 13, 17; Possible and Impossible 3; Racism 17; Reading 4; Sadness 15; School 2, 3; Sickness 2; Sports 24; Tall Tale Heroes 16; Technology 3; Trouble 3; Understanding 13; Work 2, 7; Writers and Writing 1, 17, 18

11; Mothers 7; Native Americans 5, 6, 14; Occupations 6, 7; Pollution 2; The Presidency 4; Revolutionary War 18; Sadness 5, 6, 7; Sleep 2; Smells 6; War 3, 5, 6; Wealth and Poverty 12

Decisions
See: Action 10; Love 16; The Presidency 4; Voting 12

Declaration of Independence 1-8

Deer
See: Animals 25; Differences 13; Home 10; Nature 13

Defeat
See: Civil Rights 5; Confidence 6; Determination 8; War 21; Winning and Losing 3

Democracy 1-12
See also: Voting 10

Determination 1-11

Differences 1-17
See also: America and Americans 6; Change 4; Colors 9; Democracy 7; Fame 3; Football 6; Friendship 21; Goals 13; Government 2; Libraries 3; Life 4, 13; Moon and Stars 8; Names 12; Problems and Solutions 6, 12; Racism 12; Respect 2; Thinking 10; Trouble 5; Voting 6; Words 13; Writers and Writing 11

Dignity
See: Horses 7; Mothers 3; Work 14

Disabilities 1-16
See also: Mothers 14; Thinking 13

Disappointment
See: Hope 9; Sounds 3

Discouragement
See: Birds 3; Determination 10; Home 10; Inventions and Inventors 5

Discovery
See: America and Americans 13; Clothes 4; Friendship 23; History 5; Sleep 11

Dislikes
See in this Index: Likes and Dislikes

Distrust
See in this Index: Trust and Distrust

Divorce
See: Children 14; Fathers 8; Parents 12

Dogs 1-17
See also: Beauty 1; Clothes 13; Conversation 7; Eating 10; Excellence 4; Fear 1; Food 8,

17; Friendship 14; Imagination 4; Intelligence 11, 13, 16; Language 6; Laughter 12; Learning 5; Music 3; Names 8, 11; Occupations 10; Pets 10, 12; Rabbits 3; Slavery 1; Understanding 11, 15, 16; Work 8

Dolphins
See: Sea Life 6, 11

Dragons
See: Fear 5; Manners 11; Monsters and Dragons 1, 4, 6, 7, 9, 10, 11, 12; Nature 2; Singing 7; Smells 12; Weather 11

Dreams and Nightmares 1-15
See also: Baseball 14; Food 21; Future 9; Heroes 3; Home 15; Imagination 10; Inventions and Inventors 1; Likes and Dislikes 5; Magic 6; Native Americans 1; Religion 7; Time 3; Trouble 8; War 16; Zoos 6, 7

Drugs
See: Parents 8; Problems and Solutions 3; Words 17

Duty
See: Accomplishment 6; Excellence 2; Government 12; The Presidency 8, 13; Respect 3; Responsibility 4; Right and Wrong 8; Women's Rights 3

Earth
See: World 1-15
See also: Books 3; Grandparents 3; Nature 3, 5, 7, 8; Occupations 16; Pollution 4, 8; Trees 2; Water 4; Wealth and Poverty 3; Wishes 5

Eating 1-16
See also: Baseball 2; Children 6; Death 7; Dreams and Nightmares 1, 14; Food 10; Future 5; Learning 1; Monsters and Dragons 4, 6, 7; Sickness 9; Zoos 2

Education 1-18
See also: Civil Rights 2; Determination 10; Equality 13; Women's Rights 4

Elephants
See: Animals 12, 14, 21, 29; Smells 10; Thinking 11

Elves and Hobbits
See: Adventure 8; Change 19; Lies and Lying 17; Magic 16; Music 22

Emancipation
See: Civil Rights 2

Fire
See: Animals 25; Grandparents 3; Heroes 5; Hope 4; Lies and Lying 4; Seasons 12

Fish
See: Sea Life 2, 4, 7, 8

Fishing
See: Sports 28

Flag
See: America and Americans 10, 15, 16; Differences 11; Food 24; Respect 3; Revolutionary War 7, 15

Flowers
See: Adventure 3; Advice 10; Animals 15; Appearances 7; Beauty 12; Change 6; Clothes 2; Colors 3; Family 1; Life 8; Mothers 13; Names 10; Nature 11; Seasons 12, 14; Talking 6; Zoos 1

Flying
See: Birds 2, 4; Determination 5; Dreams and Nightmares 10; Hope 2; Imagination 13; Moon and Stars 5; Pride 4; Sickness 14; Success and Failure 21, 22; Thinking 1

Folk Poems
See: Anger 1; Bugs 1; Food 1, 2, 3; Friendship 2; Lies and Lying 3, 4; Love 2; Names 1; School 1; Seasons 1; Secrets 1; Sleep 1; Understanding 1; Weather 1; Zoos 1

Food 1-24
See also: Advice 3, 19; Bugs 1; Conversation 2; Dreams and Nightmares 5; Eating 15; Fairies and Ghosts 4; Grandparents 11; Horses 9; Imagination 1; Life 9; Likes and Dislikes 4; Mice and Rats 3; Monsters and Dragons 1; Native Americans 1, 6; Pets 4; Rabbits 5; Sea Life 10; Smells 2; Trees 3; Wealth and Poverty 12, 14; Weather 2

Football 1-6
See also: Sports 5, 27

Foxes
See: Animals 3, 30

Freedom 1-19
See also: Action 11; America and Americans 10, 11, 16, 17; Birds 13; Cats 6; Constitution 7; Declaration of Independence 1, 2; Equality 9; God 6; History 2; Magic 7; Revolutionary War 1; Truth 1; Voting 5; Wealth and Poverty 12; Winning and Losing 9

Friendship (and Friends) 1-27
See also: Advice 13; Animals 20; Books 1, 8, 9, 15; Brothers and Sisters 10; Clothes 3; Disabilities 12; Equality 4; Family 14; Lies and Lying 12; Love 8; Monsters and Dragons 12; The Presidency 3; Respect 11; Revolutionary War 5; Sadness 10; Sea Life 11; Secrets 5; Tall Tale Heroes 12; Technology 8

Frogs
See: Education 16; Food 19; Words 12

Fun
See: Birds 4; Books 16; Goals 2; Grandparents 16; Occupations 3, 22; Parents 5, 10; Possible and Impossible 8; Science 11; Secrets 7; Sickness 1; Sports 25; Weather 14; Work 3, 13; Writers and Writing 16

Future 1-15
See also: Constitution 1, 7; Equality 16; Fairies and Ghosts 7; Imagination 3; Laughter 17; Libraries 6; Pollution 8; Time 14, 16; Understanding 2; Words 32

Ghosts
See: Fairies and Ghosts
See also: Fear 1; Future 2; Time 3

Gifts
See: Animals 16; Laughter 7; Life 20; Names 6; Parents 17; Talking 10; Time 19

Girls
See: Action 2; Adventure 3; Arithmetic 2; Baseball 13; Intelligence 14; Names 7; Racism 12; Sleep 3; Trees 1; Writers and Writing 18

Goals 1-14
See also: Advice 8; Life 17; Space Exploration 4; Talent 2

God 1-17
See also: Age 4; America and Americans 1, 11, 16; Animals 2, 8, 30; Beauty 6; Choices 3; Declaration of Independence 1; Differences 11; Disabilities 2; Excellence 2; Fairies and Ghosts 2; Fathers 9; Freedom 9; Hope 2; Music 10; Occupations 17; Peace 2, 3, 14; Possible and Impossible 2; Racism 7; Religion 3; Revolutionary War 2, 18; Sadness 13; Sea Life 2; Sleep 2, 3, 4; Talent 2, 6; Time 17; Trees 3, 5, 8; Trouble 4; Wealth and Poverty 1; Women's Rights 13; Work 1, 12; World 1

Golf
See: Children 15, Sports 21

Honor and Dishonor
See: Death 6; Declaration of Independence 4; Excellence 2; Friendship 9; Inventions and Inventors 12; Respect 3

Hope 1-13
See also: America and Americans 13; Change 13; Children 9; Freedom 2; Good and Bad 9; Justice and Injustice 3; Mothers 13; Problems and Solutions 1; Trouble 8; Sickness 8; Smells 1; War 5; Zoos 4

Horses 1-9
See also: Adventure 5; Conversation 8; Laughter 15; Monsters and Dragons 6; Talking 12; Tall Tale Heroes 9, 19; Water 3

Humor
See: Advice 9; Birds 17; Disabilities 12; Dogs 12; Laughter 5; Winning and Losing 17; Writers and Writing 1

Hunger
See: Dreams and Nightmares 1; Eating 5; Fear 18; Food 21; Freedom 1, 16; Good and Bad 5; School 2; World 11

Hurt
See: Lies and Lying 11, 16; Names 1

Ideal
See: Democracy 8

Ideas
See: Age 7; Beauty 1; Courage 10; Democracy 7; Eating 4; Education 1; Imagination 10; Inventions and Inventors 5; Pets 5; Reading 6; Success and Failure 19; Thinking 8

Imagination 1-13
See also: Colors 6; Disabilities 12; Education 13; Food 21; God 17; Pollution 5; Religion 5; Science 8; Singing 6; Technology 3; Water 4; Writers and Writing 8

Impossible
See in this Index: Possible and Impossible

Independence
See: Revolutionary War 1, 19

Indians
See in this Index: Native Americans

Information
See in this Index: Facts and Information

Injustice
See in this Index: Justice and Injustice

Insects
See in this Index: Bugs

Inspiration
See: Disabilities 5; Mothers 14; Reading 2; Writers and Writing 13

Integration
See: Civil Rights 6

Intelligence (and Stupidity) 1-18
See also: Anger 17; Animals 3; Appearances 5; Brothers and Sisters 6, 14; Bugs 8, Choices 2; Dogs 9; Education 2, 7; Heroes 6; Lies and Lying 12; Love 4; The Presidency 11; Pride 8; Respect 4; Sports 14, 19; Thinking 9; Wealth and Poverty 8

Inventions and Inventors 1-12
See also: Monsters and Dragons 3; Mothers 6; Sleep 11; Tall Tale Heroes 4; Words 20

Justice and Injustice 1-10
See also: America and Americans 16; Arithmetic 2; Civil Rights 2; Constitution 7; Death 27; Excellence 7; Goals 4; Government 13; Heroes 9; History 3; Parents 6

Kindness 1-8
See also: Dogs 5; Fathers 11; Love 5; Mice and Rats 10; Religion 8

Knowledge
See: Action 8; Dogs 12; Education 6; Libraries 6; Space Exploration 5; Technology 10; War 3

Language 1-8
See also: Differences 4; Home 11; Native Americans 8; Truth 9

Laughter 1-18
See also: Fathers 12; Grandparents 3; Happiness 11; Occupations 21; Religion 2; Sadness 10; Sounds 1; Tall Tale Heroes 2; Understanding 8

Leaders and Leadership
See: America and Americans 17; History 10; Responsibility 8; Voting 10

Failure 11; Time 11; Trouble 8; Voting 9;
War 17; Wealth and Poverty 1, 4, 7, 10, 12

Monsters and Dragons 1-13
See also: Dreams and Nightmares 13; Fear 5;
Manners 11; Nature 2; Respect 1; Singing 7;
Smells 12; Weather 11

Moon and Stars 1-11
See also: Animals 24; Fairies and Ghosts 1;
Future 12; Love 21; Secrets 2; Wishes 13

Mothers 1-14
See also: Beauty 9; Birds 16; Clothes 14;
Disabilities 15, 16; Dogs 17; Food 24; Goals
9; God 10; Good and Bad 7, 19; Home 13;
Pets 6, 12; Problems and Solutions 8; Sadness
6, 15; Smells 1, 8, 10; Tall Tale Heroes 16;
Trouble 9; Writers and Writing 5

Mottoes
See: America and Americans 14; Goals 8;
Learning 3; Possible and Impossible 13;
Revolutionary War 15; Winning and Losing 5

Mountain Climbing
See: Fear 7, 8; Sports 22; Winning and Losing 7

Music 1-22
See also: Confidence 5; Freedom 18;
Inventions and Inventors 8; Occupations 22;
Talking 3; Wealth and Poverty 12, 14;
Weather 10, 17

Names 1-20
See also: Appearances 10; Change 12; Grand-
parents 17; Tall Tale Heroes 5; Time 19;
Trouble 17

Native Americans 1-16
See also: Adventure 5; Clothes 15; Death 6;
Differences 4, 16; Equality 7; Hope 12;
Justice and Injustice 9; Manners 8; Moon
and Stars 7; Peace 6; Religion 3, 7; Success
and Failure 3; Tall Tale Heroes 12;
Understanding 3, 5; Writers and Writing 9

Nature 1-15
See also: Monsters and Dragons 3

Needs
See: Equality 8; Family 12; Friendship 3;
Heroes 3; Language 7; Love 12; Manners 1,
6; World 5

Nightmares
See in this Index: Dreams and Nightmares

Noise
See in this Index: Sounds

O

Obedience
See: Excellence 2; Government 12; Parents 2

Obligation
See: Animals 13; Family 15; Work 13

Obstacles
See: Disabilities 14; Excellence 8; Goals 4;
Problems and Solutions 9, 10; Success and
Failure 20; Tall Tale Heroes 20; Winning and
Losing 12

Occupations 1-23
See also: Fathers 6; Libraries 7; Science 5;
Women's Rights 4; Words 16

Old Age
See in this Index: Age

Olympic Creed
See: Sports 20

Olympics
See: Accomplishment 9; Education 9

Opinions
See: Cats 10; Grandparents 11; Home 14;
Peace 9; Teachers 7

Opportunities
See: Civil Rights 2; Courage 9; Education 15;
Equality 15; Happiness 17; History 10;
Intelligence 4; Justice and Injustice 6;
Responsibility 3; Right and Wrong 7; Sports
21; Talent 5; Women's Rights 7, 10; Work
10; Writers and Writing 1

P

Pain
See: Good and Bad 5; Laughter 7; Life 12,
20; Sports 7

Painting and Painters
See: Occupations 14; Words 25

Parents 1-17
See also: Anger 7; Brothers and Sisters 4, 7;
Children 4, 8, 14; Choices 7; Friendship 9;
Names 14, 19; Right and Wrong 16; School
7; Secrets 10; Technology 6

Patience
See: Anger 6; Cats 9; Differences 7; Laughter
13; Learning 2; Love 5; Success and Failure
17; Trouble 16

Patriotism
See: America and Americans 1, 9, 10, 11, 15, 16

Protect and Protection
See: Confidence 8; Constitution 2; Dogs 13; Future 13; Intelligence 1; Trees 11

Protest
See: Democracy 6

Proverbs
See: **African**: Accomplishment 1; Conversation 1; Dreams and Nightmares 1; Eating 1; Libraries 1; Lies and Lying 2; **African-American**: Confidence 2; **Albanian**: Cats 1; **American**: Age 2; Books 1; Government 3; Home 1; Life 1; Sounds 2; **Armenian**: Rabbits 2; **Chinese**: Anger 6; Clothes 3; Intelligence 4; Parents 4; Sea Life 4; Trees 4; **Danish**: Advice 7; Peace 5; Time 4; **Dutch**: Good and Bad 8; Language 3; Truth 4; **Egyptian**: Slavery 4; **English**: Action 7; Appearances 8; Beauty 3; Birds 7, 8; Cats 5; Dogs 4; Love 6; Right and Wrong 6; Sickness 6; Time 8; Water 5; Wealth and Poverty 6; Weather 6; Work 3; **Estonian**: Death 12; **Ethiopian**: Equality 4; **French**: Likes and Dislikes 9; **German**: Singing 5; World 7; **Greek**: Fear 6; Talent 4; **Hawaiian**: Smells 5; **Hebrew**: Time 15; **Hungarian**: Happiness 6; **Indian**: Future 8; **Irish**: Fame 6; Manners 4; Thinking 6; **Italian**: Courage 7; Friendship 15; Music 13; Seasons 9; **Jamaican**: Horses 2; **Japanese**: Children 8; Determination 4; Differences 12; Laughter 9; Teachers 4; Wishes 8; **Lithuanian**: Justice and Injustice 7; **Malayan**: Kindness 7; **Mexican**: Hope 10; **Moroccan**: Mothers 8; **Philippine**: Freedom 13; Learning 9; Respect 8; **Russian**: Colors 8; God 12; Success and Failure 15; Winning and Losing 15; **Serbo-Croatian**: Pride 6; Words 29; **Slovenian**: Bugs 9; **Spanish**: Family 14; Mice and Rats 9; Secrets 12; Sleep 10; **Swedish**: War 21; **Tibetan**: Goals 11; **Turkish**: Animals 31; Excellence 9; Trouble 16; **Vietnamese**: Brothers and Sisters 15; **Welsh**: Education 18; **Yiddish**: Choices 9; Sadness 16; Talking 15

Punishment
See: Moon and Stars 2

Rabbits 1-7
See also: Animals 25; Cats 8; Happiness 20; Pride 7; Sounds 5

Race
See: Accomplishment 8; America and Americans 7; Baseball 9; Choices 7; Civil Rights 2; Constitution 3; Differences 17; Dreams and Nightmares 12; Equality 14, 15; Grandparents 4; Music 11; Racism 6, 14, 17; Work 14

Racism 1-17
See also: Confidence 8; Excellence 11

Rain
See: Tall Tale Heroes 19; Weather 1, 2, 3, 5, 7, 14, 15

Rainbows
See: Birds 2; Differences 11; Happiness 14

Rats
See in this Index: Mice and Rats

Reading 1-9
See also: Adventure 7; Advice 11; Books 12; Goals 6; Libraries 8; Slavery 3; Talent 3; Writers and Writing 2

Relatives
See: Animals 7, 24; Differences 4; Horses 1; Names 5

Religion 1-9
See also: Equality 15

Respect 1-13
See also: Age 4; Confidence 8; Differences 3, 7; Excellence 5; Family 7; Nature 8; Religion 2; Right and Wrong 7; Spelling 6; Tall Tale Heroes 12; Voting 1

Responsibility 1-9
See also: Democracy 9; Intelligence 1; Right and Wrong 2

Revenge
See: Anger 17

Revolutionary War 1-20
See also: Declaration of Independence 8; War 5

Right and Wrong 1-16
See also: Civil War 1; Democracy 6, 10; Family 4; Food 23; Good and Bad 11, 16; Government 4; Grandparents 16; Inventions and Inventors 5; Laughter 7; Native Americans 14; Parents 2; The Presidency 10; Racism 7, 13; Respect 5; Science 1; Sounds 12; Trouble 18; War 11; Winning and Losing 1, 3; World 13

Rights
See in this index: Civil Rights and Women's Rights
See also: Action 6; Civil War 15; Declaration of Independence 1, 2; Democracy 6, 10; Education 15; Equality 12; Freedom 17; Government 12; Winning and Losing 6

Americans 3; Parents 6; Rabbits 6; Women's Rights 14

Turtles
See: Animals 9; Freedom 14; Sickness 4

Ugliness
See: Anger 9; Appearances 9; Beauty 2, 4, 13; Love 4

Understanding 1-16
See also: America and Americans 18; Beauty 13; Books 19; Civil War 14; Conversation 7, 9; Death 9; Differences 9; Fathers 9; Freedom 2; Friendship 22; Language 2; Life 8; Mothers 4; Parents 14; Peace 4, 11; Racism 6; Respect 5; Right and Wrong 8; Sadness 6; Science 2; Talent 1; Technology 3; Truth 8; World 5

United States
See: America and Americans 1-19
See also: Birds 6; Constitution 1, 2, 3, 7; Declaration of Independence 2; Family 11; The Presidency 7; Tall Tale Heroes 7

Universe
See in this Index: World

Voting 1-13
See also: Education 6

War 1-22
See also: Children 3; Declaration of Independence 3; Equality 7; Fear 2, 18; Heroes 5; Love 6; Peace 8, 11, 15; School 5, Voting 8

Water 1-7
See also: Books 17; Death 9; Future 15; Music 22; Native Americans 11; Pollution 7; World 8

Wealth and Poverty 1-14
See also: Action 13; Choices 7; Confidence 8; Courage 13; Death 12; Declaration of Independence 4; Education 1, 18; Friendship 21; God 15; Happiness 19; History 1; Learning 9; Native Americans 1, 10; Occupations 4; Pride 8; Racism 12, 15; Secrets 2; Sleep 5; Success and Failure 3; World 11

Weather 1-21
See also: Advice 13; Appearances 3; Bugs 8; Determination 1, 11; Fathers 1; Football 5; Good and Bad 2; Grandparents 11; Monsters and Dragons 12; Moon and Stars 10; Music 18, 19, 20, 22; Nature 6; Tall Tale Heroes 8, 12, 19

Whales
See: Sea Life 5, 8, 13

Wind
See: Appearances 3; Moon and Stars 10; Music 18, 19, 20, 22; Nature 6; Weather 8, 10, 11, 12, 16, 17, 21

Winning and Losing 1-19
See also: Basketball 7; Differences 15; Fame 1; Fathers 7; Football 6; Freedom 10; Life 6, 10, 17; Reading 5; Revolutionary War 11; Sports 6, 11, 14, 23; Success and Failure 1; Talent 2; Time 7; War 18; Wealth and Poverty 4

Wise and Wisdom
See: Age 2; Choices 1; Constitution 5; Disabilities 12; Love 4; The Presidency 2; Sleep 5; Teachers 8; Winning and Losing 2

Wishes 1-13
See also: Animals 22; Civil Rights 4; Dreams and Nightmares 7; Imagination 2; Parents 16; Sadness 1; War 1; Witches and Wizards 1

Witches and Wizards 1-9
See also: Change 1; Colors 11; Determination 1; Love 4; Occupations 15; Technology 1; Trees 10

Wolves
See: Advice 2; Animals 20; Appearances 11; Fear 10; Tall Tale Heroes 2

Women
See: Anger 8; Equality 2; History 7; Justice and Injustice 9; Peace 10; Pride 4; Success and Failure 7; Voting 1; Winning and Losing 8

Women's Rights 1-15
See also: The Presidency 12

Wonder Woman
See: Right and Wrong 9

Words 1-32
See also: Advice 1; Change 10; Democracy 3; Freedom 7; Happiness 7; Home 11, 15; Hope 3; Horses 4; Language 2, 6; Manners 6; Reading 2; Religion 4; Sadness 14; Talent 3; Talking 3; Understanding 3, 16; Witches and Wizards 5; World 13

Work 1-18

See also: Advice 17; Animals 13; Children 10; Clothes 2; Determination 11; Equality 1; Excellence 3, 10; Fame 9; Goals 1; Good and Bad 5; Intelligence 6; Learning 3; Life 7; Mothers 5, 10; Occupations 21; Peace 13; Smells 9; Sports 22; Success and Failure 12, 17; Talent 2; Teachers 6; Voting 1; War 1; Wealth and Poverty 1, 13; Weather 18; Wishes 5; Writers and Writing 4, 13, 16

World 1-15

See also: Accomplishment 2; America and Americans 17; Books 6; Children 6, 18; Constitution 6; Death 20, 26; Differences 5, 10; Disabilities 11; Future 13; Good and Bad 5; Happiness 12; Home 14; Hope 4, 6; Imagination 2; Justice and Injustice 7; Moon and Stars 7; Peace 11; Pollution 2, 7; Respect 13; Revolutionary War 7; Truth 6; War 14, Wealth and Poverty 2, 14; Weather 4; Wishes 12

Worries and Worrying

See: Advice 10, 19; Change 2; Children 2; Clothes 2; Death 24; Differences 15; Problems and Solutions 4; Sports 24

Writers and Writing 1-20

See also: Advice 1; Books 4, 7; Dogs 6; Occupations 8, 10; Reading 1, 2; Spelling 2; Talent 3; Truth 2; Words 8, 21; Work 14

Youth

See: Children 1-18

Zoos 1-7